SIMPLIFIED BOOK-KEEPING FOR SMALL BUSINESSES

Geoffrey Whitehead, B.Sc. (Econ.)

Formerly Senior Lecturer and
Head of Professional Studies Division
Thurrock Technical College
Essex

George Vyner Ltd.

Some firms which supply useful information or services

For the Simplex System of Book-keeping:
George Vyner Ltd. (Ref. S.B.S.B.)
P.O. Box No. 1
Holmfirth
Huddersfield
HD7 2RP

For: *Croner's Reference Book for Employers*
Croner's Reference Book for the Self-Employed
Croner Publications Ltd. (Ref. S.B.S.B.)
Croner House
173 Kingston Road
New Malden
Surrey KT3 3SS

For advice on Capital Transfer Tax mitigation schemes, through life assurance, and for Pension schemes and all financial planning:
James Lemon FLIA
23 Mulberry Close
Cambridge
CB4 2AS
(0223) 358003

For the *'Money Which' Tax Savings Guide*
Consumers Association
14 Buckingham Street
London WC2N 6DS

For advice on the formation of companies and the purchase of ready made companies:
Natcom Services,
46 St. Mary's Street,
Ely,
Cambs.,
CB7 4EY

For *Taxation Simplified* and *Smith's Taxation*
Lofthouse Publications
1 West Close
Carleton
Pontefract WF8 3NR

Foreword

The owner of a small business has no time for elaborate systems of book-keeping, yet it is essential for him to keep clear, accurate accounts. He must be able to see easily whether he is making a profit or loss so that future activities can be planned. He must also be able to produce, at any given time, the exact figures the law demands, especially for tax purposes.

The aim of this book is to give such a businessman general basic guidance on the principles of book-keeping for his enterprise, and to offer him a specific system which can be adapted to any kind of business, whether trading, manufacturing or servicing.

George Vyner Ltd's Simplex System is the original simple system of book-keeping and has been refined over the years to meet the needs of all types of businesses. It is relatively inexpensive; is stocked by most leading bookshops and stationers and offers a free advice service to those who find difficulty in using the system. It is used by so many businessmen that regular reprints are necessary, so that changes in legal requirements etc. can be quickly taken into account.

This book originally appeared as one of John Murray's Success Studybooks, *'Success in Book-keeping for the Small Business'*. I am grateful for permission to reproduce some 93 pages of that book, with additional exercises, in the present volume.

In this book I have referred to a number of organisations and firms which offer services to the owners of small business. I have listed their addresses overleaf, and would like to thank them for their cooperation at various stages. I would particularly like to thank Brian Senior of George Vyner Ltd. for his help and advice throughout the project.

Geoffrey Whitehead

Special Foreword to Teachers and College Lecturers

The Simplex System makes an ideal, practical exercise for pupils and students of all ages and all abilities. For those with a knowledge of double-entry book-keeping it shows how short-cuts may be taken with the double-entry system without destroying its underlying principles of sound record-keeping. The best time to present a module of Simplex book-keeping is the pre-Christmas and pre-Easter period when classes tend to be restless and seek something different, but which is also practical and educationally valuable. After such a module students return to their 'double-entry' with heightened interest and understanding. For those intending to take up a career in accountancy it is a useful introduction to a system many of them will spend their lives auditing.

For many pupils who show an independence of spirit, which leads teachers to conclude that they may themselves set up small businesses, the system is of great interest, while its very simplicity appeals to even the weakest of pupils, who only need to be able to add up money to keep perfect records.

Geoffrey Whitehead

Contents

Unit One

The Accounting Requirements of the Small Business

1.1 Introduction

The owner of the small business requires a system of book-keeping which displays the following characteristics:

(a) It should be simple.
(b) It should require as few books as possible.
(c) It should not take up too much time.
(d) It should satisfy the tax inspector, without the help of a professional accountant.
(e) It should comply with the Companies Acts, where appropriate.
(f) It should enable the owner to judge the success of his business.

(a) Simplicity

The system adopted must be very simple, for the proprietor of a small business usually has to keep the books personally with little if any assistance from professional accountants. He may of course employ a book-keeper, but even that person does not want to keep a full set of books or follow a complete system of double-entry book-keeping. The system needs to be clear enough for the books to be kept properly even by a person who has no previous knowledge of accounting.

(b) As Few Books as Possible

Ideally only one book should be needed. However, it is usual in most systems to keep a separate Wages Book if there are employees, and there are advantages in having a separate book for Value Added Tax.

(c) The Time Required must be Small

Book-keeping records in most small businesses can only receive attention at odd moments when there are no more pressing problems to be dealt with. This means that the system should be based on separate entries, with as little as possible 'carried forward' from one day to the next, or one week to the next.

(d) Tax Requirements

The system should be sufficiently complete to satisfy the Income Tax authorities that it is a proper record, carefully and honestly kept. It should enable the businessman to prepare his own Trading Account and Profit and Loss Account, without any need to send the records to an accountant, and to answer any questions by the local inspector of taxes so that tax assessments can be agreed quickly and confidently. There is really no need at all for the average small business to employ an accountant. With regard to the Value Added Tax, the book-keeping system must meet the requirements of the Customs & Excise authorities, and satisfy any inspection they may make to ensure that proper records are being kept.

(e) Compliance with the Companies Acts

If the firm is a company the book-keeping records must be adequate for the purposes of the Companies Acts 1948-81.

There are two kinds of company: the public company and the private company. The shares of important public companies may be bought and sold on the Stock Exchange. Public companies must keep a full set of book-keeping records, but their methods need not concern us in our study of small-business accounting. Private companies, of which there are over half a million in Britain, may not sell shares to the general public. Many of these companies are very small, with less than £1 000 of capital. Such private companies should find the simple systems of book-keeping described in this book quite adequate for their needs.

(f) Judging the Efficiency of the Business

The astute businessman will want to know how his business compares (i) this week with last week, (ii) this quarter with last quarter, (iii) this year with last year and (iv) with other investment possibilities. The owner of a shop or other small business who works sixteen hours a day for 362 days a year and is left with a profit smaller than he could earn as a bus conductor or a builder's labourer is clearly wasting his time. He needs to know this, and—with a little guidance from this textbook—the system he uses should enable him to judge his true business situation.

1.2 The Simplex System of Book-keeping

Many firms now offer simple systems of book-keeping for the small business. The system described in this book is known as the 'Simplex' system, and its copyright is held by George Vyner Ltd. This system has been selected because it is up to date, particularly easy to follow, and well suited to the needs of the small business.

The Simplex system consists of the Simplex D Account Book, with 52 weekly record pages, one for every week of the year. In addition, about ten further pages, which may be described as analysis pages, enable the businessman to analyse receipts and expenses weekly, to add up useful quarterly totals and to obtain from these quarterly totals annual figures. A set of final accounts prepared from the annual figures reveal the profit for the year. These records may then be submitted to the tax inspector, and are adequate for his purposes: there is no need to seek the services of an accountant.

Two further books—a Wages Book (if there are employees to be paid) and a VAT record book—are also available. An explanation of what is necessary to change over from an existing system of book-keeping to the Simplex system is given in Section 9.3.

Although the Simplex D (the D stands for 'decimal') Account Book is adequate for all types of businesses, George Vyner Ltd. have prepared special books for the Licensing trade (the Simplex Licensees' Account Book) and for farmers (the Simplex Everall Farm Account Book). There is also a special book for non-profit-making enterprises, the Simplex Account Book for Club Treasurers and School-Fund Treasurers. These books are described in later chapters in this book.

1.3 Separating Business Accounts from Private Accounts

A problem which applies more to the small business than to the larger firm is that of distinguishing between business moneys and one's own private finances. Difficulties are bound to arise sooner or later unless two distinct sets of records are kept.

It is very desirable to have two separate bank accounts: one for personal cheques and one for business transactions. This may of course result in additional bank charges, but the extra cost is justified by the advantages.

1.4 Professional Accountancy Services

Although many businessmen successfully prepare their own final accounts using the Simplex System, and mention has been made that professional accountancy services are not required for routine book-keeping there are of course many matters for which specialist advice may be necessary. In particular the provision of pensions for the small businessman, and provision for Capital Transfer Tax, cannot be arranged without considering alternative schemes and seeking professional financial advice.

1.5 Exercises in Simplex Book-keeping

Businessmen wishing to get used to the Simplex System before starting up in business, and schools and colleges who wish to teach this simple type of accounting will find at the end of each chapter exercises to give practice in the use of the Simplex rulings. These may be entered in a Simplex D Account Book purchased especially for that purpose. For schools and colleges packets of paper ruled correctly may be purchased at reasonable prices from George Vyner Ltd., Mytholmbridge Mills, Mytholmbridge, Holmfirth, Huddersfield. HD7 2TA.

1.6 Equal Opportunities

Small businesses are not an exclusively male province, and the Simplex System is widely used by business persons of both sexes. In this text, where the words 'he' and 'his' are used, the reader is asked to remember that 'she' and 'her' are also intended; 'businessman' may be read 'business woman' etc. (See the Interpretation Act, 1978.)

Unit Two

'Cash Flows' through the Small Business

2.1 What are 'Cash Flows'?

Before any business can operate successfully, cash must flow in; it may be in the form of capital contributions by the proprietor, or it may be borrowings made by the proprietor from a bank, building society, finance company or similar institution. Cash must flow out whenever stock is purchased or running expenses are met by the proprietor.

An accounting system, however simple, must record these 'cash flows', and enable the proprietor to compare the current cash flows with those of previous periods. Furthermore, the proprietor needs to see from these figures just how well the actual cash flows compare with the estimates he may have made when planning his present activities. A businessman who 'budgets' ahead, and then compares actual costs and takings with his budgeted figures, is likely to discover adverse price movements (and perhaps pilfering or theft from the till) more quickly than the competitor who fails to make such estimates.

Cash flows may be divided into (*a*) cash inflows, (*b*) cash outflows and (*c*) turnover flows.

(*a*) Cash Inflows

This heading covers such items as:
(i) capital contributions by the proprietor;
(ii) bank loans;
(iii) mortgages;
(iv) loans from finance houses, money-lenders, etc.;
(v) inflows from services rendered, e.g. rent received and commission received.

(*b*) Cash Outflows

The typical outflows of cash from a small business are:
(i) payments for the purchase of capital assets;
(ii) payments for the purchase of consumables, e.g. stationery and wrapping materials;
(iii) running expenses, wages, rent, rates, petrol and oil, etc.;
(iv) drawings by the proprietor (to support his personal household);
(v) tax payments to the Inland Revenue and Customs & Excise authorities.

(c) Turnover Flows

Here we include:

(i) outflows as stock in trade is purchased for resale later;

(ii) inflows when goods are sold for cash;

(iii) inflows when customers, previously supplied with goods on credit, settle their debts.

Fig. 2.1 illustrates these cash flows diagrammatically. Each type is considered in more detail in later Units when we tackle the problem of recording the flow in the book-keeping records.

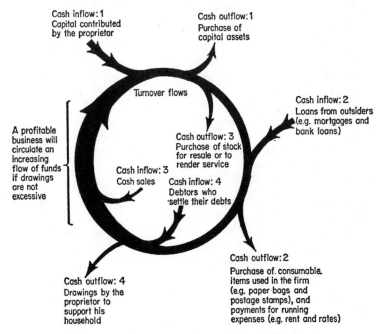

Fig. 2.1 *Cash flows in and out of the small business*

2.2 Adverse Effects on Cash Flows

An adverse effect on cash flows is anything that causes a cash flow *into* the business to be *reduced* for some reason, or a cash flow *out* of the business to be *increased* for some reason.

These adverse effects may be direct or indirect. A direct effect is one which operates on the cash itself. An indirect effect operates on the goods or assets of the business. The theft of goods is an example of an indirect effect: the end result is that the goods stolen cannot be sold, and hence cash inflows are reduced.

A businessman must always be alert to detect adverse effects on cash flows, and a preliminary list of the major items is given here to indicate areas requiring supervision.

(a) Adverse Effects which operate Directly on the Cash itself

(i) Burglary, i.e. deliberate theft by outsiders.

(ii) Theft of cash by the manager.

(iii) Theft of cash by the staff.

(iv) Incorrect change being given, either by accident or by design.

(v) Payment of fraudulent invoices or statements.

(vi) Payment of incorrect invoices or statements.

(vii) Making-up of wage packets for non-existent employees.

(b) Adverse Effects which operate Indirectly

(i) Theft of assets.

(ii) Theft of consumables.

(iii) Theft of stock by staff.

(iv) Passing-out of stock (to relatives and friends of staff).

(v) Shop-lifting.

(vi) Poor buying, e.g. wastage of perishable stock.

(vii) Excessive breakages, e.g. carelessness in the crockery department.

(viii) Excessive wear and tear on assets, e.g. use of company vehicles for private purposes.

(ix) Destruction of stock by fire, etc.

At least some of these adverse effects should be discernible from a study of your book-keeping records. Some help in their detection is given later in this book (see page 129), but it is very important to be alert at all times; to look for the assistant who is better dressed, or the manager who is more prosperous, than expected. If someone on the staff 'looks like a million dollars' it may well be *your* $1 000 000 she looks like.

2.3 Exercises on 'Cash Flows'

1. Explain the term 'cash flow' for the benefit of a young lady who proposes to set up in her local town as a florist. What sort of in-flows and out-flows of cash must she expect to meet during the first year of business life?

2. Asked by a school leaver what qualifications he needed in retail trade, the careers officer replied 'Honesty'. Why is honesty such an important qualification, and how would a dishonest employee affect 'cash flow' in any shop that employed him?

Unit Three

A Week's Accounting Records

3.1 The Simplex Page

Fig. 3.1 shows a page from a Simplex account book. The individual parts of this page will be examined in detail later; here it is only intended that the reader should note the layout, and how it is used to record the cash flows discussed in Unit 2. The illustration given in Fig. 3.1 is necessarily rather small. (The reader who is seriously considering adopting a Simplex system would be well advised to obtain a copy of the Simplex book and to study it in conjunction with the next few Units: understanding is much easier when the whole book is available full size.)

3.2 Advantages of the Weekly Layout

The most important feature of the Simplex layout is the fact that figures do not need to be carried forward from one week to another, except in the 'Weekly Cash Report' and 'Weekly Bank Report'. Here of course a balance is usually in hand at the end of each week and must be carried forward.

It is a great advantage to have the work of each week kept separate from the work of every other week. It means that you need not carry forward totals of most items from week to week. 'Carrying forward' is a tedious and time-consuming process; moreover, it prevents the records of the current week from being kept until the records of the previous week have been recorded and carried to the current week. Provided that you add up the various columns on the page, check the cash in the till and carry it forward, and carry forward what appears to be the bank figure, no other carrying forward is necessary immediately. All other items, expenses and turnover are carried from the page direct to a final summary at the back of the book. This work can be postponed until an odd minute is available, and at busy times it can be left for several weeks if necessary without any real inconvenience. Readers who have used traditional book-keeping methods, which require records to be carried forward from week to week, will see at once the advantages inherent in the Simplex system.

3.3 A Brief Look at the Various Sections

Each section of the page records a particular activity for a period of one week. These activities may be distinguished as follows.

(a) The 'Receipts' Section

Here are recorded the daily takings for each day of the week, separated off into 'Daily Takings (cash)', 'Daily Takings (cheques)' and 'Other Receipts'.

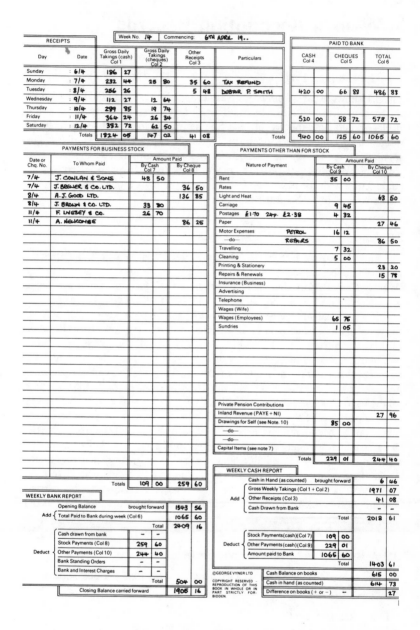

Fig. 3.1 *Layout of a Simplex page*

'Daily Takings' would be the cash flowing in from cash sales, i.e. a turnover flow. 'Other Receipts' would be chiefly debts collected, and occasionally rent paid by a sub-tenant, or tax refunds received.

A most important entry under 'Other Receipts' would be the cash or balance in the bank brought in as capital on the day the business commences. Similarly, any new funds or equipment contributed by the proprietor is really extra capital and should be recorded as an 'Other Receipt'. Another type of entry in this column would be loans received from outside bodies such as banks or finance houses, while a fourth type would be 'fees received' or 'commission received'. All such receipts should be entered at once.

Part of this 'Receipts' section is a 'Paid to Bank' column in which daily payments into the bank are recorded. Whenever cash is banked it must be recorded in the paying-in book, and the total paid in is then entered in the 'Paid to Bank' section.

The 'Particulars' column enables a short note to be made of any special items received. This is of great help when details of an item are called for at some future date—if, for example, it is queried by an inspector of taxes. Indeed, a brief note here may be self-explanatory to the inspector.

To summarize the 'Receipts' section, we can record each of the cash inflows shown in Fig. 2.1 as follows:

Table 3.1   Recording cash inflows

Inflow No.	Type of inflow	Column where recorded
1	Capital contribution	'Other Receipts'
2	Loans from outsiders	'Other Receipts'
3	Cash sales received in cash	'Daily Takings (cash)'
4	Cash sales received by cheque	'Daily Takings (cheques)'
5	Debts settled by customers	'Other Receipts'
6	Sundry earnings	'Other Receipts'

(b) The 'Payments for Business Stock' Section

In this section we record any payments made to suppliers for goods which are to be resold, or used in the business if it is a service trade. Many of these payments may be made in cash, or by cheque, direct to the carman at the time of delivery. Others will be made at a later date, depending on the credit-worthiness of the businessman and the custom of the trade. Usually the credit period is very short in trades where the goods are perishable; it is often longer for durable goods where the rate of turnover is slower.

Many businesses do not buy and sell goods, but instead offer a service. Thus a builder and decorator is not, like a retailer of electrical goods, buying appliances for resale to customers. Instead he buys bricks, lime, sand, paint, paper and other materials which will be embodied in the work done for his customers. All such purchases of stock 'to render a service' must be recorded as 'Payments for Business Stock' and will eventually appear in the Trading Account as one of the expenses to be charged against profits.

Whenever payments are made to suppliers, the name of the supplier is entered in the 'To Whom Paid' column, and the amount is entered in either the 'By Cash' or 'By Cheque' column, according to the method of payment used.

(c) The 'Payments Other than for Stock' Section

This section is used to record all payments other than 'turnover' payments for stock for resale or stock to render a service. Many of the items, such as rent and rates, are listed individually. There is a gap further down the page which separates items which are losses (or expenses) of the business from items that are not. Capital items, for example, are used permanently in the business and cannot be written off the profits except as depreciation. Drawings are not an expense of the business, nor are payments to the Inland Revenue. A more detailed explanation of these items is given later.

To summarize these payments sections, we can record each of the cash outflows shown in Fig. 2.1 as follows:

Table 3.2 Recording cash outflows

Outflow No.	Type of outflow	Section where recorded
1	Purchase of assets	Lower part of 'Other Payments' column
2	Consumable items and other expenses	Top part of 'Other Payments' column
3	Purchase of stock for resale or to render service	'Business Stock' column
4	Drawings	Lower part of 'Other Payments' column
5	Tax payments and other private payments	Lower part of 'Other Payments' column

(d) The Weekly Bank Report

The bank report opens with a balance brought forward from the previous week. To this is added the total paid into the bank during the week, and then various sums spent are deducted. These will all be cheques drawn, either for cash, payments to suppliers or payments for business expenses. There will also be deductions for any standing orders payable by the bank, and for bank charges. These items are explained more fully in Unit 16.

(e) The Weekly Cash Report

The cash report begins with a balance of cash brought forward from the previous week. To this is added the weekly takings, any other cash receipts and the cash drawn from the bank. This is then reduced by the amount of cash paid out for goods supplied and for business expenses, and by the total sums banked for the week. The balance of cash in hand is then checked against the till itself to ensure agreement. This figure in the till is entered in the 'Cash in Hand' section. Any difference between the calculated book figure and the actual cash in hand would have to be carefully investigated.

There is an important point about any 'difference on books'. If this item appears regularly the Inland Revenue are likely to take the view that it is 'hidden drawings'. After all, if cash is missing it is your job to find out why. Are staff stealing the takings? Are they so incompetent that they give wrong change? It is your job to solve these problems. If you do nothing they will conclude you are using the money personally and will add the total missing to your profits and tax it as profit you have taken as drawings, but not declared.

3.4 Conclusion

Each of the sections listed above is dealt with in detail in the next four Units. The main point of the Simplex layout is its simplicity in displaying every aspect necessary to the businessman (except his VAT commitments) on a single page each week. Special arrangements for dealing with VAT are discussed in Unit 18.

3.5 Exercises on the Layout of a Simplex Page

1. Write a sentence or two about each of the items listed below saying where you would record it on the Simplex page.
   (a) Cash takings of £195.65 on Wednesday 3rd July.
   (b) Cash takings of £272.50 and takings by cheque of £38.75 on Friday 5th July.
   (c) Goods delivered from Wholesale Supplies Ltd., for £84.50, which you paid for by giving a cheque to the delivery man on 4th July.
   (d) Payment of a month's rent, by cheque, £120.00 on 3rd July, by post.
   (e) Payment of income tax to the Inland Revenue on July 5th, £728.50.

2. Write a sentence or two about each of the items listed below saying where you would record it on the Simplex page, and how much the entry would be.
   (a) On Monday August 4th the till totals £85.60. There was a £5 float in the till at the start of the day.
   (b) A delivery man delivers goods valued at £48. You return him packing cases on which there is £4.80 refund, and the balance is paid by cheque to the delivery man.
   (c) The delivery man, whose lunchtime is due, agrees to help you move some heavy stock. You give him £1 to pay for his lunch.
   (d) The V.A.T. account for the quarter £785.60 is paid by cheque to H.M. Customs.
   (e) £220 is paid for a new till for the shop by cheque.

3. Explain why the Simplex system makes a special point of not carrying figures for receipts, payments for business stock etc., forward from week to week.

Unit Four

Recording Receipts

4.1 The Receipts Section of the Weekly Page

The section of the weekly page which is used for recording receipts is shown in Fig. 4.1. It has three columns which are directly concerned with receipts: one headed 'Gross Daily Takings (cash)', one headed 'Gross Daily Takings (cheques)' and one headed 'Other Receipts'. There is also a space for 'Particulars'. A separate column headed 'Paid to Bank' is provided for the proprietor to record any sums paid into his bank account during the week.

RECEIPTS								PAID TO BANK					
		Week No. 14		Commencing: 6TH APRIL 19..									
Day	Date	Gross Daily Takings (cash) Col 1		Gross Daily Takings (cheques) Col 2		Other Receipts Col 3		Particulars	CASH Col 4		CHEQUES Col 5		TOTAL Col 6	
Sunday	: 6/4	196	27										
Monday	: 7/4	232	44	28	80	35	60	TAX REFUND					
Tuesday	: 8/4	256	26			5	48	DEBTOR P. SMITH	420	00	66	88	486	88
Wednesday	: 9/4	112	27	12	64									
Thursday	: 10/4	299	85	19	74									
Friday	: 11/4	364	24	26	34				520	00	58	72	578	72
Saturday	: 12/4	392	72	62	50									
Totals		1824	05	147	02	41	08	Totals	940	00	125	60	1065	60

Fig. 4.1 *The 'Receipts' record on the weekly page*

Types of Receipt

The chief purpose of book-keeping records is to determine whether the business is profitable or not. In attempting to discover this, we must know about and follow certain guide-lines used since time immemorial to determine profit. These traditional criteria have been reaffirmed in recent years by decisions of the courts in inland-revenue cases. For better or worse, the profits of every business are a matter of keen interest to the Chancellor of the Exchequer and his representative—the local tax inspector. It follows that accounts prepared along unusual lines at the whim of the individual business-man can lead to disputes with the Inland Revenue authorities over the tax payable.

The basic formula in the calculation of profit is

$$\text{RECEIPTS } less \text{ EXPENSES} = \text{PROFIT}$$

However, the words 'receipts' and 'expenses' are too wide, and must be narrowed by a careful definition. For example, there are *capital receipts* which the business receives from the proprietor at the start of the enterprise, and there are *revenue receipts* which flow into the business as trading activities proceed and services are rendered to clients. Similarly, we can distinguish *capital expenditure* (such as the purchase of business assets) from *revenue expenditure* (such as the purchase of consumable items necessary to the conduct of the firm, payment of wages, telephone and motor-vehicle expenses). This distinction is important because *capital* receipts and *capital* expenditure are *not* taken into account in a proper calculation of profit. Profit is in fact determined by the formula:

REVENUE RECEIPTS *less* REVENUE EXPENDITURE = PROFIT

The separate identification of capital items and revenue items is a fundamental principle of accounting, and is essential to the keeping of correct records.

(*a*) **Revenue receipts** consist of all those receipts which result from the normal activities of the business. They may be

(i) daily takings resulting from the sale of goods,
(ii) daily takings resulting from the provision of services, or
(iii) miscellaneous receipts.

Miscellaneous receipts are those which arise from some incidental activity other than the main business activity, and which ought properly to be regarded as income of the proprietor. For example, if a businessman sub-lets part of his premises, the rent he receives represents an income to him which should be included in the profits of the business.

(*b*) **Revenue expenditure** includes all those expenses *incurred directly in the earning of the revenue receipts listed above*, provided that the benefits received from the expenditure do not last longer than one year. Thus the purchase of goods for resale is a revenue expense, but the purchase of furniture or motor vehicles is not, since these items are expected to last for longer than one year.

A full discussion of the calculation of profits will be easier to understand after we have considered receipts and expenditure, and is therefore left until Unit 21. Let us now return to examining the 'Receipts' section of the weekly page. As we do so, bear in mind that we must distinguish between those receipts of a 'revenue' nature, which will need to be used in calculating the profits, and those which can be properly disregarded when profits are worked out at the end of the financial year.

4.2 The 'Daily Takings' Column

The daily takings of the business are the total amount of cash in the tills at the end of the day, less any float which may have been put there at the start of the day. Instead of waiting until the actual moment of closing the premises to discover the daily-takings figure, it is is often more convenient to cash up a little before closing time and extract from the tills all that has been taken so far that day. Any further takings that day will be treated as takings of the following day, and will be placed in the till with the float the following morning. The daily takings are recorded in the appropriate columns of the Simplex page as shown in Fig. 4.1.

Safety Measures with Daily Takings

Business premises are a common target for thieves, and every precaution should be taken to ensure that if burglaries are unavoidable they are at any rate unfruitful. Both the daily takings and the cash floats should be removed from the tills after business hours—and the tills should be left open. (A till that is left open is less liable to be broken or even removed bodily by the thief; the loss of a till can be both expensive and inconvenient.)

The daily takings may be deposited in the night-safe of a local bank. A charge is made for this service, but it might well prove to be the most satisfactory method of safeguarding cash overnight. Takings may instead be taken home, at some risk to the proprietor, who should certainly install a good safe if this is his regular practice. The cash floats for the tills next day should also be taken home, preferably in separate bags indicating to which till they belong. Obvious safeguards, such as taking different routes to the bank each night, should never be neglected.

The Problem of Debtors

If a customer is given credit he becomes a debtor. Debtors present an accounting problem to the trader, quite apart from the usual problem of getting them to pay. The nature of the accounting problem is whether the goods should be regarded as (*a*) sold (in which case the amount of this 'credit sale' must be included in the daily takings), or (*b*) not sold until they are actually paid for (in which case the goods must be imagined as still being in stock, even though in reality the debtor has them and may be using them).

The second method is the simpler, since the goods are not yielding any profit until they are actually paid for. On the whole, however, the first method is preferable, since in law the goods become the property of the buyer at the moment that the parties intend the property to pass; it makes no difference if the payment is postponed by giving the buyer credit.

No matter which solution to the accounting problem he adopts, the trader who gives credit should keep a *debtors' record book* in which all debts are written down day by day as they occur, with the name, address, brief details of the goods, and amount. An example of such a record is shown in Fig. 4.2.

(*a*) **Regarding goods as not sold until paid for, but as 'Stock out to Customers'.** In this method credit sales are entered in a debtors' record book as described above, but are disregarded for 'takings' purposes.

When a debtor pays a debt the following action should be taken:

(i) Cross out the debt in the debtors' book by scoring it through.

(ii) Record the cash in the 'Daily Takings' column in the normal way.

This method is the simplest method for most traders.

(*b*) **Regarding goods sold on credit as 'sold'.** At the end of every week draw a clear line across the debtors' book, add up the week's debts and add the total to the week's takings before it is posted to the analysis column at the end of the book (see below).

When a debtor pays a debt the following action should be taken:
  (i) Cross out the debt in the debtors' book by scoring it through.
  (ii) Record the cash paid, not as 'Daily Takings' but as 'Other Receipts'. This ensures that the cash will not be counted twice, since we have already included the sale of the goods in the weekly takings during the week they were sold. Now that the goods are actually being paid for, the cash is entered as an 'Other Receipt'. This is explained more fully below.

19..		Paid on	£	
Nov	1	Mrs. Smith, 2, River Road	5 Nov	5	48
	1	Mrs. P. Jones , 3, Hill Road		3	25
	3	R. Tyler (Mr.), 4, Combe Close		7	28
	4	L. Brown (Miss), 27, High St.		1	52
	4	R. Johnson (Mrs), 48 Parker Place		0	48
	5	Total for week		18	01

Include this total in the week's takings

Fig. 4.2 *A simple debtors' record book*

4.3 Transferring 'Daily Takings' to the 'Weekly Summary of Takings'

At the end of each week the total figure of the 'Daily Takings' columns (cash and cheques added together) must be transferred to the 'Weekly Summary of Takings' page, near the end of the Simplex book. This is shown in Fig. 4.3.

If you allow credit to some customers, and regard the goods as sold at once (method (b) above), the total debts accepted in the week—found by adding up the debtors' record book—should be added to the total of the 'Daily Takings' columns to give the correct total sales for the week. The layout of this summary page (Fig 4.2 overleaf) in the Simplex book permits the trader to draw up quarterly and annual figures, from which he may prepare his Trading Account. (see Section 21.2). Note that if you use method (a) for debtors, the outstanding debtors at the end of the year must be added to the total sales for the year in the box provided.

What to do with Cheques received in the Daily Takings

Cheques received as part of the daily takings are entered in the 'Gross Daily Takings (cheques)' column and are then added to the cash takings to be recorded in the summary. They will of course be paid into the bank, and consequently will appear in the 'Paid to Bank' column, along with the cash paid in at regular intervals. A businessman whose takings are considerable should bank daily, using the night-safe service if necessary.

WEEKLY SUMMARY OF TAKINGS

WEEK No.	AMOUNT	WEEK No.	AMOUNT	WEEK No.	AMOUNT	WEEK No.	AMOUNT		
1	1326 42	14	1971 07	27	1784 60	40	1721 30		
2	1372 56	15	1485 90	28	1886 20	41	1562 55		
3	1428 60	16	1276 13	29	1654 40	42	1472 80		
4	1418 55	17	1732 50	30	1420 50	43	1459 60		
5	1422 30	18	1426 50	31	1428 50	44	1473 28		
6	1384 60	19	1388 60	32	1556 60	45	1426 40		
7	1372 60	20	1785 60	33	1495 90	46	1389 85		
8	1426 50	21	1685 60	34	1480 01	47	1427 30		
9	1732 80	22	1526 60	35	1630 27	48	1625 46	Total Summary for Year	
10	1688 80	23	1430 40	36	1680 48	49	1752 80	1st Qtr.	19428 03
11	1725 60	24	1480 40	37	1690 25	50	2120 50	2nd Qtr.	20403 50
12	1642 40	25	1492 60	38	1685 72	51	2750 25	3rd Qtr.	21112 03
13	1486 30	26	1721 60	39	1738 60	52	1408 39	4th Qtr.	21590 48
						53		Trade Debtors	465 50
Total 1st Qtr.	19428 03	Total 2nd Qtr.	20403 50	Total 3rd Qtr.	21112 03	Total 4th Qtr.	21590 48	TOTAL	82999 54

Fig. 4.3 *The Simplex 'Weekly Summary of Takings'*

4.4 Other Receipts

Four main types of receipt come under the heading 'Other Receipts'. These are listed below.

Type of Receipt	*Explanation*
(a) Payments by debtors	The goods being paid for may have been regarded as 'sold' when they were supplied to the debtor. If so, no action is necessary now to include the receipt in daily takings, for it will already have been included in 'takings' at an earlier date. The money received must be included in the Weekly Cash Report. If goods sold to debtors were not treated as 'sold' until paid for, the receipt must now be treated as cash takings and should therefore be included in the 'weekly takings' figure. The cash received must also be carried to the Cash Summary (or, in the case of cheques, to the Bank Summary).
(b) Capital receipts	The capital provided by the proprietor when a business is launched is obviously a capital receipt. However, many small businesses are kept going in the first few months by the proprietor paying out of his private funds for goods and services, and it is important to realize that these payments are in fact capital contributions which should be recorded as 'Other Receipts'. We may also have capital receipts from the sale of surplus assets or worn-out assets. These receipts must

Type of Receipt	Explanation
	be collected together in one place for inclusion in the capital of the business.
	A special summary column for 'Other Receipts' in the back of the Simplex D Book can be used to record these capital receipts. The column is headed 'Extra capital introduced'.
(c) Revenue receipts	These are similar to daily takings, but are not the usual type of items included under that heading. Common examples are rent and commission received. Another example is the 'Enterprise Allowance' (see page 175). Revenue receipts must be included when calculating the profits at the end of the year.
	On rare occasions we receive money which is accountable for tax purposes, because it has avoided tax beforehand. The most likely example is a 'bad debt recovered'. (Where a debt has been previously written off as bad, it has been deducted as a loss in the accounts.) If such a debtor pays up, the sum received is treated as a revenue receipt, since it is taxable.
	A special summary column for these miscellaneous receipts will be found at the back of the Simplex book. They will then be brought into the Profit and Loss Account at the end of the year.
(d) Occasional non-revenue receipts	On rare occasions we receive money which is not accountable for tax purposes, since it has been used to calculate tax already. Examples are income-tax refunds. These occasional non-revenue receipts are best recorded in the same place as 'capital receipts' (see above), since they are like profits of former years ploughed back into the business. Similarly 'Loans' arranged are not taxable, and should be taken to the special summary at the back of the Simplex book.

4.5 Summary: What to do to record Receipts

The actions to be taken by the user of a 'Simplex' system to record various types of receipt are summarized diagrammatically in Fig. 4.4 overleaf.

4.6 Payments to the Bank

Most retailers bank daily, large firms bank two or three times a day. Care should be taken when banking takings, and times and routes to the bank should be varied. The cash to be banked, and any cheques received, are listed

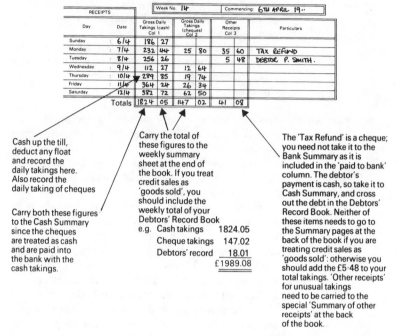

RECEIPTS		Week No. 14		Commencing: 6TH APRIL 19··			
Day	Date	Gross Daily Takings (cash) Col 1		Gross Daily Takings (cheques) Col 2		Other Receipts Col 3	Particulars
Sunday	: 6/4	186	27				
Monday	: 7/4	232	44	25	80	35	60	TAX REFUND
Tuesday	: 8/4	256	26			5	48	DEBTOR P. SMITH.
Wednesday	: 9/4	112	27	12	64		
Thursday	: 10/4	289	85	19	74		
Friday	: 11/4	364	24	26	34		
Saturday	12/4	382	72	62	50		
	Totals	1824	05	147	02	41	08	

Cash up the till, deduct any float and record the daily takings here. Also record the daily taking of cheques

Carry both these figures to the Cash Summary since the cheques are treated as cash and are paid into the bank with the cash takings.

Carry the total of these figures to the weekly summary sheet at the end of the book. If you treat credit sales as 'goods sold', you should include the weekly total of your Debtors' Record Book e.g. Cash takings   1824.05
Cheque takings   147.02
Debtors' record   18.01
                          £1989.08

The 'Tax Refund' is a cheque; you need not take it to the Bank Summary as it is included in the 'paid to bank' column. The debtor's payment is cash, so take it to Cash Summary, and cross out the debt in the Debtors' Record Book. Neither of these items needs to go to the Summary pages at the back of the book if you are treating credit sales as 'goods sold': otherwise you should add the £5·48 to your total takings. 'Other receipts' for unusual takings need to be carried to the special 'Summary of other receipts' at the back of the book.

Fig. 4.4 *Recording receipts under the Simplex system*

RECEIPTS		PAID TO BANK					
Day	Date	CASH Col 4		CHEQUES Col 5		TOTAL Col 6	
Sunday	: 6/4						
Monday	: 7/4						
Tuesday	: 8/4	420	00	66	88	486	88
Wednesday	: 9/4						
Thursday	: 10/4						
Friday	: 11/4	520	00	58	72	578	72
Saturday	: 12/4						
	Totals	940	00	125	60	1065	60

Daily lodgements as per bank paying-in book

Combined total is transferred to both the Weekly Cash Report (reducing the cash balance) and the Weekly Bank Report (increasing the bank balance)

Fig. 4.5 *The Simplex 'Paid to Bank' column*

in the paying-in book and the total figure is inserted in the 'Paid to Bank' column of the Simplex book (see Fig. 4.5). The weekly total of takings banked is then transferred to both the Weekly Bank Report and the Weekly Cash Report. It represents an increase in the 'Bank' balance and a decrease in the 'Cash' balance in hand.

4.7 Exercises on the Recording of Receipts

Using some of the special paper ruled for Simplex accounting (obtainable from George Vyner Ltd., at reasonable prices) enter the following items in the Receipts section, and total the necessary columns. Compare your answer with the Answer Section at the back of the book.

1. Tom Brown uses the Simplex D Account Book. It is week No. 27 and the week commences on Sunday 1st October. Sales in cash each day are as follows: Monday £117.20; Tuesday £185.50; Wednesday £48.90; Thursday £386.50; Friday £477.25 and Saturday £562.00. On Monday he also sold goods for a cheque £73.65. On Wednesday he is notified that he has won £728.50 on the Football Pools and decides to put £500 in as extra capital. He banks on Tuesday £200 cash and a cheque for £73.65, and on Friday Cash £750 and the football pools money, a cheque for £500 from his personal bank account. Make all these entries and total the various columns.

2. M. Lipton uses the Simplex D Account Book. It is Week No. 15 and the week commences on July 9th. Sales in cash each day are as follows: Monday, £48.65; Tuesday £72.65; Wednesday £84.50; Thursday £229.75; Friday £347.50; Saturday £492.85.

He also takes a cheque on Tuesday for £100.00. On Friday he received a sum of money by cheque from a tenant for rent £52.00. He pays £200 into the bank on Wednesday consisting of cash £100.00 and cheques £100.00 and on Friday he pays in £402.00, made up of cash £350 and cheques £52.00. Make all these entries and total the various columns.

3. R. T. Crafty uses the Simplex D Account Book. His week No. is 52 and the week commences on 26th March. Sales in cash each day are as follows: Monday £137.50; Tuesday £246.20; Wednesday £384.50; Thursday £74.00; Friday £386.50; Saturday £296.55.

He also takes a cheque on Thursday for £118.45. On Friday he receives a sum of money in cash from A. Debtor £18.25. He pays £350.00 into the bank on Wednesday, consisting of cash only. On Friday he pays in £400.00 made up of cash £281.55 and cheques £118.45. Make all these entries and total the various columns.

4. Anne Accountant uses the Simplex D Account Book. It is Week No. 17 and the week commences on 23rd July. Fees received are mostly paid by cheque and each day are as follows: Monday £25.00; Tuesday £482.50; Wednesday £36.50; Thursday nil; Friday £28.50. Only Friday's payment was in cash.

She also receives a cheque on Wednesday for £42.50 from a debt collection agency. On Friday she receives a sum of money in cash £14.50 for the use of a machine loaned to a fellow accountant. She pays £586.50 into the bank on Thursday, all in cheques. Make all these entries and total the various columns.

Unit Five

Recording Purchases of Stock for Resale or to Render a Service

5.1 Purchases

The word 'purchases' has a special meaning in book-keeping. In everyday language anything that is bought is a 'purchase', but in business use the word is understood to mean 'a purchase of goods for resale or to render a service'. Depending on the type of business, it is the opposite of the word 'sales' or the opposite of the phrase 'fees for services rendered'. 'Purchases' come into the business, and require to be paid for by the proprietor; 'sales' go out of the business, and are paid for by the customer. The difference between the two gives the profit of the enterprise, and is found by the formula

$$\text{SALES} - \text{PURCHASES} = \text{PROFIT}$$

However, the cost of its 'purchases' is far from being the only expense that a business incurs: there are of course running costs and overheads to be considered. Similarly, sales are not the only receipts. Accountants talk therefore about 'gross profit' and 'net profit'. Gross profit means 'fat' profit, or total profit. Net profit means 'clean' profit, or clear profit.

$$\text{GROSS PROFIT} = \text{SALES} - \text{PURCHASES}$$
$$\text{NET PROFIT} = \text{GROSS PROFIT} + \text{MISC. RECEIPTS} - \text{EXPENSES}$$

In Unit 4 we saw that the daily takings, or 'sales', are recorded in the 'Receipts' section of the Simplex page. The 'purchases' are recorded in the 'Payments for Business Stock' section of the Simplex page, as shown in Fig. 5.1.

5.2 Recording Purchases

When goods are purchased they may be paid for in cash or by cheque. Payment may be made to the carman who delivers the goods, or by post. There will usually be some document available to inform the businessman of the value of the consignment, and on which a receipt can be obtained. Cheques are, in themselves, receipts once they have been stamped 'paid' by the banker, but the trader is still entitled under the Cheques Act, 1957, to ask for a receipt for the sum paid. The types of document used in the transactions are described in detail below. Here we are solely concerned with the record made of payments for purchases.

As shown in Fig. 5.1 the amounts paid are recorded by writing down the name of the payee, and the amount. If the payment was a cash payment it is recorded in the 'By Cash' column. If the payment was by cheque it is recorded in the 'By Cheque' column. At the end of the week the two columns are totalled. The two amounts, 'total cash paid' and 'total cheques paid', are added together and entered in the 'Weekly Summary of Payments for Goods Purchased' (see Fig. 5.2) as the total purchases for the week. Once again the

Date or Chq. No.	To Whom Paid	Amount Paid	
		By Cash Col 6	By Cheque Col 7
7/4	J. CONLAN AND SONS	48 50	
7/4	J. BREWER & CO LTD		36 50
8/4	A. J. GOOD LTD		136 85
8/4	J. BROWN & CO LTD	33 80	
11/4	F. LIVESEY & CO	26 70	
11/4	A. NEWCOMBE		86 25
	Totals	109 00	259 60

PAYMENTS FOR BUSINESS STOCK

Fig. 5.1 *The recording of 'purchases' in the Simplex system*

system permits quarterly totals and an annual total to be prepared. This annual total is transferred to the Trading Account, where it is used to find the Gross Profit of the business.

5.3 Documents for Goods Purchased

(a) **Invoices.** An invoice is defined as 'a document which is made out by the seller when he sells goods to a customer'. Most suppliers use a multi-copy system of invoices similar to the batch shown in Fig. 5.3. Such a multi-copy system enables the supplier to start in motion the various activities that are required to deal with the fulfilment of an order. The distribution of invoices from the popular five-copy system is as follows:

WEEKLY SUMMARY OF PAYMENTS FOR GOODS PURCHASED

WEEK No.	AMOUNT		WEEK No.	AMOUNT		WEEK No.	AMOUNT		WEEK No.	AMOUNT	
1	285	50	14	368	60	27	880	60	40	860	25
2	292	70	15	572	32	28	884	40	41	526	30
3	324	26	16	426	24	29	552	60	42	539	45
4	315	30	17	380	50	30	380	42	43	542	60
5	444	25	18	515	30	31	520	32	44	532	75
6	385	00	19	472	40	32	640	62	45	674	50
7	362	60	20	658	20	33	806	82	46	779	25
8	358	60	21	800	50	34	1240	20	47	638	40
9	327	20	22	572	40	35	820	15	48	1268	27
10	1236	40	23	786	30	36	430	24	49	1272	30
11	295	55	24	980	42	37	840	25	50	1428	50
12	1226	30	25	825	30	38	400	60	51	1784	25
13	801	40	26	1406	12	39	480	45	52	1210	20
									53		
Total 1st Qtr.	6655	06	Total 2nd Qtr.	8764	60	Total 3rd Qtr.	8877	67	Total 4th Qtr.	12057	02

Total Summary for Year

1st Qtr.	6655	06
2nd Qtr.	8764	60
3rd Qtr.	8877	67
4th Qtr.	12057	02
Purchases Creditors	142	50
TOTAL	36496	85

Fig. 5.2 *The Simplex weekly summary of payments for goods purchased*

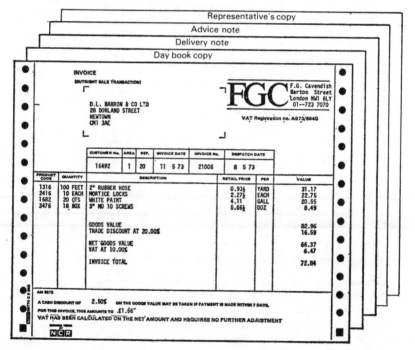

Fig. 5.3 *A set of invoices for goods purchased*

(i) The *top copy* is sent by post to the customer to notify him that the order is in hand and should be delivered shortly.

(ii) The second copy or *day-book copy* is sent to the supplier's accounts department. Here it is used to debit the customer's account now that he has become a debtor.

(iii) and (iv) The third copy or *delivery note* is sent with the fourth copy or *advice note* to the stock department. Here they are used to authorize the removal of the goods from stock, and to send them with the documents to the dispatch department. The advice note is packed with the goods, to inform the buyer of the contents of the parcel or consignment. The delivery note is given to the carman, who gets a signature for the goods on delivery.

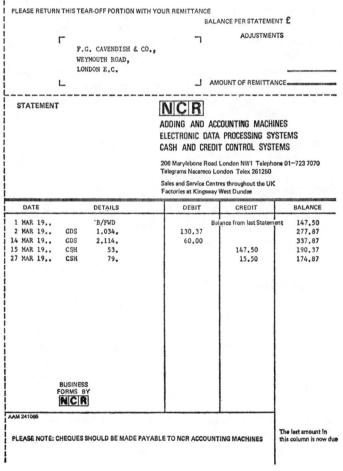

Fig. 5.4 *A mechanized statement of account*

This acknowledgment of safe delivery is returned to the stock department or dispatch department.

(v) The fifth copy or *representative's copy* is sent to the commercial traveller who took the order to inform him that it has been fulfilled.

Invoices should always be preserved, either in an indexed lever-arch file or in a 'concertina' file. Since the trader usually receives two copies—the top copy and the advice note—he should clip them together when both are available.

(b) **Credit Notes.** A credit note is a document made out whenever one person returns goods to another. The credit note is always made out by the seller, who is now receiving back the goods which are unsatisfactory for some reason. It leads to a reduction in the debt of the customer or, if he pays cash, to a reduction in the amount payable on the next occasion that he places an order. Credit notes should be filed in the same way as invoices in a lever-arch file or a concertina file.

(c) **Statements.** A trader who is given credit is expected to pay, not on delivery, but when a *Statement of Account* is rendered—usually at the end of the month. These days statements are often prepared on a book-keeping machine at the same time that the ledger card for the customer is up-dated. A trader who receives this mechanized type of statement can use it to check his own records of the goods invoiced to him in the trading period covered by the statement. Returns credited to him should also be shown as a reduction in the amount owed. A typical statement of account is shown in Fig. 5.4.

5.4 Purchases taken from Stock for Use by the Proprietor

An item which indirectly affects the 'Payments for Business Stock' is the taking home of goods for use by the proprietor. The method of dealing with this item is given later (see Section 21.2).

5.5 Transferring 'Payments for Business Stock' to the 'Weekly Summary of Payments for Goods Purchased'

As with the Weekly Summary of Takings the Weekly Summary of Goods Purchased (Fig. 5.2 p.22) enables the trader to collect together the total quarterly and yearly figures for purchases. The 'purchases' for the year will then be used to work out the profits of the business in the Trading Account. Note that if there are any trade creditors, whose bills have not yet been paid, they must be included in the final figures by recording the total trade creditors in the box provided before adding up the total for the year.

5.6 Exercises in Recording Payments for Business Stock

1. M. Phillips records on his Simplex page under the heading 'Payments for Business Stock' the following items during the week.

July   7.   Paid to R. Corbett by cheque £25.74 and to S. Tims in cash £5.40.
July   8.   Paid to McKrill Biscuit Co., by cheque £85.50 and to Prepared Foods Ltd., £46.50 by cheque.

July 9. Paid to R. Masterson by cheque £27.25 and to The Mineral Water Co. Ltd., in cash £25.85.

July 13. Paid to M. Laws by cheque £17.25.

Enter these items and total the 'cash' and 'cheque' columns.

2. R. Walford records on his Simplex page under the heading 'Payments for Business Stock' the following items during the week.

Aug. 14. Paid to M. Rogerson by cheque £27.55 and to B. Laker by cheque £13.50.

Aug. 16. Paid to A. Waterson in cash the sum of £25.80 for materials supplied.

Aug. 18. A delivery from R. Cook & Co., is valued at £48.50 but returns amounting to £7.25 are given by Walford to the van driver. The net amount is paid in cash.

Enter these items and total the 'cash' and 'cheque' columns.

3. Mary Toft records on her Simplex pages under the heading 'Payments for Business Stock' the following items during the week.

Oct. 7. Paid to T. Ludd by cheque £28.74 and to S. Thames in cash £5.46.

Oct. 8. Paid to Water Biscuit Co. Ltd., by cheque £88.50 and to Novel Foods Ltd., £48.50 by cheque.

Oct. 9. Paid to R. Smiley by cheque £112.00 and to Fresh Vegetables Ltd., in cash £7.35.

Oct. 13. Paid to M. Lawson by cheque £14.25.

Enter these items and total the 'cash' and 'cheques' columns.

4. R. Bliss records on his Simplex page under the heading 'Payments for Business Stock' the following items during the week.

May 24. Paid to M. Lawrence by cheque £24.25 and to K. Mayman by cheque £27.20.

May 26. Paid to R. Brett in cash the sum of £13.25.

May 28. A delivery from Utopia Ltd., is valued at £42.80 but returns amounting to £5.00 are given by Bliss to the van driver. The net amount is paid in cash.

Enter these items and total the 'cash' and 'cheques' columns.

Unit Six

Recording Payments Other than for Stock

6.1 Payments Other than for Stock

We have already seen in Unit 5 that stock for resale and stock to render service is purchased throughout the year and is recorded in the 'Payments for Business Stock' section of the weekly page. In addition, many items which are not for resale, but are for use in the business, are purchased when required. These may be either *consumable items* (such as petrol and oil, office stationery and postage stamps) or *capital items* (such as machinery, typewriters, furniture and fittings). A third kind of payment is that made for *services rendered* to the business (such as wages, rent and insurance).

Nature of Payment	Amount Paid			
	By Cash Col 8		By Cheque Col 9	
PAYMENTS OTHER THAN FOR STOCK				
Rent			180	00
Rates				
Light and Heat			70	67
Carriage	7	56		
Postages £1·70 54p £3·18	5	42		
Paper			27	54
Motor Expenses PETROL	18	56		
—do— SERVICING	83	50		
Travelling	7	42		
Cleaning	8	50		
Printing & Stationery			23	25
Repairs & Renewals			78	56
Insurance (Business)				
Advertising				
Telephone				
Wages (Wife)				
Wages (Employees)	87	50		
Sundries PAPER BAGS	1	05		
VALUE ADDED TAX			2107	50
Private Pension Contributions				
Inland Revenue (PAYE + NI)			83	66
Drawings for Self (see Note. 10)	80	00		
—do—				
—do—				
Capital Items (see note 7) SHELF UNIT	32	00		
Totals	331	51	2571	18

Fig. 6.1 *Recording payments other than for stock*

All these payments, which may be called *working expenses*, must be recorded on the weekly page, in the section shown in Fig. 6.1.

Finally there are some rather specialized items, such as payment of income tax to the Inland Revenue, of Value Added Tax to the Customs & Excise, and drawings by the proprietor. These are not 'working' expenses, but are recorded on the weekly page in the same way.

6.2 Recording Working Expenses

Working expenses, i.e. payments for consumables and services received, may be paid in cash or by cheque. It will often be the case that only one entry per week appears under each heading. For example, rent is unlikely to be paid twice in one week; possibly it will only be paid once a quarter or once a month. But some items (such as postage) are paid more frequently than once per week. In this case it is usual to jot down at some convenient spot on the page such items as they occur. The total can then be entered in the cash or cheque column on the last day of the week. This method may be seen on the 'postages' line in Fig. 6.1.

Summarizing the Expenses of the Business

The Simplex weekly page is designed to record each week's receipts and payments on a single sheet of paper. To calculate the profits of the business we must collect together all these items into an annual figure. We have already seen how the daily takings are summarized (see Section 4.3) and how purchases of business stock are summarized (see Section 5.2).

Fig. 6.2 shows the 'Summary of Payments for Expenses' page which appears near the end of the Simplex book. The weekly figures are transferred from the 'Payments Other than for Stock' columns (Fig. 6.1) to this summary, where they are added together to give quarterly totals. The quarterly totals are eventually added to give annual totals, which can then be transferred to the Profit and Loss Account to determine the profits for the year.

6.3 Recording Capital Items

The 'Payments Other than for Stock' section is divided by the printer into two parts, the top part being used to record payments for working expenses, and the lower part for other payments. Capital items, which are unlikely to occur very frequently once the business is actually under way, are recorded at the bottom of the page. Some indication of the item purchased should be written in the space next to the words 'Capital Items'. Thus (taking an example from Fig. 6.1) a typical entry might be: 'Shelf unit . . . £32. It does not matter whether the item is new or second-hand: provided that it is one of permanent use to the trader in the conduct of his affairs, and likely to last more than one year, it is treated as a capital asset.

Capital expenses are not losses of the business, and are not therefore summarized in the same way as expenses. There will not be many of them,

28 Recording Payments Other than for Stock

Week No.	Rent and Rates	Light and Heat	Carriage and Postages	Paper	Motor Expenses	Motor Expenses	Travelling	Cleaning	Printing and Stationery	Repairs and Renewals
1	520 00		12 36					32 00		
2			4 56		16 95			32 00		
3	236 50		7 32		9 12			32 00		
4			6 15		13 15			39 50		
5		86 26	5 29		16 12			32 00		36 25
6		42 60	2 34	27 63			13 24	32 00		
7			13 75		14 10			32 00		
8			12 94		15 12			32 00		
9			4 25		11 27			42 50		
10			6 25		36 19			32 00	36 38	
11			7 13		14 12			32 00		
12			8 01		15 06			32 00		
13			9 94		13 72			35 00		
1st Qtr.	756 50	128 85	100 29	27 63	174 92	– –	13 24	437 00	36 38	36 25
14			11 36		17 46			32 00		
15	520 00		5 17		12 37			32 00		
16			8 64				23 68	32 00		
17			6 25		8 54	168 54		34 50		
18		62 30	17 83	27 63	18 49			32 00		127 32
19		35 14	1 75		13 28			32 00		
20			24 40				16 28	32 00		
21			13 25		11 63			32 00		
22			16 01		9 17			39 50		
23			19 14	14 92	19 51			32 00		
24			14 60		14 42			32 00		
25			1 75		11 72			42 50		
26			7 99		16 58			32 00		
2nd Qtr.	520 00	97 44	148 14	42 55	153 17	168 54	39 96	436 50	– –	127 32
27	520 00		14 27		15 24			35 00		
28			3 18				14 92	41 25		
29			2 46		18 57			35 00		
30			15 25		27 32			35 00		
31	236 50	44 60	6 13	28 14	12 54			36 00	47 22	
32		25 50	5 73		14 46			46 25		
33			28 82				16 25	35 00		
34			7 87		16 68			35 00		
35			19 54		23 17			40 30		
36			6 75		45 76			35 00		
37			11 46	28 32	39 24			35 00		
38			4 21		15 76			35 00		
39			12 54	15 04	21 83			35 00		
3rd Qtr.	756 50	70 10	138 21	71 50	250 57		31 17	477 80	47 22	– –
40			4 42		23 74			35 00		
41	520 00		14 86		12 49			35 00		
42			7 71		14 61			35 00		
43			19 39	28 32	25 57			35 00	18 15	
44			7 19				86 71	48 50		
45			13 58		26 38			35 00		
46		79 85	12 88		10 26	131 26		35 00		28 94
47		62 80	2 29		12 43			39 50		
48			3 84		27 51			35 00		
49			8 14		15 17			35 00		
50			4 12	15 14	19 36			43 25		
51			14 61		18 20			35 00		
52			17 16		11 44			35 00		
53										
4th Qtr.	520 00	142 65	130 19	43 46	217 17	131 26	86 71	481 25	18 15	28 94
Annual Total	2553 00	439 04	516 83	185 14	795 83	299 80	171 08	1832 55	101 75	192 51

Fig. 6.2 *Summary of*

FOR EXPENSES

Week No.	Insurance (Business)	Advertising	Telephone	Sundries						Wages	Inland Revenue	Total
1										68 00		632 36
2										68 00		121 51
3										68 00		352 94
4										68 00	148 50	275 30
5	50 00									78 00		303 91
6			324 00							78 00		519 81
7										85 00		144 85
8		272 50								85 00	156 20	573 76
9				24 30						165 00		247 32
10										165 00		275 82
11										165 00		218 25
12										165 00	176 30	396 37
13										165 00		223 66
1st Qtr	50 00	272 50	324 00	24 30						1423 00	481 00	4285 86
14										165 00		225 82
15										165 00		734 54
16										165 00	176 30	405 62
17				1 52						165 00		384 35
18			423 00							124 50		833 07
19				3 56						124 50		210 23
20										124 50	138 20	335 38
21		86 40								124 50		267 78
22				29 62						124 50		218 80
23										168 00		253 57
24										168 00	143 40	372 42
25										168 00		223 97
26										168 00		224 57
2nd Qtr	—	86 40	423 00	34 70						1954 50	457 90	4690 12
27										168 00		752 51
28										168 00	159 90	387 25
29										168 00		224 03
30										168 00		245 57
31			375 00							168 00		953 13
32	95 20									168 00	86 54	441 68
33										85 55		165 62
34				29 85						85 55		174 95
35										85 55		168 56
36										85 55	112 25	285 31
37										85 55		199 57
38										85 55		140 52
39										85 55		169 96
3rd Qtr	95 20	—	375 00	29 85						1606 85	358 69	4308 66
40										173 40	147 27	383 83
41										173 40		755 75
42				12 17						173 40		242 90
43			416 00							173 40		715 83
44										173 40	169 50	485 30
45		163 60								173 40		411 96
46										173 40		471 59
47				14 97						173 40		305 39
48										173 40	108 24	347 99
49										173 40		231 71
50										168 00		249 87
51										168 00		235 81
52										168 00	106 71	338 32
53												
4th Qtr	—	163 60	416 00	27 14						2238 00	531 73	5176 25
Annual Total	145 20	522 50	1538 00	115 99						7222 35	1829 32	18460 89

payments for expenses

and those there are will merely add to the value of the assets of the business. They are recorded near the back of the Simplex book in a table headed 'Capital Expenses Incurred During The Year'. This is shown in Fig. 6.3.

DATE	NATURE AND FULL DETAILS OF EXPENSE	INVOICE TOTAL		NET VALUE OF ASSET		VAT	
19.. JAN 31	WEIGHING MACHINE (REF 2/5/17405)	234	75	204	14	30	61
JUNE 7	ELECTRONIC TILL (MICROLEADER 4/732/5A)	438	20	381	04	57	16
NOV 7	SHELF UNITS (6 × 6FT × 6 SHELVES)	136	00	118	26	17	74

CAPITAL EXPENSES INCURRED DURING THE YEAR

Fig. 6.3 *Recording additions to assets during the year*

6.4 Recording Drawings for Self

The proprietor of a business draws sums of money in expectation of profit, for the support of himself and his family. These payments by the business to the proprietor are therefore quite different from any other type of payment. A full explanation of these drawings is given later; at the moment it is only necessary to note that they are recorded in the lower part of the 'Payments Other than for Stock columns, just above capital items. The drawings are then carried to a Summary of Drawings for Self, as shown in Fig. 6.4 opposite. Space is available for up to three partners.

6.5 Recording Tax Payments

Every trader is liable to pay tax on his profits twice during the year, on January 1st and July 1st. Companies are liable to pay Corporation Tax on January 1st in a single lump sum. A businessman who is also an employer must deduct tax from employees' wages and remit it to the Inland Revenue monthly (or quarterly if the sums involved are small). In addition, all businessmen whose turnover exceeds £19 500 per annum must charge their customers with Value Added Tax and account for it to the Customs & Excise at the end of each quarterly taxation period. (A full description of Value Added Tax is given in Unit 18, including, the Special Schemes for Retailers.)

Whenever such payments are made they are recorded in the Simplex system in the 'Payments Other than for Stock' section, as shown in Fig. 6.1. The total sums paid in this way are collected together for convenience on the 'Summary of Payments for Expenses' sheet (see Fig. 6.2), but they are different from other

SUMMARY OF DRAWINGS FOR SELF

Week No.	Partner 1		Partner 2		Partner 3	Week No	Partner 1		Partner 2		Partner 3	Yearly Summary Partner 1		
1	150	00				27	150	00						
2	150	00				28	150	00	750	00		1st Qtr	1950	00
3	150	00				29	150	00						
4	150	00	750	00		30	150	00				2nd Qtr	4124	00
5	150	00				31	150	00						
6	150	00				32	150	00	750	00		3rd Qtr	1950	00
7	150	00				33	150	00						
8	150	00	750	00		34	150	00				4th Qtr	1950	00
9	150	00				35	150	00						
10	150	00				36	150	00	750	00		Total	9974	00
11	150	00				37	150	00						
12	150	00	750	00		38	150	00				Yearly Summary Partner 2		
13	150	00				39	150	00						
1st Qtr	1950	00	2250	00		3rd Qtr	1950	00	2250	00		1st Qtr	2250	00
14	150	00				40	150	00	750	00		2nd Qtr	5106	00
15	150	00				41	150	00						
16	150	00	750	00		42	150	00				3rd Qtr	2250	00
17	150	00				43	150	00						
18	150	00				44	150	00	750	00		4th Qtr	3000	00
19	150	00				45	150	00						
20	150	00	750	00		46	150	00				Total	12606	00
21	150	00				47	150	00						
22	150	00				48	150	00	750	00		Yearly Summary Partner 3		
23	150	00				49	150	00						
24	150	00	750	00		50	150	00				1st Qtr		
25	150	00				51	150	00				2nd Qtr		
26	150	00				52	150	00	750	00				
TAX	2174	00	2856	00		53						3rd Qtr		
2nd Qtr	4124	00	5106	00		4th Qtr	1950	00	3000	00		4th Qtr		

Fig. 6.4 *Summary of drawings for self—two partners shown*

payments. VAT and employees' Tax payments can be regarded as expenses of the business and are deductible from profits. The treatment of tax in the final accounts is described in Section 20.3.

6.6 Recording Payments of Wages

For our present purpose it is necessary only to notice that wages, and the National Insurance contributions which an employer must pay, are recorded in the 'Payments Other than for Stock' columns as shown in Fig. 6.1. They represent an expense of the business which may be deducted when calculating the profits for the year. If the number of staff exceeds two, their wages should also be entered in a separate Wages Book (see Unit 17).

Where a wife is employed in a family business, the payments made to her are treated like ordinary wages of other employees; they are deductible from the profits of the business. However, this wage paid to the wife has to be included in her earnings as part of the income of the household when tax is being calculated. Sometimes the wife opts for separate assessment from her husband, but it is debatable whether this is advantageous—it depends entirely on individual circumstances. In any case, since the earnings of the wife must be known, it is usual to record them separately as shown in Fig. 6.1. Some explanation of the tax position is given in Unit 22.

Where the wife is a partner in the business, the sums she is paid are not wages but 'drawings'. They are recorded just like the drawings of any other proprietor as outlined in Section 6.4.

6.7 Conclusion

We have now seen how to record on the Simplex page the following matters:

(*a*) The daily takings ('sales') and other receipts.

(*b*) The purchases of goods for resale or to render service ('business stock').

(*c*) The payments for consumable items and for services rendered to the business.

(*d*) The purchases of capital assets.

(*e*) The payment of tax.

(*f*) The drawing of cash by the proprietor.

It only remains to calculate the cash balance and the bank balance, by recording our receipts and payments in the 'Weekly Cash Report' and 'Weekly Bank Report'.

6.8 Exercises in Recording Payments Other than for Stock

Using suitable paper ruled as in Fig. 6.1 (obtainable from George Vyner Ltd.,) make the following entries in the 'Payments Other than for Stock' section.

1. Martin Brown is in business as a greengrocer. In Week 42 he pays the following items in cash: rent £45; postages 27p, 32p, 46p and £1.40; petrol £8.75 and insurance £15.20. He also pays wages £37.50 in cash. He pays by cheque for a weighing machine £69.75 and for sundries £8.50. He also draws for his own use the sum of £60.00 by cheque. Enter the above items and total the two columns to find the total 'Cash' and 'Cheque' payments.

2. Ella Goodtaste is in business as a fashion designer. In Week 37 she pays the following items in cash: postages £2.47 and £1.32; art materials £4.65 and travelling £12.50. She also pays wages £32.50 in cash. She pays by cheque for stationery £7.42 and a telephone bill for £281.74. She also draws for herself the sum of £100 in cash. Enter the above items and total the two columns to find the total 'Cash' and 'Cheque' payments.

3. Michael Beltaine is in business as a chiropodist. In Week 37 he pays the following items in cash: postages 27p, 32p, 66p and £1.46; advertising £32.50 and sundries 25p. He also pays travelling expenses £13.28 in cash. He pays by cheque for rates £48.50, VAT to Customs and Excise £65.60, and also draws for his own use the sum of £35.00 by cheque. Enter the above items and total the two columns to find the total 'Cash' and 'Cheque' payments.

Unit Seven

The Weekly Cash and Bank Reports

7.1 Introduction

At the end of each week's work it is advisable to check on the cash and bank positions. For this reason the Simplex system incorporates a 'Weekly Bank Report' and a 'Weekly Cash Report'. These two sections of the weekly page enable you to check the accuracy of your cash record, your record of cheques drawn and your daily entries in the 'Paid to Bank' column. Assuming that they have been kept in the manner shown below, the weekly reports can be compared with the actual cash in the till and with the statement as rendered by the bank. Any discrepancy should of course be investigated.

7.2 The Weekly Bank Report

A typical 'Weekly Bank Report' is shown in Fig. 7.1. It starts with the opening balance brought forward from the previous week. This is then increased by the total amount paid in during the week, which is found from the 'Paid to Bank' column (see Section 4.6). These two figures are then added, and their sum gives the total amount in the bank account.

WEEKLY BANK REPORT				
	Opening Balance	brought forward	2736	54
Add {	Total Paid to Bank during week (Col 4 + Col 5)		1895	60
		Total	4632	14
	Cash drawn from bank	—	—	
	Stock Payments (Col 7)	428	56	
Deduct {	Other Payments (Col 9)	165	72	
	Bank Standing Orders	—	—	
	Bank and Interest Charges	—	—	
		Total	594	28
	Closing Balance carried forward		4037	86

Fig. 7.1 *The Weekly Bank Report*

From the total in the bank account we must now deduct the total of cheques drawn. This is made up of the cheques drawn for 'Payments for Business Stock', plus the cheques drawn for 'Payments Other than for Stock', plus the total (if any) of cash drawn from the bank. It may also be necessary to deduct any standing orders that have been paid by the bank, and also any bank charges and interest charges. These items are explained below. Deducting the total paid out from the bank from the total in the account gives the 'Closing

Balance carried forward'. This is taken over to the next page, ready to start the new week.

Although the result of these calculations gives us the balance to carry forward, there are still two points to be borne in mind: one concerns 'bank reconciliation statements', the other concerns overdrafts.

(a) Bank Reconciliation Statements

In fact, although we have found the balance on the bank account according to our records, the bank may not agree with us for a number of reasons. First, the bank deducts 'charges' for keeping our account. Secondly, it automatically makes payments by 'standing orders' or 'direct debits' which we have authorised. Recurrent charges such as rates, mortgage repayments and annual subscriptions are often dealt with in one of these two ways. All such deductions will be made on our account without the bank informing us. Similarly, the bank may receive money into our account from customers who pay hire-purchase instalments or trade debts to us by 'credit transfer'. The result is that we may either have more money or less money in the bank than we think. The actual position will be known when we inspect our bank statement, which we usually receive monthly.

The process of reconciling the 'Weekly Bank Report' with the bank statement is explained in Section 16.4. It requires us to draw up a 'bank reconciliation statement' after checking the various differences between the two sets of records.

(b) Overdrafts

It is important to note that if you are trading on overdraft, the balance brought forward will be an 'overdraft balance', i.e. one that you *owe* to the bank. Therefore sums paid in will reduce the overdraft balance (instead of increasing a credit balance), and sums paid out must be added to the overdraft balance (instead of being deducted from a credit balance). Consequently you must reverse the words 'Add' and 'Deduct', as shown in Fig. 7.2. In this

WEEKLY BANK REPORT				
~~Add~~ DEDUCT {	Opening Balance	brought forward	2150	00 DR
	Total Paid to Bank during week (Col 4 + Col 5)		1895	60
		Total	254	40
~~Deduct~~ ADD {	Cash drawn from bank	—	—	
	Stock Payments (Col 7)	428	56	
	Other Payments (Col 9)	165	72	
	Bank Standing Orders	—	—	
	Bank and Interest Charges	—	—	
		Total	594	28
	Closing Balance carried forward		848	68 DR

Fig. 7.2 *The 'Weekly Bank Report' when trading on overdraft*

example the overdraft is converted to a favourable credit balance when the total paid in is deducted from it, and reconverted to an overdraft by the sums paid away in the week. (*Note:* DR means it is a debtor balance.)

7.3 The Weekly Cash Report

The 'Weekly Cash Report' shown in Fig. 7.3 is very similar to the 'Weekly Bank Report'. It starts with the opening balance (cash in hand) brought

WEEKLY CASH REPORT				
	Cash in Hand (as counted) brought forward			4	27
Add	Gross Weekly Takings (Col 1 + Col 2)			2124	75
	Other Receipts (Col 3)			25	00
	Cash Drawn from Bank			—	—
			Total	2154	02
Deduct	Stock Payments (cash)(Col 6)	132	25		
	Other Payments (cash)(Col 8)	121	12		
	Amount paid to Bank	1895	60		
			Total	2148	97
©GEORGE VYNER LTD	Cash Balance on books			5	05
COPYRIGHT RESERVED – REPRODUCTION OF THIS BOOK IN WHOLE OR IN PART STRICTLY FORBIDDEN.	Cash in hand (as counted)			4	36
	Difference on books (+ or −)			—	69

Fig. 7.3 *The weekly cash report*

forward from the previous week. To this cash in hand we add the combined totals of the 'Daily Takings' and 'Other Receipts' columns. Any cash that has been drawn from the bank for office use is also added. Now we must deduct, first, the 'Payments for Business Stock' which were made in cash, secondly, the 'Payments other than for Stock' which were made in cash, and finally the total 'Paid to Bank'. What remains after these deductions is the *cash balance* to be carried forward.

This cash balance is now checked by counting the cash balance actually in the tills. If this total agrees with the cash balance of the weekly report, all is well. Any disagreement between the balance and the cash available must be investigated to discover the error, or the cause of the cash loss from the till.

7.4 Withdrawing cash from the Bank

At times a business runs short of cash, or draws cash from its current account at the Bank to meet a particular requirement such as paying wages, or going to a sale of a bankrupt's assets etc. In these circumstances the trader merely draws a cheque to 'cash', and the only entries required are those in the Weekly Bank Report' (cash drawn from Bank) which deducts the money from the Bank Account and the entry in the Weekly Cash Report (cash drawn from Bank) which adds the money drawn to the 'Cash in hand'.

7.5 Withdrawing Cash from a Deposit Account

Many businessmen find it is advantageous to place sums on Deposit Account at the Bank. In this way the money earns a reasonable rate of interest, yet is available at seven days notice when required. In fact the bank will usually make it available at once, but charge seven days interest on it if notice is not given. Certain sums of money which are only paid intermittently, such as Income Tax (payable twice yearly), Value Added Tax (payable quarterly) Corporation Tax (payable annually) etc., are best accumulated in this way so that they are not confused with Current Account moneys. At the back of the Simplex D Account Book in the latest edition there is a section headed 'Movements in and out of Deposit Account'. It is in the style shown in Fig. 7.4. Occasionally it is necessary to balance off the account to find the amount still available for use. Banks now add interest every three months to this type of account, and when notified by a Bank Statement that interest has been added this should be entered on the Simplex record.

Movements in and out of Deposit Account								
Deposits					Withdrawals			
Date		Details	£	p	Date		Details	£	p
JAN.	1	Balance at Start	2374	24	JAN.	7	INLAND REVENUE (TRANS TO CURR A/c)	1850	=
"	31	DEPOSIT	648	50	FEB.	28	V.A.T. (TRANS TO CURR. A/c)	364	50
FEB.	28	"	775	50	MAR.	31	BALANCE (CARRIED DOWN)	2407	94
MAR.	31	"	824	20					
			£ 4622	44				£ 4622	44
MAR.	31	BALANCE (BROUGHT DOWN)	2407	94					

Fig. 7.4 *Deposit Account*

Where a Deposit Account *is not part of the business accounts*, but is the personal account of the proprietor, any sum of money taken from the Deposit Account and put into the business is like extra capital contributed. It should therefore be entered in the 'Other Receipts' section and carried to the 'Extra Capital Contributed' summary at the end of the book.

In any case, the sum transferred from Deposit Account will come into the Weekly Bank Report as an extra sum of money in the Current Account. It should be added into the sum marked 'Total Paid to Bank during Week'.

7.6 Problems with Cheque Payments

Many customers today pay by cheque, and since the development of the credit card system there is no real reason for a businessman to refuse payment of small sums by cheque if the customer has a credit card from his bank. The banks will always honour a cheque up to the limit stated on the credit card, which at the time of writing is usually £50. The acceptance of cheques in payment of sums greater than the limit on the card is unwise, unless the goods are being withheld until the cheque has been cleared.

Despite this guarantee of eventual payment cheques can still be inconvenient if they are not properly made out, and staff should be trained in the checking of cheques. Sometimes the proprietor or a floor manager insists on personally confirming that a cheque is correctly made out before goods are wrapped. The chief difficulties are:

(a) Incorrect date or no date at all

(b) Incorrect name on the line which begins "Pay . . . ." The name should be the correct business name, either of the Company, or the partnership or the Sole Trader. If the business trades under a name which is not the same as the name of the trader(s) the correct name is the name displayed at the business premises, under the new rules laid down in the Companies Act 1981. A leaflet about this is available from Companies House, 55 City Road, London, EC1Y 1BB.

(c) The wording of the amount and the figures of the amount should be the same.

(d It is frequently the case that the word 'pounds' is left out; the drawer of the cheque writing 'Thirty seven 21' instead of 'Thirty seven pounds 21'.

(e) The cheque may not be signed. Even if it is signed the signature should be compared with the signature on the credit card and any doubts raised with the drawer. He may be asked to sign it a second time.

(f It is best to cross the cheque if it is not crossed, or ask the drawer to do so.

(g) Any alterations should be initialled, or a full signature is even better.

Dishonoured Cheques

Dishonoured cheques are a problem both from the book-keeping point of view and the pursuit of the debtor. From the viewpoint of keeping the books correct the difficulty is that the cheque has been included in the Daily Takings and carried to the Weekly Summary of Takings. This will mean that the total takings for the year is eventually too high. The best thing to do is to enter the cheque in red on the day it is received in the Other Receipts Particulars Column, explaining that it has been dishonoured. Then carry this red ink entry to the Weekly Summary of Takings and deduct it from the quarterly total. The problem of dishonoured cheques will be much reduced if cheques are only accepted from customers who have a banker's credit card.The dishonoured cheque should then be entered in the Debtors' Record Book, to record the debt, and suitable action taken to 'refer the cheque to the drawer'. This means approach him and ask him what he means by it. In most cases he will be suitably apologetic, phone his bank and make arrangements for the cheque to be honoured. It is then re-presented as part of the 'Daily Takings' of the day it is paid in for the second time. If no satisfaction can be obtained it is of course an offence to write cheques knowing they will not be honoured and the police may be informed. If the sum is trivial and the businessman wishes to avoid publicity he may prefer not to pursue the matter, and the debt will then become a bad debt, which may be written off the profits at the end of the year. (see page 150).

7.7 Exercises in Preparing Weekly Bank Reports and Weekly Cash Reports

1. Tom Smith is in business as a builder. At the end of Week 15 his bank transactions have been as follows: Opening Balance £1,727.46; total paid to bank during week £498.50; Stock payments £84.95 and payments other than for stock £176.50. He also knows that his Bank deducts a mortgage payment of £84.50 during this week, as a standing order. Work out the Weekly Bank Report on special paper ruled as in Fig 7.1 (obtainable from George Vyner Ltd.,) and thus discover the 'Closing Balance' to be carried forward to week 16.

2. Mary Baker owns a restaurant. At the end of week 23 her bank transactions have been as follows: Opening Balance £2,725.62; total paid to bank during week £895.50; Stock payments £326.56 and Payments other than for stock £48.50. She also knows that bank charges of £38.50 were charged on certain investment dealings during the week. Work out the Weekly Bank Report on the special paper, and thus discover the 'Closing Balance' to be carried forward to week 24.

3. Ivor Waywivem is in business as a garage owner. At the end of week 45 his bank transactions have been as follows: Opening Balance £3,728.52; total paid to bank during week £985.70; Stock payments £525.60 and Payments other than for stock £824.65. He also knows that he withdrew cash from the bank £150 during the week. Work out the Weekly Bank Report on the special paper, and thus discover the 'Closing Balance' to be carried forward to week 46.

4. Martin Reed is in business as a thatcher. At the end of week 36 his cash transactions have been as follows: Cash in hand (brought forward from previous week) £7.52; total weekly takings £165.50; Other Receipts £15.00. Payments for stock were £38.25 and other payments in cash came to £44.50. He had paid £75.00 into the bank. Using special paper ruled as for Fig. 7.3 (obtainable from George Vyner Ltd.,) work out the Weekly Cash Report and hence discover the Cash Balance. How would you check, if you were Martin, that his balance was correct?

5. Alison Knitwell is in business as a draper. At the end of Week 4 her cash transactions have been as follows: Cash in hand (brought forward from previous week) £15.56; total weekly takings £78.75; other receipts £8.40. Payments for stock were £32.50 and other payments in cash came to £4.35. She had paid £32.00 into the bank. Using the special paper work out the Weekly Cash Report and hence discover the Cash Balance. How would you check, if you were Alison that this balance was correct?

6. Alan Groves is in business as a funeral director. At the end of week 37 his cash transactions have been as follows: Cash in hand (brought forward from previous week) £45.00; total weekly takings £762.00; Other receipts £34.00. Payments for stock were £198.00 and other payments in cash came to £236.00. He had paid £300 into the bank. Using the special paper work out the weekly Cash Report and hence discover the Cash Balance. How would you check, if you were Alan that this balance was correct?

Unit Eight
The Simplex System and Various Types of Business

8.1 Introduction—Which Type of Business is Yours?

Into which of the following categories does your business fall?

(*a*) A **farm, livestock** or **market-garden** business, which has for its main aim the raising of produce for sale to the general public.

(*b*) A **manufacturing** business, which has for its main activity the conversion of purchased raw materials into a finished product which is then sold at a profit.

(*c*) A **trading** business, which derives its main profit from the buying and selling of goods.

(*d*) A **service** business which requires purchase of materials *as well as* the use of skills. A typical example is the builder and decorator who must purchase materials and work them into the customer's property or assets to produce a visible final effect.

(*e*) A **pure service** business, where your expertise or skill in making arrangements is the vital part of the business, and little or no material is required to provide the service.

The Simplex system is suitable for each of these types of business. The following list is designed to help you decide which type of business yours is. There are bound to be some businesses which overlap and could come under two or more different headings. If this is so in your case, it is advisable to read as many of Units 9–14 as are appropriate. You will need to read every Unit if your business is concerned with all five kinds of activity.

8.2 Farms, Livestock and Market-garden Businesses

Read Units 9 and 10 if your type of business is like any of those named below:

beekeeper	livestock breeder
budgerigar breeder	market gardener
bulb grower	mushroom grower
chicken raiser	nurseryman
dairy farmer	pig breeder/dealer
dog breeder	potato grower
farmer	poultry farmer
fisherman	seedsman
fruit grower	smallholder
hatchery	soft-fruit grower

stud farm   turkey farmer
turf supplier   vegetable grower

8.3 Manufacturing Businesses

Read Units 9 and 11 if your type of business is like any of those named below:

bacon curer   pallet manufacturer
boat builder   paper-bag maker
button manufacturer   plastics manufacturer
cabinet maker   pottery
garden craftsman   rubber-stamp maker
garment manufacturer   rustic woodworker
gown maker   saddler and harness maker
foundry   sail maker
ice-cream manufacturer   sea-moss dyer/processor
loose-cover maker   wrought-ironwork manufacturer
packing-case maker

8.4 Trading Businesses

Read Units 9 and 12 if your type of business is like any of those named below:

antique dealer   draper
aquarium supplier   dress shop
artist's sundriesman   fashions shop
automobile trader   filling station
babyware shop   fish and chip shop
bait and tackle shop   fish merchant
baker   fishing-tackle shop
boats and small-craft dealer   florist
bookseller   fruiterer
boutique   furniture retailer
butcher   garage
camping-equipment shop   garden centre
car-accessory dealer   general store
car breaker   gift shop
car salesman   gown shop
carpets and rugs   greengrocer
'cash and carry'   greetings-card shop
chemist   grocer
china and glassware shop   hardware shop
Chinese restaurant   hatter
confectioner   health-food shop
dairy   hobby shop
decorator's merchant   home-improvement centre
do-it-yourself shop   horticultural sundriesman

ice-cream parlour
infants' wear
ironmonger
jeweller
ladies' wear
leather-goods shop
lingerie shop
milk bar
milliner
newsagent
night club
off licence
office-equipment seller
outfitter
paint and wallpaper shop
pet shop
petrol station
philatelic dealer
public house
radio and electrical-goods shop
rag merchant

record shop
restaurant
salvage dealer
scrap merchant
seed merchant
snack bar
sports shop
stamp dealer
stationer
supermarket
surplus store
tea room
television supply and servicing
timber supplier
tobacconist
tropical-fish shop
typewriter supplies
wallpaper merchant
wine and spirit merchant
wrought-ironwork trader

8.5 Service Businesses which require Materials

Read Units 9 and 13 if your type of business is like any of those named below:

aerial (TV) installer
agricultural contractor
amusement machinery
animal boarding
antique restorer
architectural-model maker
assembler and fabricator
automobile service
barber
beauty salon
blacksmith
boarding-house
boat builder
book binder
bricklayer
builder and decorator
café
car hire
car park
caravan park

caterer
cleaner
cobbler
copying service
crop-spraying contractor
decorator
dentist
doctor
double-glazing firm
duplication and office services
electrical contractor
electroplater
engineer
exhaust replacement service
fencing contractor
floor-laying service
furrier
garden contractor
glazier
hairdresser

health farm
heating contractor
hi-fi sales and service
home improver
hotel
insulation contractor
insurance agent
insurance broker
label printer
laboratory
milliner
motor-vehicle service/repairs
office-cleaning contractor
paint sprayer
painter and decorator
pawnbroker
photocopying service
photographer
plasterer
plumber
pregnancy-testing service
printer
rat-catcher
refrigeration engineer
roofing contractor

school (private)
shoe repairer
shopfitter
sign maker
sign writer
silver plater
slater
stonemason
swimming-pool supplier
tailor
tar paving contractor
television repairs/service
thatcher
tiler
tiling contractor
timber preservation
turf contractor
tyre service
upholsterer
vacuum-cleaner repairs
van hire
vending machines
welder
windscreen replacement
woodworm control

8.6 Pure Service Businesses

Read Units 9 and 14 if your type of business is like any of those named below:

abattoir
accommodation agency
accountant
advertising agency
air-charter service
architect
artist
auctioneer
author
baby-sitter
band
boat hire
bookmaker
business consultancy
business-transfer agent
camping hire

chimney sweep
chiropodist
chiropractor
cleaning contractor
coach service
composer
credit trader
dance band
dancing teacher
day nursery
debt collector
dental surgeon
dental technician
detective agency
dog breeder
dog handler

domestic agency
drain clearer
driving school
dry cleaner
educational consultancy
electrician
embalmer
employment agency
entertainer
estate agent
flying school
funeral director
furniture remover
golf professional
golf school
'group' (musical)
gutter cleaner
haulage contractor
heating consultant
holiday accommodation
horse trainer
inquiry agent
journalist
kennels
ladder hire
land clearer
landscape gardener
laundrette
library
literary agent
lithographic platemaker
loudspeaker hire
magician
mail-order firm
management consultancy
manufacturer's agent
marriage bureau
mercantile-protection agency
minibus hire
money-lender
motel
musical arranger
music teacher

musician
nursery school
nursing home
oculist
optician
osteopath
piano tuner
plant hirer
private detective
public-address equipment hire
public-relations consultancy
quantity surveyor
riding school
road haulage
scaffolding
school (private)
security firm
self-drive cars
singing teacher
site clearing
solicitor
staff bureau
steeplejack
stock-taking service
tarpaulin hire
taxis
tent hire
towing service
travel agent
tree feller
trichologist
typing bureau
undertaker
valuer
van hire
veterinary service
vocalist
waste clearance
watch repairer
window cleaner
woodworker
yacht hire

After reading the Units that apply to your type of business, you should proceed to Units 15-26.

Unit Nine

Opening a Simplex System

9.1 Introduction

Because of the unequivocal advantages and reliability of the Simplex system, it is likely that many readers who are already in business will be thinking of changing over to it from their present method of book-keeping. If you are among these readers, proceed as in Section 9.3. However, if you are starting up in business for the first time, you will need to follow the simple instructions given in Section 9.2.

9.2 Simplex at the Formation of a Business

(a) Prepare a list on a piece of paper of everything you are bringing into the business: cash, money at the bank and other assets of various sorts. A typical list might be as follows:

Assets Contributed

	£
Cash in hand	25
Cash at bank	625
Motor-car	350
Shop fittings	55
Stock	230
Capital contributed	£1 285

Do not count the price of your house as a business asset, even if it is your place of business. (You will be allowed to claim some expenses for this later.)

(b) On the first weekly page of your Simplex book, enter the 'cash-in-hand' sum in the 'Cash in hand brought forward' part of the Weekly Cash Report, and enter the 'cash-at-bank' sum in the 'Opening Balance brought forward' part of the Weekly Bank Report.

(c) Turning to the 'Capital Expenses Incurred During The Year' page, near the back of the Simplex book, enter details of all other capital assets that you have contributed. These assets are not being purchased, but must be recorded to show that you have contributed them to the business.

(d) Also near the back of the book, you will find a 'Summary of Other Receipts', the end column of which is called 'Extra Capital Introduced'. In the first line of this column enter the total value of all the items on your list. This is of course the capital contributed to the business. Some people think 'Capital' just means money, but 'Capital' is what the business owes back to the owner, and it is the total value of all the assets he contributes.

9.3 Simplex and the Established Business

The procedure here is very similar to the steps indicated in Section 9.2, but as you have already been in business some time you need to draw up a very careful list of all the assets of your business before you make the entries. Enter your cash and bank balances in the Weekly Cash Report and Weekly Bank Report. Next, record details of non-cash assets in the 'Capital Expenses Incurred During The Year' page. You have now recorded your total contribution of assets, but this is not necessarily the same as your contribution of *capital*. The reason is that some of your assets may have been obtained either on credit or by using loan money. To find your capital contribution you must therefore deduct these items (if any) from your total asset value.

Typical figures are shown below.

Assets		£
Cash in hand		31·50
Cash at bank		872·50
Shop fittings		750·00
Stock		1 800·00
Motor van		625·00
Debtors		50·00
Total assets		4 129·00
Liabilities		
Trade creditors	55·00	
Bank loan	2 000·00	
		2 055·00
Capital contributed		£2 074·00

Now enter the 'capital contributed' figure in the 'Extra Capital Contributed' column at the back of the book in the 'Summary of Other Receipts Section'. Enter the Bank Loan in the 'Summary of Loans and Repayments' section.

One final point here is that it is desirable to enter the 'trade creditors' figure somewhere. As there is no special place for this at the back of the Simplex book, it is best to write it as a 'note' on the 'Capital Expenses Incurred during the Year' summary. It would read something like this:

Note: On the first day of starting this Simplex Account Book, there was a sum of £55.00 owing to Trade Creditors.

9.4 The Opening Balance Sheet of a Business

At this point it is very helpful to consider the opening 'Balance Sheet' of the business. Strictly speaking it is not essential to produce the Balance Sheet of most small businesses at any time, but if you are operating as a limited company the Companies Acts (1948-81) do require you to keep proper books of account, and this includes the preparation of a Balance Sheet. For other businesses there is also the point that it is an offence under the Bankruptcy Act 1914 to fail to keep proper books of account. Thus the small trader who does not keep proper accounts but who keeps solvent will not face any charges, but if he commits an act of bankruptcy (by failing to pay his debts for example) he may find himself facing criminal charges for failing to keep proper books of account.

A Balance Sheet is a very simple idea, first suggested by Simon Stevin of Bruges in 1536. He called it a **Statement of Affairs;** a term which is still used in bankruptcy proceedings. A Balance Sheet is a list of the assets and liabilities of a firm at a particular moment in time. It can therefore be drawn up at any moment, but usually it is prepared at the start of a business (an Opening Balance Sheet) or at the end of the financial year (an Annual Balance Sheet) or at the close of a business (a Closing Balance Sheet).

We have all the figures we need in 9.3 above to draw up the Opening Balance Sheet of this imaginary firm. For convenience the assets are usually divided into two groups **Fixed Assets** and **Current Assets.** Fixed assets are assets which are required for use in the business, and cannot be sold without interfering with its activities. They are sometimes called *capital assets*, and are permanently required for use in the business. The commonest are *Land and Buildings, Plant and Machinery, Furniture and Fittings* and *Motor Vehicles.* Current assets are assets which can be turned into cash without damaging the business, indeed that is what they are for. Thus *Stock-in-Trade* is bought only to be sold again, and *Debtors* are taken on only because we expect them to pay. These, with *Cash at Bank* and *Cash in Hand* are the most usual 'Current Assets'.

The liabilities of a business are of three sorts. **Current Liabilities** are those due to be settled very soon in the course of the current year's business, i.e. in less than twelve months. **Long Term Liabilities** are those due to be settled under some special contract which lasts for more than a year. Thus a Bank Loan, or a Mortgage may be repaid over several years. The final type of liability is the **Capital,** which is repayable to the owner when the business finally ceases to trade. It is therefore very long term indeed.

Figure 9.1 shows the Opening Balance Sheet of the firm mentioned in 9.3 above.

Balance Sheet
(as at January 1st, 19..)

	£			£
Capital		*Fixed Assets*		
At start of business	2 074·00	Shop Fittings		750·00
		Motor Van		625·00
				1 375·00
Long Term Liabilities		*Current Assets*	£	
Bank Loan	2 000·00	Stock	1 800·00	
		Debtors	50·00	
Current Liabilities		Cash at Bank	872·50	
		Cash in Hand	31·50	
Trade creditors	55·00			2 754·00
	£4 129·00			£4 129·00

Fig. 9.1 The 'Opening Balance Sheet' of a business

Finally, let us note that the United Kingdom, and countries which originally learned their book-keeping by links with the United Kingdom, prepare their Balance Sheets as shown above. This is the way Simon Stevin of Bruges first presented it. Actually the sides are the wrong way round, the assets should be on the left and the liabilities on the right. Readers in other countries who use the proper system should not change back to the United Kingdom way. The error, which really followed an Act of Parliament of 1856 where the Balance Sheet was wrongly displayed, has become traditional.

Where do you keep your Opening Balance Sheet. The answer is on a sheet of paper in the front of your first Simplex Account book. At the end of the year you will be preparing your annual Balance Sheet on the pages at the back of the book, and can compare the two.

9.5 The Weekly Page

There are slight differences in the way the weekly pages are kept, according to the type of business you are running. The routine for each kind of business will be found in the following Units:

Unit 10—for farms, livestock and market-garden businesses.
Unit 11—for manufacturing businesses.
Unit 12—for trading businesses.
Unit 13—for service businesses which require materials.
Unit 14—for pure service businesses.

9.6 Exercises on Opening Balance Sheets

1. Prepare an Opening Balance Sheet (as at January 1st, 19..) for Tom Walker's business

	£
Cash in hand	480·00
Money at Bank	2 350·00
Stock in Trade	5 500·00
Land and Buildings	16 000·00
Office Furniture	3 500·00
Bank Loan	2 000·00
Creditors	1 750·00
Capital (at Start)	24 080·00

2. Prepare a Balance Sheet of A. Northerner's affairs from the following information, as at January 1st, 19..:

	£
Cash in hand	25·00
Cash in Bank	1 850·00
Stock	4 970·00
Office Equipment	850·00
Land and Buildings	14 250·00
Capital (at Start)	14 245·00
Debtors	425·00
Creditors	1 625·00
Mortgage on premises	5 000·00
Bank Loan	1 500·00

3 and 4 On the last two Balance Sheets given in the table below you will have to work out the Capital. Remember that assets are divided into fixed assets and current assets. Liabilities are in three parts, current liabilities, long-term liabilities and Capital. To find the capital at the start use the formula given below.

Capital at start = Total of assets – total of 'current' and 'long-term' liabilities.

Proprietor	No. 3	No. 4
	Tom Sawyer	Huckleberry Finn
Date	1st January 19..	1st January 19..
	£	£
Cash in Hand	50·00	180·00
Cash at Bank	2 350·00	4 760·00
Trade Debtors	1 155·00	2 375·00
Stock	7 250·00	14 945·00
Motor Vehicles	2 500·00	7 500·00
Furniture	1 850·00	4 850·00
Plant and Machinery	3 000·00	6 500·00
Land and Buildings	15 825·00	27 850·00
Creditors	2 700·00	1 650·00
Wages Due to Workers	–	550·00
Mortgage	8 000·00	12 000·00
Bank Loan	2 000·00	–
Capital	?	?

Unit Ten

The Weekly Page for Farms, Livestock and Market-garden Businesses

10.1 Receipts

(a) Gross Daily Takings

Whenever you receive money (either cash or cheques) for goods or stock which you have sold, put it in the till. At the end of each day cash up the till, deduct any float you may have used to start the till off, and enter the 'Daily Takings' in the appropriate column (cash or cheques) of the 'Receipts' section of the weekly page.

(b) Debtors

Where goods are being supplied on credit there are, as we have seen in Section 4.2, two ways of looking at the problem. If you adopt the recommended method, which is to record the credit sale in a debtors' record book and regard the goods as sold, you must remember to add the weekly total of 'debtors supplied during the week' to the week's takings when you transfer the latter to the 'Weekly Summary of Takings'.

(c) Other Receipts

(i) *Capital contributions.* Any extra money you put into the business, such as payments out of your private funds to keep the business going in its early days, represents an additional contribution of capital and should therefore be recorded in the 'Other Receipts' column. If, as is often the case, you make this contribution to pay a specific bill or purchase a specific item, you must record it as an 'Other Receipt' as well as making the relevant entry in the 'Payments for Business Stock' or 'Payments Other than for Stock' columns.

(ii) *Loans from outsiders.* Since loans become liabilities of the business, they have to be recorded as 'Other Receipts'.

(iii) *Debts settled.* If you have adopted the method referred to above for dealing with debtors, the cash you receive when the debt is settled should be entered as an 'Other Receipt'. It must not be included in 'Daily Takings' as this would result in the sale being counted twice in the takings.

(iv) *Sundry earnings.* Examples of sundry earnings include rent received from a sub-tenant, commission received, receipts from credit-card companies and repayments of VAT from HM Customs & Excise. All of these should be entered as 'Other Receipts'.

(d) Particulars Column

You may find it useful to record the names of debtors who paid, the source of 'other receipts' such as VAT refunds, and similar details for future reference.

10.2 Paid to Bank

This column, where you record day by day all sums paid into your bank account, enables you to prepare your Weekly Bank Report at the end of the week. It also helps you very much with your bank reconciliation statement (see Section 16.4).

10.3 Payments for Business Stock

Farmers, livestock dealers, market gardeners and those in similar kinds of business need to consider the 'Payments for Stock' columns in some detail.

(a) You may 'buy in' certain lines expressly to sell again. Thus a chicken hatchery might at times buy in day-old ducklings in season for customers who require them, and a nurseryman will often buy in trees and plants for resale. Such purchases are just like stock bought for resale by a trading enterprise, and are dealt with in Unit 12.

(b) Many other items will be purchased and worked into the stock finally sold. A nurseryman may buy timber to 'knock up' into seed boxes, or a bee-keeper may buy sugar to feed his bees through the winter months. These items come under the heading of 'stock to render a service'. As they are an expense of the business, they must of course be recorded at their full cost price.

Both types of item should be recorded as they occur, in date order, using the cash or cheque column according to which method of payment was used. If you receive goods and do not pay for them at once, because for example you pay on monthly credit terms, put the invoice or delivery note in your filing system until the 'statement' arrives from your supplier. Record the payment in your Simplex book only when you actually pay it.

10.4 Payments Other than for Stock

Payments made by a business 'other than for stock' comprise the running expenses, capital items and special items. Most of the entries made under this heading are perfectly straightforward, but some are listed below as worthy of special mention.

(a) **Rent.** If your place of business is separate from your own home, then all the rent, lighting and heating costs, etc., incurred at this place of business are expenses of the business and may be deducted from the profits at the end of the year. Just record them in the 'By Cash' or 'By Cheque' column, which-ever is appropriate.

Special rules apply if you operate from your own home. You may claim only a proportion of the rent, cost of heating, etc. (The actual portion may be calculated on floor area.) Often about one-fifth or one-sixth of such ex-penses are chargeable against profits. It is obviously a benefit to claim allow-ances in this way, but note that, if you ever sell your house, you may be liable to pay capital gains tax on one-fifth or one-sixth of any profits you make on the sale of the property. Normally an owner-occupied house is not liable to capital gains tax, so this is a distinct disadvantage. At present capital gains tax stands at 30 per cent, so that tax of 30 per cent of one-sixth of the gain would be payable.

(b) **Motor Expenses.** If a vehicle is used exclusively for business purposes, the whole of the running costs are an expense of the business. This includes fuel, servicing, repairs, road tax and insurance. An allowance for depreciation may be given as well; your inspector of taxes will advise on how much.

If a vehicle is used for both private and business purposes, the expenses will have to be apportioned between the two in some agreed ratio, perhaps two-thirds to one-third or half and half. Your inspector of taxes will advise you on this point when he goes through the accounts at the end of the year.

(c) **Telephone.** If you work from your own home, an appropriate portion of the telephone bill may be charged as a business expense. Once again this must be by arrangement with the tax inspector.

(d) **Value Added Tax.** All businesses whose turnover exceeds £17 000 per annum are obliged to register for VAT, and become agents for the Government in the collection of VAT. Full details of this procedure are given in Unit 18. Because the tax collected has to be paid quarterly to the Customs & Excise authorities, there will be a 'Customs & Excise (VAT)' entry once every three months in the 'Payments Other than for Stock' section. (For traders dealing largely in zero-rated goods there may be a monthly refund from the VATman instead, in 'Other Receipts').

(e) **Wages of Employees.** Wages of employees, national insurance deductions (including the employer's part) and any Trade Union subscriptions or charitable contributions that are deducted from wages and sent off to such organisations should be counted as wages paid out; the sums sent off need not be entered in your Simplex page since they are really coming from the employees. Alternatively you may prefer to enter the net wages and put other items in as 'Wages (Trade Union subs.)', etc., on a separate line.

(f) **Wages (wife).** The wages of a wife are no different from any other wages, and may be deducted from the profits at the end of the year. They are recorded separately however, because the wife will need to declare them at the end of the year as 'Income' on her Income Tax Return. If she does not make a separate return you will have to include this item on your return as 'Wife's income'. It might appear that there is no point in this process, but it is beneficial, since a working wife receives an extra earned income relief (at present it is £1 565) which means a possible tax saving of over £400. Where a wife is not employed in the business, but *is a partner of the business,* her wages are not really wages, but 'drawings' and must be shown as such.

(g) **National Insurance.** The NIC payments of employees and wives are like extra wages payable, and are chargeable against the profits at the end of the year.

Your own insurance contribution is not. It is regarded as drawings, and should be included in the 'Drawings for Self' figure (see below).

(*h*) **Inland Revenue.** Payments to the Inland Revenue usually come under one of three headings:

(*i*) *Your own tax payments.* These are due in two parts: on January 1st and July 1st each year. We regard income tax payments made by the proprietor as extra 'Drawings for Self'. He has drawn these amounts to satisfy the tax requirement, and on the Balance Sheet these sums will be added to his total drawings for the year.

(*ii*) *PAYE payments.* These are the tax deductions made from the pay packets of employees. Since they are a part of the wages you pay to employees, they should be included in the wages figure at the end of the year.

(*iii*) *Corporation Tax.* Your business will only be liable to pay Corporation Tax if it is trading as a company. The tax is payable on January 1st each year in one lump sum and at a rate prescribed in the Budget. Since 1973 this has been fixed at 52% for large companies, but a special rate of 40% applies to small companies. A 'small company' is one that makes less than £90 000 profit. To prevent hardship to companies in the band of profits immediately above this cut-off figure, a special marginal relief is given on profits from £90 000 to £225 000. This has the effect of gradually raising the profits from 40% to 52% but it does have the effect of taking a very heavy tax cut from the sums of profit between £90 000 and £225 000. If you pay Corporation Tax the amount should be entered in the 'Payments Other than for Stock' section of your Simplex book.

(*i*) **Drawings.** When the proprietor draws from the business sums of money for living expenses, some people say he is drawing out his capital. But this is not strictly true; what he is drawing out are the *profits* he hopes the business is making. Since profits are not finally calculated until the end of the year, he does not know for certain that he has made any profits. We therefore say that drawings are 'in expectation of profits made'.

Since partners need to keep their drawings separate, three 'Drawings for Self' lines are provided in the Simplex book. Note that if your wife is a true partner in the firm you must regard her remuneration as drawings and not as wages.

One further point is this. However you draw cash, for your personal use, whether you take it from the till, or from a cash dispenser at the bank or if you draw it by cheque from the bank, enter it in Column 8 as a cash withdrawal. The actual removal of the money from the bank, whether by cash dispenser or by cheque will then appear on the Weekly Bank Report and Weekly Cash Report as cash drawn from the bank. This takes it out of the Bank Account and into the Cash Box.

Column 9, amounts paid by cheque would only be used for such payments as income tax and national insurance contributions where you do actually send the Inland Revenue Department a cheque.

(*j*) **Capital Items.** Every purchase of a capital asset, whether new or second-hand, must be entered on the 'Capital Items' line. The details of each purchase should also be recorded in the 'Capital Expenses Incurred During The Year' page near the back of the Simplex book. It is wise to include serial numbers of all machines, office equipment, etc., since these may be required for police purposes in the event of burglaries.

(*k*) **Other Items.** Spare lines are provided in the 'Payments Other than for Stock' columns so that you can record any expenses which are additional to those listed. An example is commission paid on odd occasions to someone who has rendered a service. Many such extraordinary expenses may occur which are legitimate charges against the profits of the business.

10.5 The Weekly Cash Report

Some businessmen do not understand why a 'Weekly Cash Report' is necessary. They assume that by simply counting the cash in the till they know how much cash they have got, and that is all they need to know. Of course this is not good enough. Errors on the till can occur by cashiers who give the wrong change, either deliberately or because they are incompetent when handling money. Theft from tills is one of the commonest petty crimes, and millions of pounds a year are stolen in this way.

It is also very easy to overlook an entry. If you pay money out and do not record it, or receive money and do not put it into your receipts section, then clearly your cash balance will not be right at the end of the week.

Details of how to keep the Weekly Cash Report are given in Section 7.3, and you should refer to this section as you make your entries. Any difference between the expected cash balance and the actual till balance as counted should be investigated.

10.6 The Weekly Bank Report

Instructions for completing the Weekly Bank Report are given in Section 7.2. Remember that, while theft from your bank account is less likely than theft from your till, you should never leave cheque-books or bank credit cards lying about where members of staff or the public might be able to steal them. In one recent trial it was revealed that a burglar who found both a cheque book and an 'Access' card on the mat in a house he was burgling purchased goods worth over £4 000 in a few weeks. Although the bank concerned accepted full responsibility, it shows how important it is not to leave such items around.

Remember too, that you cannot check your bank account as easily as your till. You should therefore know how to draw up a 'bank reconciliation statement' (see Section 16.4).

10.7 What to do at the End of the Week

Various book-keeping activities have to be carried out at the end of each week's trading—although some can be postponed if necessary. Since these activities are the same for all types of business, they are discussed collectively in Unit 15.

10.8 Exercises on Keeping the Weekly Page

1. R. Johnson is a market gardener and keeps his Simplex D Account book to record all the details of his day-by-day transactions. Enter the following items for Week 4 April 30th-May 6th 19...

  (a) *Cash Receipts* Monday £49·50; Tuesday £72·60; Wednesday £156·50; Thursday £238·20; Friday £256·70; Saturday £425·25. *Other Receipts* Wednesday Rent from sub-tenant £45·00 in cash.
  (b) *Paid to Bank* Wednesday Cash £200; Friday Cash £300.
  (c) *Payments for Business Stock* May 3rd T. Nelson & Co. Ltd. Cheque £146·50; May 5th R. Bloom £230·25 cheque.
  (d) Other Payments Postages 27p, 35p, £1·35; Motor Expenses (cheque) £34·86; Wages £42·50 cash.
  (e) *Weekly Cash Report* began with Balance of £5. *Weekly Bank Report* began with balance £2 975·97.

Total the items at the end of the week and do the Cash and Bank Reports.

2. Mary Shaw keeps poultry and uses her Simplex D Account Book to record all her day-by-day transactions. Enter the following items in her weekly page, which is Week 38, December 16-22 19...

  (a) *Receipts* Monday 17th., cash £84·50; Tuesday cash £133·50; cheque £5·55; Wednesday cash £17·25; Thursday cash £345·25, cheque £160·00; Friday cash £278·50; Saturday cash £360·00. *Other Receipts* – dividend cheque from Linenwick Building Society £38·74 received on Wednesday.
  (b) *Paid to Bank* Monday Cash £200; Friday Cash £500·00, cheques £204·29.
  (c) *Payments for Business Stock* Monday Corn & Maize Co. Ltd. £23·40 cash; Thursday A. Naylor and Co. Ltd. £185·55 by cheque.
  (d) *Other Payments* Postages 78p, 24p, 85p; Timber poultry house purchased (capital item) £140·00 cheque. Drawings in Cash £60·00.
  (e) *Weekly Cash Report* began with a balance of £132·50. *Weekly Bank Report* began with a balance of £3 484·29.

Total the times at the end of the week, and do the Cash and Bank Reports.

Unit Eleven

The Weekly Page for Manufacturing Businesses

11.1 Receipts

The rules for making entries in the 'Receipts' column are exactly the same for a manufacturing business as for any other kind of business. The relevant information will be found in Section 10.1.

11.2 Paid to Bank

Record in this column any amounts paid to bank, on the day you pay them in. You will find the 'Paid to Bank' column of great help when you come to prepare a bank reconciliation statement (see Section 16.4). It also enables you to prepare your Weekly Bank Report at the end of the week.

11.3 Payments for Business Stock

Manufacturing businesses do not often purchase stock for resale, since the vast majority of their purchases are raw materials and components which are embodied in the product during manufacture. Therefore the usual items to be entered in this section will be raw materials and components to render services in manufacture. When you do 'buy in' finished goods from suppliers (for example, because your own production capacity cannot meet a sudden demand) you should still record such purchases as 'stock for resale'.

Record all purchases of stock, whether to render a service or for resale, in date order as they occur. Use the 'cash' or 'cheque' column according to which method of payment is used. If you receive goods on credit, as when you are trading with your suppliers on monthly terms, do not make any entry in the Simplex book at this stage. File the invoice or advice note and, when the 'statement' arrives from your supplier, use it to check that the statement is correct. The money paid for the month's supplies should be recorded in your Simplex weekly page at the time you actually pay the statement.

11.4 Payments Other than for Stock

The method of recording 'Payments Other than for Stock' is exactly the same for all types of business. A detailed account of the entries under this heading is given in Section 10.4.

11.5 The Weekly Cash Report

The reason why a 'Weekly Cash Report' is necessary is explained in Section 10.5.

In Section 7.3 you will find a detailed description of how to prepare the Weekly Cash report, and you should refer to it as you make your entries. Any difference between the expected cash balance and the actual till balance as counted should be investigated.

11.6 The Weekly Bank Report

The Weekly Bank Report should be completed in accordance with the instructions given in Section 7.2. Remember that cheque-books and bank credit cards are a temptation to thieves: the danger of leaving them lying around is stressed in Section 10.6.

Finally, you should refer also to Section 16.4 so that you will know how to draw up a bank reconciliation statement.

11.7 What to do at the End of the Week

Various book-keeping activities have to be carried out at the end of each week's trading—although some can be postponed if necessary. Since these activities are the same for all types of business, they are discussed collectively in Unit 15.

11.8 Exercises on Keeping the Weekly Page

1. R. Coppersmith is a manufacturer and keeps his Simplex D Account book to record all the details of his day-by-day transactions. Enter the following items for week 5, May 7th-13th.
   - (a) *Receipts* All by cheque Monday £149·50 Tuesday £172·60 Wednesday £186·50 Thursday £438·20 Friday £356·70. Other Receipts Wednesday Rent from sub-tenant £445·00 by cheque.
   - (b) *Paid to Bank* Wednesday Cheques £508·60 Friday Cheques £1 239·90.
   - (c) *Payments for Business Stock* May 8th Metal Supplies Ltd. Cheque £166·50 May 10th Components Ltd. £85·25 cheque.
   - (d) *Other Payments* Postages 85p, 85p, £1·35; Motor Expenses (cheque) £48.86; Wages £142.50 cash; Drawings £50 in cash.
   - (e) *Weekly Cash Report* began with balance of £45. Cash drawn from bank on Friday £200·00. *Weekly Bank Report* began with balance £2 989·98.

   Total the items at the end of the week and do the Cash and Bank Reports.

2. Anne Overton is a fashion designer with a small factory. She keeps her Simplex D Account Book to record all her day-by-day transactions. Enter the following items in her weekly page, which is Week 37, December 9-15th.
   - (a) *Receipts* Monday 10th., cash £15·29; Tuesday cash £26·30, cheque £1054·70; Wednesday cash £15, cheques £84·50; Thursday cash £14·80,

cheque £42·50; Friday cash £184·50; Saturday cash £132·50. Other receipts – Thursday VAT refund £39·74 by cheque.

(b) *Paid to Bank* Friday cash £100, cheques £1 221·44.

(c) *Payments for Business Stock* Monday Newstyles & Co. Ltd. £326·50 by cheque; Thursday Colourful Accessories £14·25 by cheque.

(d) *Other Payments* Postages 85 pence; Sundry Expenses £2·75 cash; Wages £84·20 cash; Drawings £100 by cheque.

(e) *Weekly Cash Report* began with a balance of £36·50. *Weekly Bank Report* began with a balance of £1 472·75.

Total the items at the end of the week and do the Cash and Bank Reports.

Unit Twelve

The Weekly Page for Trading Businesses

12.1 Receipts

The rules for making entries in the 'Receipts' column are exactly the same for a trading business as for any other kind of business. The relevant information will be found in Section 10.1.

12.2 Paid to Bank

This column, where you record day by day all sums paid into your bank account, enables you to prepare your Weekly Bank Report at the end of the week. It also helps you very much with your bank reconciliation statement (see Section 16.4).

12.3 Payments for Business Stock

Trading businesses make their profits by purchasing goods *for resale*. The vast majority of the items purchased are simply passed on to the consumer after the traditional retailer's function of breaking bulk has been performed. Just occasionally a retailer may purchase items which are worked up into some new form before being passed on to the customer. Chemists, for example, buy oil to make up into lotions and ointments; cafés buy bread which they resell in the form of sandwiches. Such purchases of raw materials may be described as purchases *to render service*.

Both these types of stock purchases are entered in the 'Payments for Business Stock' columns, in date order as they are paid for. Record the amount paid in either the 'By Cash' column or 'By Cheque' column, whichever is appropriate. If you receive goods and do not pay for them at once (perhaps because you deal on monthly credit terms with your supplier), you should file the invoice or advice note until you are rendered a statement by the supplier. Then enter the total payment for the month on the Simplex weekly page.

12.4 Payments Other than for Stock

The 'Payments Other than for Stock' section is exactly the same for the trading business as for all other firms. A full description of the entries to be made under this heading is given in Section 10.4.

12.5 The Weekly Cash Report

The reason why a 'Weekly Cash Report' is desirable is explained in Section 10.5. A detailed description of how to prepare the report will be found in Section 7.3, and you should refer to this section as you make your entries. Any differences between the expected cash balance and the actual till balance as counted should be investigated.

12.6 The Weekly Bank Report

The Weekly Bank Report should be completed in accordance with the instructions given in Section 7.2. Remember that while it is not likely that theft can occur from your bank account, you should never leave cheque-books or credit cards lying about. The importance of such safeguards is stressed in Section 10.6.

Finally, you should refer also to Section 16.4 so that you will know how to draw up a bank reconciliation statement.

12.7 What to do at the End of the Week

Various book-keeping activities have to be carried out at the end of each week's trading—although some can be postponed if necessary. Since these activities are the same for all types of business, they are discussed collectively in Unit 15.

12.8 Exercises on Keeping the Weekly Page

1. A. Upson keeps a corner shop in Newtown. He keeps his Simplex D Account book to record all the details of his day-by-day transactions. Enter the following items for Week 6 May 14th-20th.

   (a) *Cash Receipts* Monday £149·55; Tuesday £172·80; Wednesday £158·60; Thursday £438·20; Friday £356·70; Saturday £725·60. *Other receipts* Wednesday Rent from sub-tenant £25·00 in cash.
   (b) *Paid to Bank* Wednesday Cash £200; Friday Cash £500.
   (c) *Payments for Business Stock* May 16th T. Knowles Co. Ltd. cheque £196·50; May 18th T. Luke £330·25 cheque.
   (d) *Other Payments* Postages 37p, 85p, £4·35; Motor Expenses (cheque) £48·86; Wages £62·50 cash. The Bank deduct £14·50 for charges on investment work on Upson's behalf.
   (e) *Weekly Cash Report* began with Balance of £54. *Weekly Bank Report* began with balance £3 816·42.

   Total the items at the end of the week and do the Cash and Bank Reports.

2. M. Grainger is a newsagent and keeps her Simplex D Account Book to record all her day-by-day transactions. Enter the following items in her weekly page, which is Week 40, December 30th-Jan. 5th 19...

   (a) *Receipts* Monday 31st, cash £42·65; Tuesday cash £38·25; cheque £15·00; Wednesday cash £47·62; Thursday cash £83·66, cheque £5·00;

Friday cash £93·75. Saturday cash £127·28. Other receipts – commission for sale of motor vehicle £15·00 cheque – Wednesday.

(b) *Paid to Bank* Friday Cash £200·00; cheques £35·00.

(c) *Payments for Business Stock* Monday Wholesalers Co. Ltd. £495·00 by cheque Thursday Weekly Press Ltd., £225·50 cheque.

(d) *Other Payments* Postages 85p; Wages to delivery boys and girls £36·50 in cash; Rates £48·95 by cheque.

(e) *Weekly Cash Report* began with a balance of £86·59. *Weekly Bank Report* began with a balance of £2 478·36.

Total the items at the end of the week and do the Cash and Bank Reports.

The Weekly Page for Service Businesses Which Require Materials

13.1 Receipts

(a) Gross Daily Takings

The takings of this type of business consist of fees received for services rendered; usually they will be received at the end of the job, when the work has been completed to the customer's satisfaction. Enter all such items in the 'Gross Daily Takings (cash)' or 'Gross Daily Takings (cheques)' column. If several such items are received in a single day, a till will be necessary; the *total* takings should then be entered as one figure in each column at the end of the day.

(b) Debtors

Any customer who is given goods or (in your case) services on credit will become a debtor of your business. There are two ways of dealing with this problem (see Section 4.2). If you adopt the preferred method, which is to record the debt in a separate debtors' record book, remember to include the weekly total of 'debtors supplied during the week' in your total takings figure when you transfer it to the Weekly Summary of Takings.

(c) Other Receipts

(i) *Capital contributions.* Any extra money you put into the business, such as payments out of your private funds to keep the business going in its early days, represents an additional contribution of capital and should therefore be recorded in the 'Other Receipts' column.

(ii) *Loans from outsiders.* Loans must be recorded as 'Other Receipts'. They become liabilities of the business.

(iii) *Debts settled.* If you have adopted the method referred to above for dealing with debtors, the cash you receive when the debt is settled should be treated as an 'Other Receipt'. It must not be included in the daily takings, otherwise it will be counted twice.

(iv) *Sundry earnings.* Any earnings which are not the result of normal 'services rendered' should be entered as 'Other Receipts'. Examples include rent received from a sub-tenant, tax refunds, and receipts from credit-card companies.

(d) Particulars Column

You may find it useful to record the names of debtors who paid, the source of 'other receipts', and similar details for future reference.

13.2 Paid to Bank

This column, where you record day by day all sums paid into your bank account, enables you to prepare your Weekly Bank Report at the end of the week. It also helps you very much with your bank reconciliation statement (see Section 16.4).

13.3 Payments for Business Stock

Businesses which offer a service where materials are necessary to provide the finished effect required by the customer, may be said to purchase those materials 'to render a service'. Decorators, for example, buy paint and wall-paper for use in the premises of their customers; garages buy oil and brake-fluid to service cars. All such items are *stocks purchased to render a service*. At the same time, you may occasionally buy things to sell at a profit to your customer: these are *stocks purchased for resale*. Both these types of stock should be entered in date order in the 'Payments for Business Stock' section of the weekly page, using the 'By Cash' or 'By Cheque' column as appropriate. If you do not in fact pay immediately for these goods, perhaps because you deal with your supplier on a monthly credit basis, do not make any entry until the statement is received from your supplier. Simply file any invoices or advice notes which you are given. On the date when you actually settle the account, at the end of the month, enter the amount in your 'Payments for Business Stock' column.

13.4 Payments Other than for Stock

The method of recording 'Payments Other than for Stock' is exactly the same for the service business as for all other businesses. A detailed account of the entries to be made under this heading is given in Section 10.4.

13.5 The Weekly Cash Report

The advantages of having a weekly cash report are explained in Section 10.5. A detailed description of how to prepare the report will be found in Section 7.3, and you should refer to this section as you make your entries. Any difference between the expected cash balance and the actual till balance as counted should be investigated.

13.6 The Weekly Bank Report

The Weekly Bank Report should be completed in accordance with the instructions given in Section 7.2.

While it is unlikely that thefts will occur from your bank account, you should appreciate the risk of leaving cheque-books and credit cards lying about (see Section 10.6).

Finally, you should know how to draw up a bank reconciliation statement. Details are given in Section 16.4, and any reader who is not familiar with banking practice should study the whole of Unit 16.

13.7 What to do at the End of the Week

Various book-keeping activities have to be carried out at the end of each week's trading—although some can be postponed if necessary. Since these activities are the same for all types of business, they are discussed collectively in Unit 15.

13.8 Exercises in Keeping the Weekly Page

1. M. Lucas is a builder. He uses his Simplex D Account book to record full details of his day-by-day transactions. Enter the following items on the weekly page, for Week 15, 12th July 19..-18th July 19... At the end of the week total the various sections and complete the Cash and Bank Reports.

Receipts Wednesday Cash £15·50; Thursday cheque £285·65; Friday cheque £342·65; Saturday Cash £50.

Other Receipts Extra capital contributed by Lucas £500 cheque, Wednesday.

Paid to Bank Friday £1 128·30, all cheques.

Payments for Business Stock 14th July Cement Co. Ltd. £108·50 cheque; 16th July United Timber Ltd. £87·55 cheque; General Electric Stores Cash £8·42.

Other Payments Wages cheque £84 Drawings cheque £60 VAT payment by cheque £136·52 Motor Expenses Cash £18·54 Sundries £23·62 cash.

Weekly Cash Report Began with a balance of £42·50. Cash drawn from Bank £200.

Weekly Bank Report Began with an overdraft of £230·50.

2. R. Tobermory is a decorator. He uses his Simplex D Account book to record full details of his day-by-day transactions. Enter the following items on the weekly page, for Week 18, 2nd August-8th August, 19... At the end of the week total the various sections and do the Weekly Cash and Bank Reports.

Receipts Wednesday Cash £16·50; Thursday cheque £85·85; Friday cheque £42·65; Saturday Cash £50.

Other Receipts Extra capital contributed by Tobermory £1 000 cheque on Wednesday.

Paid to Bank Friday £1 128·50 cheques.

Payments for Business Stock Decorators' Suppliers Ltd., were paid £84.60 by cheque on Thursday; Wallpapers Ltd. were paid £26·50 in cash on Saturday.

Other Payments Motor vehicle expenses, cheque £15·65; Lucas bought a ladder (capital item) £27·84 by cheque; Wages £72·50 cash.

Weekly Cash Report Began with a balance of £5·00. Cash drawn from Bank £100·00.

Weekly Bank Report Began with an overdraft of £327·50.

Unit Fourteen

The Weekly Page for Pure Service Businesses

14.1 Receipts

(a) Gross Daily Takings

The takings of this type of business consist of fees received for services rendered. The sums received should be put into a till if they are numerous, and the *totals* should then be entered each day in the 'Daily Takings' column.

(b) Debtors

Where services are given and credit is allowed to the customer, that customer becomes a debtor of your business. There are two ways of dealing with this problem (see Section 4.2). If you adopt the recommended method, which is to record the debt in a separate debtors' record book, remember to include the weekly total of 'debtors supplied during the week' in your total takings figure when you transfer it to the Weekly Summary of Takings.

(c) Other Receipts

(i) *Capital contributions.* If you put extra money into the business, for instance if you make payments out of your own pocket to keep the business going in the early days, you are in fact contributing additional capital, and this should be recorded in the 'Other Receipts' column.

(ii) *Loans from outsiders.* These should be recorded as 'Other Receipts': they become liabilities of the business.

(iii) *Debts settled.* If you have adopted the method referred to above for dealing with debtors, the cash you receive when the debt is finally paid must be treated as an 'Other Receipt'. If you were to record it under 'Daily Takings' it would be counted twice.

(iv) *Sundry earnings.* Any earnings which are not the result of normal 'services rendered' should be entered as 'Other Receipts'. Examples of sundry earnings include rent received from a sub-tenant, tax refunds, and receipts from credit-card companies.

14.2 Paid to Bank

In this section you record any amounts paid to bank, on the day you paid them in. This helps you with your bank reconciliation statement (see Section 16.4) and also enables you to prepare your Weekly Bank Report.

14.3 Payments for Business Stock

Businesses which offer a pure service rarely if ever buy stock for resale, and do not use materials to render a service. If your business is of this 'pure service' type, you may not need to make any entries at all in the 'Payments for Business Stock' section. If you do occasionally buy goods for resale, or to be worked into your service product in some way, enter them in date order as you make them, recording cash payments in the 'By Cash' column and cheque payments in the 'By Cheque' column.

Be careful not to enter capital purchases, such as office equipment or tools, in this section. They are recorded in the 'Payments Other than for Stock' columns.

14.4 Payments Other than for Stock

The method of recording 'Payments Other than for Stock' is exactly the same for the 'pure service' business as for all other businesses. A detailed account of the entries to be made under this heading is given in Section 10.4.

14.5 The Weekly Cash Report

The reasons for keeping a Weekly Cash Report are explained in Section 10.5. A detailed description of how to prepare the report will be found in Section 7.3, and you should refer to this section as you make your entries. Any difference between the expected cash balance and the actual till balance as counted should be investigated.

14.6 The Weekly Bank Report

The Weekly Bank Report should be completed in accordance with the instructions given in Section 7.2.

While it is not likely that theft can occur from your bank account, cheques are easily lost or stolen. The risks of leaving cheque-books and credit cards lying about are stressed in Section 10.6.

Remember, too, that you cannot check your bank account as easily as your till. You should therefore know how to draw up a bank reconciliation statement; this is explained in Section 16.4.

14.7 What to do at the End of the Week

Various book-keeping activities have to be carried out at the end of each week's trading—although some can be postponed if necessary. Since these activities are the same for all types of business, they are discussed collectively in Unit 15.

14.8 Exercises in Keeping the Weekly Page

1. M. Reagen is an osteopath. He uses his Simplex D Account Book to record details of his day-by-day receipts and payments. Enter the following items and total the weekly totals for Week No. 21, 23rd August–29th August 19...

Receipts Monday Cash £35·00, cheques £27·00; Tuesday Cash £42·00; Wednesday Cash £38·00, cheques £41·00. Thursday Cash £56·00; Friday Cash £48·00, cheques £17·00; Saturday Cash £36·00. On Friday a bad debt of £37·50 was recovered, by cheque.

Paid to Bank Wednesday £37 cash, cheques £57·00, Friday £80 cash, cheques £65·50.

Payments for Business Stock 24th August Masseurs Ltd, cheque £19·27, Rex Pharmacy £5·50 cash.

Other Payments Rent £128·00 by cheque. Sundries £5·80 cash Wages (wife) £25·00 cash. Drawings Cash £60 Secondhand X-ray machine (capital item) £280 by cheque.

Weekly Cash Report Opening balance £85·50.

Weekly Bank Report Opening balance £4 759·50.

2. Pat Sterling is a beauty consultant. She uses her Simplex D Account Book to record details of her day-by-day receipts and payments. Enter the following items and total the weekly totals for Week No. 24, 13th September–19th September 19...

Receipts Monday Cash £24 cheques £42·00; Tuesday Cash £28·50; Wednesday Cash £17·50, cheques £41·50; Thursday cash £48·00; Friday Cash £27·50, cheques £184·00; Saturday Cash £48.

Paid to Bank Tuesday £40·00 cash, cheques £42·00; Friday £74·50, cash cheques £225·50.

Payments for Business Stock Beauty Care Ltd, cheque £103·50 on 17th September.

Other Payments Rent £50·00 by cheque. Sundries £15·80 cash. Wages £35·00 cash. Drawings cash £60.

Weekly Cash Report Opening balance £85·50.

Weekly Bank Report Opening balance £1 760·50.

Carrying the Weekly Figures to the Summaries

15.1 Detailed Instructions for the End of the Week

The activities described below will be necessary at the end of the week. If you are using the Simplex system, however, they need not *all* be performed before the next week's records can be commenced. Activities that should be carried out as soon as the business closes for the weekend are listed in Section 15.2. Activities that may be postponed if necessary until there is a slack period in the following week, or even until the following weekend, are listed in Section 15.3.

The important point is that daily and weekly records must be made at the time they occur, but the carrying of the weekly totals to the summary pages at the back of the Simplex book may be postponed if necessary.

15.2 Activities that should be Carried Out At Once

On closing the business for the weekend, you should:

(*a*) Add up all the columns on the weekly page.

(*b*) Complete the Weekly Cash Report, and find the balance of cash in hand according to the book records.

(*c*) Check the till, and ensure that it agrees with the book-keeping balance. If it does not, discover the cause of the discrepancy—perhaps an entry in the cash payments has been overlooked. Note that any difference on books should be recorded in between the two lines. There is a good reason for this. If there is a regular disparity between the two figures the Inland Revenue will feel that it indicates a general slackness either in the book-keeping or in the supervision of the tills. It may be due to the proprietor taking money which is not being recorded as drawings. They may therefore regard the total difference on the books for the year as being an extra sum to be recorded as profit—the amount having actually been extracted as drawings. It cannot be too strongly emphasised that keeping correct records is vital in establishing a sound relationship with the Inland Revenue Department.

(*d*) When you have reconciled these figures, carry the cash figure forward to the next week, remove the cash from the till and take it home. Leave the till open so that it will not be damaged by any burglar trying to find out if there is cash in it.

(*e*) Similarly complete the Bank Report. You cannot of course check this book-keeping record with your bank record unless you carry out a bank reconciliation (see Section 16.4). Carry the closing balance forward ready for the start of next week's work.

Your book-keeping system is now ready for the following week. The activities listed in Section 15.3 still remain to be performed, but you need not worry about them until a spare moment is available.

15.3 Activities that may be Postponed Until Later

These items involve carrying the weekly figures to the analysis columns at the end of the Simplex book, so that they may be used to determine the profits of the business. The stages, which are described below, take only a few minutes; it will take you longer to read this page than it will to do the actual work once you get thoroughly familiar with it. Proceed as follows:

(a) Transfer the total daily-takings figure to the 'Weekly Summary of Takings'. In order to find this figure you must add together the following items:

    (i) the gross daily takings (cash),

    (ii) the gross daily takings (cheques),

    (iii) the debts recorded in the debtors' record book for the week, if you are using this system.

Now enter this total in the summary.

(b) Examine the 'Other Receipts' items. If they are debtors you need not record them in the weekly summary of takings if you are using the 'debtors' record book' method. If they are miscellaneous receipts or extra capital contributed or VAT repayments record them in the Summary of Other Receipts at the back of the Simplex D book. If a Loan has been received record it in the Summary of Loans and Repayments at the back of the book.

(c) Add together the totals of the 'By Cash' and 'By Cheque' columns in the 'Payments for Business Stock' section. The combined total is then carried to the 'Weekly Summary of Payments for Goods Purchased' page.

(d) Carry all the 'Payments Other than for Stock' to their appropriate summaries on the 'Summary of Payments for Expenses' pages. Sometimes a column has more than one item, e.g. 'Rent and Rates', and you must of course add these items together before entering them in the summary. In this summary there are several spare lines which can be used for expenses not listed on other lines, but peculiar to your business. Note that employees' National Insurance Contributions and PAYE tax deductions are really all part of wages. You can either gross up the Wages to the full figure or show the net figure in the 'Wages' column and put the total paid to Inland Revenue each month as one of the expenses of the business in the Inland Revenue column. It will then go in the Profit and Loss Account at the end of the year.

(e) Enter drawings in the 'Summary of Drawings for Self' section.

(f) Because of a House of Lords decision goods taken for own consumption have to be charged to the proprietor at selling price. Enter such items in the summary 'Goods for own Consumption' at the back of the book.

(g) Carry the capital items to the summary headed 'Capital Expenses incurred during the Year', recording in careful detail the reference numbers of any equipment or machinery purchased.

15.4 Quarterly Summaries

Every thirteen weeks you will come to the end of a quarterly period. You should then add up the quarterly totals, and carry them to the annual summary if one is provided. It is always interesting to see how one quarter compares with the next, but as the years go by you can compare the Spring Quarter, for example, with the previous Spring Quarter. This is even more interesting, since you are comparing figures which really should be similar as far as sales and expenses go. You can then see how your business is expanding or contracting.

15.5 The Further Development of this Book

You now know how to keep your weekly record and carry the entries to the summaries at the back of the Simplex book. It only remains to learn how to prepare the 'final accounts' at the end of the year. These accounts enable you to find the profit you have made in the trading period. Before proceeding to this final section, there are three important matters to which we must turn our attention. These are Bank Reconciliation Statements (Unit 16), Wages Books (Unit 17) and Value Added Tax (Unit 18).

Unit Sixteen

Bank Reconciliation Statements

16.1 Introduction

The word 'reconcile' means 'to make friends again'. It frequently happens in business that two sets of figures which should agree, for some reason do not. The commonest of all such situations is the apparent discrepancy between the bank balance shown in our Weekly Bank Report, and the actual balance as shown in the bank's ledger and notified to us when the bank sends us a 'bank statement'. When we show that these two seemingly conflicting figures are in fact compatible, we are effecting a reconciliation. The major British banks have recently adopted a computerized system which has changed the way in which bank statements are rendered to customers, but this is unlikely to affect the need for 'bank reconciliation statements' as described in the next few pages. In order to understand why reconciliation is necessary we must consider branch banking practice.

16.2 Practical Banking

When a customer opens a current account he is able to make and receive payments through the cheque system; the bank, for obvious reasons, does not undertake to correspond with the customer every time a transaction takes place. Some banks hardly ever write to their customers, except when an account is overdrawn. Similarly, the customer never writes to the bank to tell them he is making out a cheque. Every now and then the customer may ask for a bank statement, or the bank, feeling that a sufficiently large collection of paid cheques has accumulated on its files, will render a statement to the customer.

16.3 Why a Bank Statement usually Differs from our Weekly Bank Report

In practice it will rarely be the case that the bank's statement shows the same balance as our own Weekly Bank Report. The differences are always due to a lack of knowledge of what the other person has been doing. For example, there may be

(a) differences arising from the bank's actions, about which we have not been notified, or

(b) differences arising from the time-lag which is inevitable whenever cheques are sent in payment of debts, or are received and paid into the bank for clearing through the Bankers' Clearing House, or

(c) errors, either by the bank or by ourselves. Such errors are unlikely to occur frequently, because the banks usually institute careful checks on their figures, and we naturally do our best to avoid mistakes in our own book-keeping records. Inevitably though, mistakes do occur from time to time.

Fuller explanations of the first two causes of difference are desirable at this point.

(a) Lack of Knowledge of What the Bank has Done

There are many occasions when the bank does not bother to inform us that it has taken money from, or has credited money to, our account. It either sends us automatically, or expects us to ask for, a statement at regular intervals, usually on the last day of the calendar month. Not until we receive this statement do we learn that the bank has taken certain actions. The most common items discovered on the bank statement are as follows:

(i) Removal of sums for bank charges, or for interest on overdrafts.

(ii) Payment of standing orders and direct debits we have arranged in the past. Most people remember to deduct these sums from the bank account if they are monthly payments, for example mortgage payments or payments for rates. The less regular ones may be overlooked, such as annual subscriptions to trade associations and professional bodies.

(iii) Receipt of sums by credit transfer. Numerous debtors will use the credit-transfer system as a convenient method of paying sums directly into our bank account. The only problem is that until we receive our bank statement we usually have no idea that the debt has been settled. Such items will appear on the statement as a deposit increasing the balance.

When such items are discovered on a bank statement, they must at once be entered on the weekly page of the Simplex book. Any receipts by credit transfer, either from customers or investments, should be entered in the 'Other Receipts' section. Any deductions by the bank, either for bank charges or interest on loans, should be entered in the 'Payments Other than for Stock' section, in the 'By Cheque' column. Although a cheque has not been written out, the loss has been deducted from the bank account. Any standing orders which have been overlooked must be similarly entered in the 'Payments Other than for Stock' section.

(b) Delays Inevitable in the Cheque System

(i) Imagine that we send a cheque for £50·00 to the Betta Biscuit Company in Scotland. Before posting the letter containing the cheque, we enter the item in the 'Payments for Business Stock' section. It will probably be at least two days before that letter arrives, and when it does arrive the Betta Biscuit Company may take a day to get to the bank and pay it in. There will then be a further delay while the cheque is passed through the bank's head office in London, or the Bankers' Clearing House if two different banks are involved. During this time-lag, our Weekly Bank Report will show that we have deducted the cheque from our available funds, but the bank will think that we still have this money. Sometimes, when a creditor puts a cheque in his pocket and forgets to pay it in, several months may pass by before the bank statement and our Weekly Bank Report agree on this point. *Neither of them is wrong*, and it would be a mistake to 'correct' them or take any action—we must simply wait for the Betta Biscuit Company to put the matter right by paying the cheque into their account. Such a situation would be made clear in the *bank reconciliation statement*, which as its name implies, is a written statement explaining a difference between the two records.

(ii) Now imagine that it is the last day of the month, that we are going to collect a bank statement which the bank has already prepared for us, and while we are at the bank we will pay in some cheques which arrived in the morning mail. Before setting off we record these cheques in the 'Paid to Bank' section in our Simplex book, and list them in the paying-in book. When we receive our bank statement and examine it, we find of course that it is not completely up to date, because the cheques just paid in do not appear on it. If the cashier could stop work to up-date our bank statement, there would be no problem—but this is asking too much. Instead we shall have to explain the difference between our Weekly Bank Report and the bank statement by a sentence or two in a *bank reconciliation statement*.

16.4 How to draw up a Bank Reconciliation Statement

Consider the following bank statement as supplied by Barclays Bank to A. Ryder, on January 30th, 19... At this date the Weekly Report in Ryder's Simplex book showed a balance of £449·39.

A. Ryder—Bank Statement

In account with Barclays Bank Ltd.

Date	Details	Dr.	Cr.	Balance
		£	£	£
1.1.19..	Bal. c/fwd			508·40
3.1.19..	Cheque	14·16		494·24
5.1.19..	Sundries		62·80	557·04
12.1.19..	,,		75·00	632·04
14.1.19..	Standing Order	30·50		601·54
14.1.19..	Sundries		12·56	614·10
15.1.19..	Cheque	60·00		554·10
19.1.19..	Sundries		35·00	589·10
26.1.19..	,,		85·00	674·10
29.1.19..	Cheque	48·00		626·10
30.1.19..	Charges	4·55		621·55
30.1.19..	International Inventors (transfer)		12·80	634·35

The following points are of interest:

(a) The account is kept on a 'running-balance' method, by which the balance is shown on the account every day.

(b) Credit items are items paid in by Ryder, or credit transferred by someone who owes Ryder money (such as the transfer from International Inventors on January 30th). These items increase the balance on the account, because the bank owes Ryder more money.

(c) Debit items are cheques drawn by Ryder, and also charges deducted or standing orders paid. All these items reduce the balance on the account.

Ryder must now compare these items with his Weekly Bank Reports for the last month. Let us imagine that he finds the following items to be a source of difficulty:

(i) On January 30th Ryder paid into the bank a cheque for £14·94 received from R. Loring. This cheque has not yet been cleared by the bank so it does not appear on this bank statement. It is a 'time-lag' item.

(ii) The £12·80 which has been transferred by International Inventors to Ryder's account is assumed to be the payment of a debt and needs to be entered in his 'Other Receipts'. Ryder was not aware that the bank had collected this money on his account.

(iii) A cheque for £71·65 paid to T. Wilson on January 2nd has not yet been presented by him for collection through the Bankers' Clearing House. It does not appear on the bank statement at all. This is a time-lag item and will need to be explained in the bank reconciliation statement.

(iv) On January 30th the bank deducted £4·55 from Ryder's account for 'bank charges'. This needs to be entered in the 'Payments Other than for Stock' section, since it is the first Ryder has heard about the bank's action.

(v) On January 31st a cheque for £120·00 was made out to Anne Employee, but has not yet been presented for payment. Like Wilson's cheque in (iii) above, this is a time-lag item.

The first thing to do to reconcile the bank statement with Ryder's Simplex book is to make entries at once in the current Simplex Weekly page to take account of the bank's actions. We must enter Bank Charges in Payments other than for Stock, £4·55 and £12·80 in "Other Receipts" with "Payment by International Inventors" in the particulars column. This means that our next Weekly Bank Report will take account of these differences. In the meantime we can justifiably claim that our Simplex page balance has changed from £449·39 to £457·64. This is because we deduct £4·55 – leaving £444·84 – and then add £12·80, giving a new balance of £457·64. We now have to reconcile this balance of £457·64 with the Bank Statement figure of £634.35.

We can now draw up a 'reconciliation statement' as shown below:

BANK RECONCILIATION STATEMENT

(as at January 31st, 19..)   £

Balance as per Bank Report (amended)   457·64

deduct Cheque paid in, not yet cleared (*because the bank
does not know we have this money*)   R. Loring   14·94
                                                                                     ———
                                                                                     442·70

add Cheques drawn but not yet presented for payment (*because
the bank thinks we still have this money*) T. Wilson   71·65
                                                            Anne Employee 120·00
                                                                                     ———
                                                                                     191·65
                                                                                     ———
Balance as per bank statement   £634·35

The statement above satisfactorily reconciles the Weekly Bank Report with
the bank statement, and we may therefore feel confident that no errors on the
bank's part or Ryder's part have occurred.

The Bank Reconciliation Statement could just as easily have been written out
the opposite way, starting with the 'Balance as per Bank Statement' and ending
with the 'Balance as per Bank Report'. The explanations of course would be the
other way round, as shown below:

BANK RECONCILIATION STATEMENT

(as at January 31st., 19..)   £

Balance as per Bank Statement   634·35

deduct Cheques drawn but not yet presented for payment (*The Bank
thinks we still have this money but we know we have paid it out*)
                                                            J. Wilson   71·65
                                                            Anne
                                                            Employee   120·00
                                                                                    ———
                                                                                    191·65
                                                                                    ———
                                                                                    442·70

add Cheques paid in but not yet cleared (*because the Bank does
not yet realise we have received this money, but we know we have
paid it in*)   R. Loring   14·94
                                                                                    ———
Balance as per amended Bank Report   £457·64

It only takes half an hour every month to go through the bank statement and prepare this simple type of agreement between your records and the bank's. A neat copy of the bank reconciliation statement should be written out and filed away for reference purposes.

16.5 Paid Cheques as Receipts

Since the Cheques Act, 1957, declared cheques marked 'Paid' to be receipts, the customary method of giving a receipt when accounts are settled has fallen into disuse. Often the paid cheque is the only available proof that payment has been made, and it may need to be produced in support of the accounts. Few banks today, however, will return paid chqeues to their customers automatically—even though it is plainly desirable that this important evidence of payment should be on hand. You are therefore strongly urged to request your bank to return all paid cheques along with your bank statement. A small charge may be made for this service.

16.6 Exercises in Preparing Bank Reconciliation Statements

1. A. Cole's Bank Statement reads as follows for the months of March 19. .

Date	Details	Dr	Cr	Balance
		£	£	£
1.3.19..	Balance C/fwd			427·40
3.3.19..	Cheque	31·30		396·10
5.3.19..	Sundries		300·00	696·10
12.3.19..	Cheque	181·50		514·60
14.3.19..	Sundries		400·00	914·60
14.3.19..	Cheque	28·80		885·80
15.3.19..	Sundries		250·00	1135·80
19.3.19..	Sundries		350·00	1485·80
26.3.19..	Cheque	346·24		1139·56
29.3.19..	Sundries		350·00	1489·56
30.3.19..	Charges	12·50		1477·06
30.3.19..	Bank of England (transfer)		33·80	1510·86

On March 31st his Bank balance according to the Weekly Report in his Simplex D book was £1735·80. Checking through the month's records he finds the following differences between the bank statement and his Simplex D records.

The Bank charges he did not know about, and decides to enter them in the coming week.

The Bank of England transfer (dividend on Government Stock he holds) he also did not know about. He decides to enter this as an 'Other Receipt' in the coming week.

The £346·24 cheque paid out on 26th March was paid to Miller Services Ltd., for repair work. He had entirely forgotten to enter this in his Simplex D book. To save altering entries he decides to enter it in the coming week on his next Simplex Page.

Finally the payment into the bank on 19th March was recorded in error in his Simplex book as £250 like the previous entry. This error he also decides to put right by putting an extra entry of £100 in the Paid to Bank section next week.

Draw up a Bank Reconciliation Statement with suitable explanations.

2. The following statement was received from the bank indicating P. Marshalls position during January.

Bank Statement (as at January 31st 19. .)

Date	Details	Dr	Cr	Balance
Jan		£	£	£
1	Balance			411·55
3	Sundries		380·00	791·55
5	Direct Debit	104·50		687·05
9	Credit Transfer (J. Jones)		38·50	725·55
10	Cheque	221·65		503·90
13	Cheque	139·25		364·65
17	Sundries		584·50	949·15
20	Standing Order	60·05		889·10
22	Cheque	48·35		840·75
25	Cheque	72·64		768·11
29	Cheque	384·26		383·85
30	Sundries		580·00	963·85

Comparing these items with his Simplex D book Marshall finds that he had forgotten to deduct the Standing Order from his books and was not aware that J. Jones had transferred £38·50 to his account. He decides to make these the first entries in his next weekly page. In the meantime his Weekly Bank Report shows his Bank Balance as £985·40. Do the Bank Reconciliation Statement.

3. Here are the entries made by J. Wilson in his Simplex Account book for the last week of June. Opening Balance £3621·50; Paid to Bank Tuesday £425·00; Thursday £385·55; Friday £462·85; Cheques drawn A. Summer, £26·50; B. Greystone £134·48; M. Lord £85·80; personal Drawings £300·00; Final Balance £4348·12.

The Bank statement sent to him on June 30th reads:

Date	Details	Dr	Cr	Balance
June		£	£	£
25	Balance			3621·50
26	Sundries		425·00	4046·50
27	Cheque	26·50		
	Cheque	134·48		3885·52
29	Sundries		385·55	4271·07
	Cheque	300·00		3971·07
	Direct debit (rates)	89·92		3881·15

(a) What should J. Wilson do about the direct debit for rates?

(b) Draw up a Bank Reconciliation Statement.

4. Here are the entries made by B. Senior in his Simplex Account book for the last week in July. Opening Balance £423·78; Paid to Bank Wednesday, £495·28; Friday £584·94; Cheques drawn T. Morgan £31·75; M. Rice £42·55; R. Logan £178·62; Personal Drawings £160·00; Final Balance £1091·08.

His Bank Statement sent to him on July 31st reads:

Date	Details	Dr	Cr	Balance
July		£	£	£
26	Balance			505·50
	Cheque	81·72		423·78
28	Sundries		495·28	919·06
	Cheque	31·75		
	Cheque	178·62		708·69
30	Sundries		584·94	1293·63
	Direct Debit (Rates)	89·95		1203·68

Draw up a Bank Reconciliation Statement as at July 31st 19...

Unit Seventeen
The Wages Book

17.1 Introduction

In most countries today the employer is expected not only to pay the wages of his workers but also to act as an agent for the government in the collection of various forms of taxation. Welfare and social security services have grown to such an extent that it is quite impossible to finance them all by taxation on a few luxury goods, as in former times. Today every employee must pay contributions to National Health and Insurance schemes, and many must also pay income tax and pension contributions. Many also make voluntary contributions to savings schemes and to charitable organizations. These contributions are deducted from the employee's gross wages, and the employer is responsible for paying the collected totals over to the Inland Revenue Authorities, National Savings Movement, or whoever is to receive them.

17.2 The Simplex Wages System

The "Wages Book" illustrated in Fig. 17.1 is a companion to the Simplex D Account Book. It is suitable for any small business having up to 28 employees.

The book includes a list of employees at the front, 52 weekly pages, and summary pages at the back. Since the weekly pages are cut shorter than the first page, the list of employees is visible all the year round.

Columns are provided for gross pay, statutory sick pay, and for deductions (pensions, tax, etc). These deductions are then totalled, and when deducted from

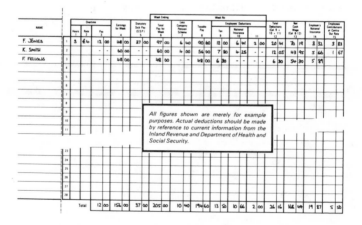

Fig. 17.1 *A Simplex wages book*

the gross pay give the net wage payable. Columns are also provided for the employer's contributions, and the sub-totals provided each week give the necessary entries to go into the weekly page of the Simplex accounts book.

For comparison with previous weeks and months, a 'Summary of Wages' is provided at the back of the wages book; the first half-year of such a summary is shown in Fig. 17.2.

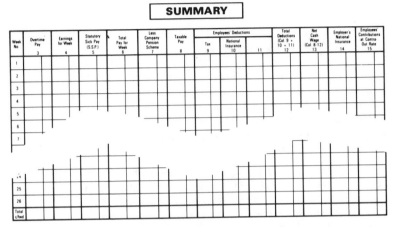

SUMMARY

Fig. 17.2 *The first half-yearly summary of wages*

17.3 Pay As You Earn

As far as employees are concerned, income tax in Britain is collected by a 'pay-as-you-earn' system—usually abbreviated to PAYE. This is much the most convenient system for the ordinary employee, since he does not have to save money in order to pay his income tax. Instead the tax, and various other deductions, are removed before his pay packet is prepared; the net 'take-home' pay is the residue which is available for the employee's own use. There are suggestions that this PAYE system will be ended shortly, but over the years it has proved an efficient and cheap method of collection.

PAYE is based on the following arrangements:

(a) **Code numbers.** Every employee is given a *code number,* based on the allowances to which he is entitled. These include *personal allowances* (for single and married persons), *dependent relatives allowances, daughter's services, housekeeper's services,* and other small allowances for disablements such as blindness. A person with heavy responsibilities has large allowances and hence a high code number; a person with few responsibilities has a low code number and is taxed more heavily. A change in circumstances, for instance the assumption of duties to help a dependent relative results in a change of code number as soon as it is reported.

(*b*) **Tax tables.** These are prepared by the Inland Revenue and issued to employers. They enable the employer, by consulting the tax table, to determine exactly how much tax should have been deducted by that week in the year. He can then compare this figure with the total tax paid already up to the previous week. The difference must be the amount that is to be deducted from the current week's pay packet. If a change of circumstances has resulted in an employee's code number being raised, he may already have paid more tax than is now due. This will be revealed by the tax tables. If a refund is due to the employee, it is put at once into the pay packet.

The total sums deducted from pay for taxation are payable each month by the employer to the Inland Revenue authorities.

(*c*) **Other important tax records.** The 'P45' is a form which is given to employees who change employment. Before the new employer can deduct the correct tax, he must know the amount deducted by the previous employer and the total pay earned in the previous appointment. This information is supplied to him by the old employer on Form P45 given to the employee when he terminated his employment.

The 'P60' is a form given to all employees at the end of the tax year. It shows the total pay received, the tax deducted, the National Health and other payments made, and the net pay. It is widely used as part of the social security system, and should be preserved by the employee in case he, or his family, wish to claim benefits such as student grants.

Supplies of these forms are available from your local tax office.

WEEK No.	PAYE		Eee. Nat. Ins. Contr.		Eer. Nat. Ins. Contr.		TOTAL		Less S.S.P. Reclaimed		NET PAYABLE	
	Col. 9		Col. 10		Col. 14				Col. 5			
Total Due to Inland Revenue												
Date Paid:							Cheque No.:					

Fig. 17.3 *Summary of Payments to Inland Revenue*

(d) Since 1975 when National Insurance cards were abolished, all sums due for both PAYE and National Insurance contributions (both employee's and employer's contributions) are payable monthly to the Inland Revenue Authorities. To assist the employer the Simplex Wages Book includes at the back twelve monthly 'Summaries of Payments to Inland Revenue' where the weekly sums due can be recorded and added together to give the monthly total due, the date of payment and the cheque number. One of these summaries is shown in Fig. 17.3.

17.4 Keeping the Wages Book

The work of keeping a wages book is completed in the following stages:

(a) Enter the name of employees on the first page of the book.

(b) Record each employee's wages, contributions, etc. each week on the line opposite his name. If statutory sick pay is included this should be shown separately.

(c) Add up the columns to obtain the weekly totals; carry these totals to the summary at the end of the book.

(d) Obtain the necessary cash from the till or the bank, and make up the wages envelopes.

(e) Enter in the Simplex account book the total wages paid.

(f) If it is the correct week to remit PAYE etc to the Inland Revenue Authorities, and to reclaim statutory sick pay, complete the summary at the back of the Simplex Wages Book, make the necessary payment and enter it in the Simplex D account book.

17.5 Croner's Reference Book for Employers

Employers have many responsibilities to employees besides the payment of wages. *Croner's Reference Book for Employers,* now in its 25th year, is intended to provide an up-to-date guide to such matters.

Further information may be obtained from Croner Publications, whose address is given in the Foreword to this book.

17.6 Wages and Self-Certified Sickness Payments

Changes in United Kingdom sick pay legislation are transferring responsibility for payment of sickness benefits to employers. Since April 1983 the first eight weeks of sick pay have had to be paid by the employer. In order to reclaim this money employers must keep 'self-certified sickness' records. Forms for this purpose are available from Formecon Services Ltd, Gateway, Crewe, CW1 1YN.

17.7 Exercises in Keeping the Wages Book

Four exercises for keeping the Wages Book appear overleaf. These exercises require special ruled paper which may be obtained at an economical price from George Vyner Ltd., at the address shown in the front of this book. Please write for a supply if you wish to use these exercises in schools or colleges.

For exercises see page 82.

Notes: (a) Gross Wage for week = Weekly wage + overtime pay
(b) Taxable Pay = Gross Wage for Week − Pension Contribution
(c) Nett Wage = Taxable Pay − Total Deductions

Name	Overtime Hours	Rate (£)	Wage for week (£)	Company Pension Contribution (£)	Tax (£)	National Insurance (£)	Employer's Nat. Insurance (£)	Employee's Contribution at contracted out rate
Question 1								
Mr. A.	2½	1·30	56	2·00	—	2·81	6·12	1·67
Mr. B.	4	1·50	52	2·00	—	2·77	6·03	1·63
Miss C.	—	—	42	1·50	4·20	2·13	4·59	0·99
Question 2								
Mr. G.	4	1·30	68	3·00	2·60	3·37	7·38	2·23
Mrs. H.	—	—	75	3·50	8·50	3·45	7·56	2·31
Mr. J.	5½	2·20	48	1·50	2·00	2·85	6·21	1·71
Question 3								
Mr. P.	3½	1·50	56	2·00	—	2·89	6·30	1·75
Mrs. Q.	3½	1·50	52	2·00	—	2·73	5·94	1·59
Miss R.	5	0·95	48	1·50	3·20	2·55	5·53	1·41
Question 4								
Mrs. X.	3	1·80	60	3·00	4·50	3·05	6·66	1·91
Mr. Y.	8	1·30	78	3·50	2·00	3·97	8·73	2·83
Miss Z.	4	1·50	54	2·00	4·20	2·85	6·21	1·71

Unit Eighteen

Value Added Tax

18.1 Introduction: How VAT Works

Value Added Tax was introduced in April 1973 as a new form of taxation, replacing Purchase Tax and Selective Employment Tax. It brings the British tax system to some extent into line with Common Market tax systems, but in truth there is no uniform system of Value Added Tax. The British system is based on a 15 per cent tax on the majority of goods and services required by ordinary consumers. Certain items are 'zero-rated', which means that they are taxed but the rate of tax is zero. Other items are 'exempt', which means that in theory the consumer does not pay tax on these items. In fact there is a hidden tax item even when goods or services are exempt. This is because the exempt items, for example dental services, have to be supplied by professional people who will pay VAT on almost all supplies they use in their services. These higher costs will have to be passed on to the consumer in higher prices.

The basic idea of VAT is that tax is added at every stage of production as value is added to the product. The word 'production' is being used here in its economic meaning. Economists say that an article has not been completely 'produced' until it reaches the final consumer. Thus a typical chain of production might read as follows:

GROWER → MANUFACTURER → WHOLESALER → RETAILER → CONSUMER

Let us consider a tree cut down in a Forestry Commission plantation and made into a ladder which eventually is purchased by one Inigo Jones, a do-it-yourself enthusiast. The ladder costs Jones £10, but in fact the Forestry Commission charged £3 for the tree; the Wemakem Ladder Co. charged £6 for the ladder to Distribution Ltd., who charged Adam Smith (Hardware & Ironmongery) £8 for it. The value *added* in each stage was £3, £3, £2 and £2, respectively. VAT would be levied all the way along the 'production' line at 15 per cent of the added value. Thus the Forestry Commission would charge the Wemakem Ladder Co. an extra 45 pence tax; Wemakem would charge Distribution Ltd. 90 pence; Distribution Ltd. would charge Smith the retailer £1·20, and Smith would charge the final consumer Jones £1·50 in tax.

The tax paid by a purchaser as goods come into his business is called *input tax*. The tax collected as goods go out of his business is called *output tax*. The output tax should usually be higher than the input tax, because the businessman has 'added' value to the goods—even if he merely adds his profit margin. Thus in the example above, the Wemakem Ladder Co. has input and output taxes as follows:

	Input Tax	Output Tax
	15% of £3	15% of £6
	= 45 pence	= 90 pence

Its tax liability is therefore $(90 - 45) = 45$ pence.

Note that the tax which the firm must pay over to HM Customs & Excise finishes up as 15 per cent of the value it has added. But the Ladder Co. has not really paid this tax; it collected it from Distribution Ltd. Distribution in turn collect it from Smith the ironmonger, and he in turn collects it from the customer. In fact the only person who really pays tax is the final consumer. The firms who pay tax over to HM Customs & Excise only do so as the agents for the Government in the collection of the tax. They are not paying it out of their own pockets. A full explanation is given in Fig. 18.1.

	Forestry Commission	Wemakem Ladder Co.	Distribution Ltd.	A. Smith (ironmonger)	I. Jones (consumer)
Cost price without tax	—	£3·00	£6·00	£8·00	£10·00
Selling price without tax	£3·00	£6·00	£8·00	£10·00	—
Value added	£3·00	£3·00	£2·00	£2·00	—
Cost price with tax	—	£3.45	£6.90	£9.20	£11.50
Selling price with tax	£3.45	£6.90	£9.20	£11.50	—
Input tax	—	45p	90p	£1.20	£1.50
Output tax	45p	90p	£1.20	£1.50	—
VAT payable to Customs & Excise	(45 – 0)p 45p	(90 – 45)p 45p	(£1.20 – 90)p 30p	(£1.50 – £1.20)p 30p	—

Fig. 18.1 How Value Added Tax works. Note that the final consumer (Jones) pays £1.50 tax to the retailer. This £1.50 reaches the Customs and Excise as a succession of payments by all those businesses where value has been added, i.e.

$$as\ 45p + 45p + 30p + 30p = £1.50$$

18.2 Registration for VAT

Any businessman who supplies goods and services which are not exempt and whose turnover exceeds £20 500 per year, or £7 000 in the last calendar quarter, or who believes that turnover in the next year will exceed £20 500 must register as a taxable person. Deregistration is permitted, since the limits of registration were raised, if turnover is expected to be less than £19 500 in the year ahead. Persons who feel that registration will be advantageous to them, even though their turnover is less than the agreed level, are permitted to register voluntarily, but are required to remain on the register for at least two years.

Special cases, listed in Schedule 5 of the Act, are land, insurance, postal services, betting, gaming and lotteries, finance, education, health, and burial or cremation services. Firms in these fields need not register and need not keep records, but will not be able to deduct input taxes paid on goods purchased for use in the business. They are therefore effectively being treated like consumers, subject to tax. This is by no means advantageous.

To register you complete Form VAT 1, obtainable from your local office of HM Customs & Excise. Once registered you have the following duties to perform:

(a) To record your inputs.

(b) To record your outputs or keep records for an appropriate Small Retailers' Scheme.

(c) To complete your VAT return (Form VAT 100) at intervals, specifying in it which (if any) of the special retailers' schemes you are using.

(d) To keep records and accounts adequate for these purposes.

(e) To pay the tax as it falls due, if it exceeds £1. Payment by cheque, bank giro or National Giro should accompany the return form.

A trader who sells zero-rated goods to consumers will usually be entitled to a refund of tax rather than be liable to pay tax. Sometimes this may mean positive hardship to a retailer who has paid tax but cannot obtain a refund for three months. In such cases it will be possible to obtain refunds of tax monthly, by arrangement with your local Customs & Excise office.

18.3 Special Schemes for Retailers

'Retailers' are not necessarily shopkeepers, but anyone who supplies goods and services to the public without tax invoices. Such businesses may find it difficult to comply with the legal requirement to calculate the output tax on every supply that they make, as it takes place. Clearly this would be quite impossible for many shopkeepers at busy peak periods. Special schemes have therefore been devised to enable the retailer to calculate his output tax at the end of the tax period without recording every sale separately. (There are no special schemes for *input* tax; retailers will almost always be supplied by wholesalers who give tax invoices which will enable them to calculate the input tax easily.) These special schemes are characterised below, (details are given later in this Unit). In these brief descriptions reference is made to 'rates of tax'. At present there are only two rates of tax, *zero rate* (0 per cent) and *standard rate* (15 per cent). At one time a *higher rate* was also used. Any rate above zero rate is referred to as a *'positive'* rate of tax.

Scheme A. This scheme is designed for retailers who only sell goods at one rate of tax.

Scheme B. This scheme may be used by retailers who sell goods at two rates of tax only, but not at more than two rates. Zero counts as a separate rate. The condition is that the goods sold at the lower rate of the two, do not form more than one half (50 per cent) of the total. If they do form more than one half another scheme must be chosen. It can also be used for services provided the services are taxed at the higher of the two rates in use.

Scheme C. This scheme is for retailers with a small turnover (less than £50 000 a year) whose Trade Classification is from 8 201-8 239. This number is shown on the retailers Certificate of Registration (Form VAT 4).

Scheme D. This scheme is for retailers whose taxable turnover is less than £125 000 per year. The proportion of goods bought at each rate of tax is applied to the selling price (gross takings) to find out how much output tax has to be accounted for.

Scheme E. This scheme is suitable for large scale retailers who can keep detailed records of the total amount, including VAT, which customers will be paying for goods received by the retailer, at each positive rate of tax.

Scheme F. Is suitable for retailers whose goods and services are supplied at more than one rate of tax, but who can separate the sales at each rate of tax at the point of sale.

Scheme G. This scheme is suitable for the small retailer who wants to keep his records as simple as possible. No output records are necessary except gross daily takings; the calculations of output tax are based on the cost of goods to the retailer. After the tax has been calculated by the method explained later, it has to be raised by one eighth, as experience has shown this method slightly understates the VAT payable. For businesses only concerned with two positive rates of tax the addition is only one-twelfth. This rule can be taken advantage of by retailers who sell only a tiny quantity (less than 2 per cent of turnover) of zero-rated items.

Scheme H and Scheme J. These schemes are only suitable for multiple shops and other retail outlets where exact details of the quantities of each different line can be recorded consistently. It follows that most small businessmen will not select these schemes.

Note: One final point on these schemes is that where a retailer has several departments or shops, and is able to keep separate records for them, he may choose to account for one field of activity on one Scheme and another field of activity on a different scheme. The rules for this are given in Notice No 727 Section 25.

18.4 Choosing a VAT Method and a Definition of Gross Takings

Before you can begin to keep your VAT records you need to decide which method you are going to use and how you are going to define your 'gross takings'.

(a) Which Method?

The *normal* method of calculating VAT is by keeping a record of tax inputs and tax outputs, using the 'tax invoices' received from suppliers or given to customers. If you are issuing tax invoices (see Fig. 18.2) you will keep your records by this normal method. If you are not using tax invoices you will have to keep records by one of the *special schemes for retailers*.

Fig. 18.3 tabulates the schemes and enables you to choose the one that seems best for your business. The last column of Fig. 18.3 indicates how you should use the rest of this Unit to solve your VAT problems. Whichever choice you make, you must identify the method selected in the space provided on your VAT Account when you submit it to HM Customs & Excise.

(b) Which Definition of Gross Takings?

There are two methods of calculating 'gross takings' for the period, the **standard definition** and the **optional definition.** The standard definition is based on payments received in the period and is most useful to those who do not sell on credit,

---

SALES INVOICE No. 74   14 August 1979
To A Retailer Ltd.
48 North Road, London N12 5NA.
From: Foundation Trading (UK) Ltd.
Bowman Street, Chester.   VAT Regd. No. 987 6543 21
Sale

Quantity	Description and Price	Amount exclusive of VAT	VAT Rate	VAT Net
		£	%	£
6	Radios, SW14 at £21.30	127.80		
12	Record Players P38 at £9.80	117.60		
6	Amplifiers J27 at £11.80	70.80		
		316.20	15	45.06*
	Delivery (strictly net)	6.00	15	0.90
Terms: Cash Discount of 5% if paid within 14 days		322.20		45.96
	VAT	£45.96		
Tax Point: 14/8/1979	TOTAL	£368.16		

*This is calculated on the discount price

Fig. 18.2 *A tax invoice (courtesy of HM Customs & Excise)*

and consequently have no debtors. The optional definition is based on the sales figure, both in cash and on credit. It follows that with this method the retailer pays VAT on sales even though he may never be paid by some of his debtors. Clearly this is disadvantageous to the retailer. It is now possible for retailers to claim VAT where the debtor is formally deemed to be insolvent. The rules provide that the retailer will claim as a creditor in the bankruptcy proceedings for the net amount of debt only, and claim the VAT refund in his VAT accounts. This will reduce the disadvantage of the optional definition to some extent, though it will give no relief in the large number of cases where traders do not pursue debtors as far as formal bankruptcy proceedings.

If you decide to use this alternative definition you must notify the Customs and Excise Authorities in writing before you start the scheme. A full description of these definitions is given later.

The Simplex VAT Book

The Simplex VAT book, a companion volume to the Simplex account book, has been designed to cater for any small business, of whatever type, and whatever scheme it is using. The following points are of interest:

(a) The book is intended for the sole purpose of keeping VAT records as required by the VAT regulations. It is not meant for recording financial accounts, which must still be kept separately.

(b) The records should be entered daily.

(c) The book is divided into four quarters, or VAT periods.

(d) Each quarterly part contains:

(i) Thirteen pages of input account, for recording 'input' tax invoices received from suppliers.

(ii) Ten pages of output account, for recording 'output' tax invoices sent to customers, and output hire-purchase or credit-sale agreements.

(iii) One page, of which half is for recording returns sent out to suppliers and half is for recording returns by customers.

(iv) Three pages each of which is given over to one month's Daily Takings records. Thus the trader dealing chiefly in zero-rated sales who wishes to claim a VAT refund each month is able to find his monthly 'Gross Takings' total easily, while the trader who only sends in a quarterly return simply adds the three monthly totals together.

(v) Three pages each given over to calculations and a VAT Return, from which the actual VAT Return Form 100 can be prepared, either monthly or quarterly.

All these records must be preserved for three years, unless a shorter period has been agreed by HM Customs & Excise.

You should now consult Fig. 18.3 and decide which method of VAT records is appropriate to your business. The suitability of the various schemes is given in the second column.

When you have decided which method or scheme you are going to use, you will find it helpful to study the third column, which tells you what records it is necessary to keep. The last column then tells you which part of the text you should read for a description of your particular method. Fig 18.3 starts below.

18.5 VAT by the Normal Method

(a) The Input Account

You should record in the Input Account details of all invoices in respect of purchases of goods or services made by you. It is to your advantage to record such invoices immediately they are received, even if you do not pay them immediately. You are obliged to identify separately (i) goods for retailing and (ii) services (your general business overheads, including business stationery, etc.), taxable at different rates. Columns have therefore been provided in the Simplex VAT book to enable this to be done (see Fig. 18.4). For convenience we have imagined a multiple rate system using Standard Rate 15%, Positive Rate A 25%, Positive Rate B 40% and zero rated items. Until a multiple-rate system is introduced columns A and B should be left blank.

The totals at the end of each page are to be carried forward to the next page. Seven pages are provided in all, which should be adequate for most small

(continues on page 91)

Note: Fig 18.3 starts here and continues on pages 90-91.

Method	*Who is it suitable for?*	*Records to be kept*	*Remarks*
Normal Method	Suppliers of goods or services, for which proper tax invoices are issued to customers.	(a) Figures for all taxable inputs (b) All taxable outputs of goods (c) All taxable outputs of services (d) Goods applied to personal use (e) Taxable self supplies (f) Credits for returns in or out	Read Section 18.5 in the main text Can be used for services, hirings etc.
Scheme A	Suppliers of goods and/or services at the standard rate of tax	(a) Daily gross takings	Read Section 18.6 and 18.7 in the main text

Method	Who is it suitable for?	Records to be kept	Remarks
Scheme B	Firms which supply goods without tax invoices at two rates of tax only. Services may be included if they are at the higher rate of the two. The goods sold at the lower rate must not be more than half (50 per cent) of taxable turnover.	(a) Gross daily takings for all goods (lower rate goods need not be recorded separately) (b) Cost price plus profit margin and VAT (if any) of all goods at the lower rate of the two (c) Sales figures for HP (etc.) goods (d) All goods applied to personal use	Read Sections 18.5, 18.6 and 18.8 in the main text See first column about services under this Scheme
Scheme C	Firms in trades 8201-8239 and whose taxable turnover is less than £75 000. Not to be used for goods grown or manufactured, or for services.	(a) The cost to you (including VAT) of all the things bought at a positive rate of tax (b) The cost to you of all zero rated items (c) If growing or man-manufacturing you must use some other scheme for these items and keep records accordingly—or use the normal method	Read Section 18.9 in the main text For (c) read Section 18.5 in the main text, or see other schemes
Scheme D	Firms where sales at different rates cannot easily be distinguished; and where total turnover is less than £200 000 per year. This scheme may not be used for services.	(a) Gross daily takings (b) Cost (including VAT) of all goods purchased (c) Sales figures for HP (etc) goods (d) All goods applied to personal use	The scheme calls for an annual scheme adjustment. Read Sections 18.5, 18.6 and 18.10 Not to be used for goods grown or manufactured, or for services.

Method	Who is it suitable for?	Records to be kept	Remarks
Scheme E	Multiple shops and other retailers who can consistently record all types of goods at selling price	Details of these schemes may be obtained from your local VAT office	Not described in this text
Scheme F	Firms which supply the following without tax invoices: (*a*) services, and/or (*b*) goods, where sales at standard and zero rates can be clearly distinguished	(*a*) Separate gross daily takings for all standard-rate, and zero-rate goods or services (*b*) Sales figures for HP (etc) goods (*c*) All goods applied to personal use	Read Sections 18.5, 18.6 and 18.11 in the main text Can be used for services, hirings etc.
Scheme G	Same as D above but this scheme is for businesses whose turnover exceeds £200 000. Cannot be used for services or for goods grown or manufactured.	(*a*) Cost (inc. VAT) of stock in hand at at start, with a separate total for each rate of tax (*b*) Cost of goods purchased (including VAT) for each rate of tax (*c*) Gross daily takings (*d*) Sales figures for HP (etc) goods (*e*) Taxable outputs of services (*f*) All goods applied to personal use	Read Sections 18.5, 18.6 and 18.12 in the main text
Schemes H and J	See E above	See E above	See E above

Fig. 18.3 *Choosing the most appropriate method of VAT for your business*

businesses. Returns should then be deducted by taking away the totals carried from the 'Input Returns' account. The final total in the right-hand column labelled 'Carry this total to the VAT Account' is then ready to be carried to the VAT account, either monthly or quarterly.

Number all invoices in the order in which you receive them, and keep them in your filing system.

According to Fig. 18.4 you have received a VAT invoice from one of your suppliers, Smith & Jones, for standard-rate goods to the value of £50 (on which you have been charged VAT of £7.50), positive rate A goods of £40 (tax £10) and positive rate B goods of £100 (tax £40). Zero rated goods value £5 have also been supplied. Subsequently you have returned goods to the value of £6 (tax 90 pence). At the end of the period the total of the returns on the Input Returns section will be deducted from the total purchases for the quarter, to give the final total of deductible VAT input tax.

Input records are used in some of the Special Schemes for Retailers as the basis for output tax. For example, if a retailer cannot separate off the amounts sold at different rates of tax himself, the Customs & Excise will assume that what he sells must be what he buys. Therefore, if they can tell from the Input Records what he buys at Standard Rate and Zero Rate it is fairly easy to work out what he sells at these rates. This is explained more fully in Sections 18.9, 18.10 and 18.12 below.

INPUT ACCOUNT—PURCHASES OF GOODS AND SERVICES

Invoice Date	Invoice Number	From whom purchased	Invoice Total		Cost of Goods (excluding VAT) Standard Rate		Positive Rate 'A'		Positive Rate 'B'		Zero Rated Goods		Input Services		Exempt and non deductible (incl. VAT)		Deductible VAT Input Tax	
APR 3	00214	SMITH & JONES	252	50	50	00	40	00	100	00	5	00					57	50
		Totals carried forward to next page																

If this page is your last for the current VAT period, do not use the 'Totals carried forward' line but complete your records below

Totals for accounting period			31807	08	13450	00	4017	50	5268	00	3757	50			185	00	5129	08
Less totals from 'Input returns (credits) account'			506	48	108	00	44	70	221	00	17	00					115	78
Grand totals for accounting period			31300	60	13342	00	3972	80	5047	00	3740	50			185	00	5013	30

Carry this total to the VAT Account ➤

INPUT RETURNS—(CREDITS) ON GOODS PURCHASED

Invoice Date	Invoice Number	From whom received	Credit Note Total		Cost of Goods (excluding VAT) Standard Rate		Positive Rate 'A'		Positive Rate 'B'		Zero Rated Goods		Input Services		Exempt and non deductible (incl. VAT)		Deductible VAT Input Tax	
APR 7	00310	SMITH & JONES	6	90	6	00											90	
		Totals to be carried to 'Input Account'	506	48	108	00	44	70	221	00	17	00					115	78

Fig. 18.4 *The Simplex VAT input records*

(b) The Output Account

If you are recording VAT by the normal method, details of all VAT invoices issued by you during the account period have to be entered in the Output Account section of the VAT book. The details should be recorded in the columns shown in Fig. 18.5, according to the column headings. If you are using one of the small retailer's schemes you should only record in the Output Account invoices issued in respect of goods or services that fall *outside* the scheme. The invoices should be numbered and recorded consecutively.

Numbered copy invoices should be kept. Two spare columns for Positive Rate A and B have been provided for use if the Chancellor should introduce a multi-rate system; until then they should be left blank.

If you sell goods under written hire-purchase or credit-sale agreements, appropriate documents must be issued and the details recorded in the relevant columns of the Output Account. The totals at the end of each page are to be carried forward to the next page.

OUTPUT ACCOUNT—INVOICED SALES, SERVICES, WRITTEN HP & CREDIT SALE TRANSACTIONS

Date	Number	To whom sold	Gross Invoice Total	Standard Rate	Positive Rate 'A'	Positive Rate 'B'	Liable at Zero Rate	Exempt	Export Sales	V.A.T. Output Tax
APR 1	0001	R.T. Brown	317 00	80 00	60 00	100 00	10 00			67 00

| Totals carried forward to next page | | | | | | | | | |

If this page is your last for the current VAT period, do not use the 'Totals carried forward' line but complete your records below:

Totals for accounting period	58016 06	26146 00	8211 41	9765 00	4012 90			9880 75
Less totals from 'Output returns (Credits)' account	669 15	325 00	48 00	160 00	11 40			124 75
Grand totals for accounting period	57346 91	25821 00	8163 41	9605 00	4001 50			9756 00

Carry this total to the VAT Account ⟶

OUTPUT RETURNS—(CREDITS) ON GOODS SOLD

Date	Number	To whom given	Credit Note Total	Standard Rate	Positive Rate 'A'	Positive Rate 'B'	Liable at Zero Rate	Exempt	Export Sales	VAT Output Tax
APR 7	0012	R.T. Brown	11 50	10 00						1 50

| Totals to be carried to 'Output Account' | 669 15 | 325 00 | 48 00 | 160 00 | 11 40 | | | 124 75 |

Fig. 18.5 *The Simplex VAT output records*

According to Fig. 18.5 you have sold and invoiced R.T. Brown for standard-rate goods value £80 (on which you have charged VAT of £12), positive rate A goods of £60 (tax £15) and positive rate B goods of £100 (tax £40). Zero rated goods value £10 have also been supplied. Subsequently you have had returned to you by Brown standard rated goods worth £10 (tax £1.50). At the end of the period the returns in the Output Returns section will be deducted from the total outputs to give the net total of outputs to be carried to the VAT Account.

(c) The VAT Account

At the end of each VAT period the figures of input tax and output tax are carried from the Input and Output Accounts to the VAT Account, and are then used to complete the VAT Return which you will receive from HM Customs & Excise. A 'normal' VAT Account is shown in Fig. 18.6.

18.6 Gross Daily Takings

The whole idea of the small retailer's schemes is to enable small businesses, which do not give their customers tax invoices, to account for VAT in a relatively simple way. All these schemes require the businessman to know his

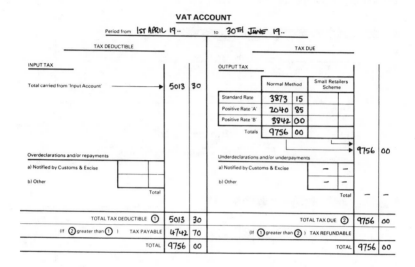

Fig. 18.6 *A VAT Account by the normal method*

quarterly total of gross daily takings. There are two methods of calculating this: (*a*) the 'Standard Method', based on the payments actually received from customers in the tax period, and (*b*) the optional method which is based on supplies during the tax period whether payment was received or not.

(*a*) The Standard Method

Gross daily takings for the purpose of VAT special schemes means the total value of all the supplies made by the retailer *inside* the scheme. Any items he sells on hire-purchase, credit-sale or conditional-sale terms, having completed a proper agreement under the Hire Purchase Acts, are *outside the scheme* and should be accounted for by the 'normal' method (see Section 18.5). Any services (as opposed to goods) are outside Schemes C, D, E, G, H and J, and if they are at lower rate they are outside Scheme B as well and must be accounted for either by the normal VAT method or by Schemes A or F. Goods applied to your own use are inside the scheme, and should be included in the gross daily takings at selling price, including tax. So are any goods sold against Barclaycard, Access and other credit cards. You must also include the face value of all trading checks, coupons, vouchers, book tokens, record tokens and gift tokens which you exchange for goods. If you run your own trading-stamp scheme and exchange stamps for goods, you do not include these in takings.

Add all these items together on the 'Daily Takings' page of your VAT book, as shown in Fig. 18.7, and then deduct from the total figure all items which reduce your takings, for example cash refunds to customers who return goods or present trading stamps for redemption *in cash*. (If they redeem trading stamps in goods, you have already disregarded these in working out your takings.) You also deduct takings on written HP agreements, payments to trading-stamp companies for stamps supplied, and all the services supplied unless you are using Schemes A or F or Scheme B in certain circumstances.

When you have subtracted the total of these deductions from the total takings, you are left with your 'Gross Daily Takings' figure.

(b) The Optional Method

The calculation is the same as in the standard method already described except that sales made on credit must be included (+ VAT) in the daily takings figure. This means that later on, when they actually pay, the settlement payments are left out of the calculation. Also left out of the calculation are payments received in the trading period for goods supplied before the trader starts to use the optional method.

Other Points of Interest

The records of gross daily takings must be made every day. Many of the columns will only require an entry occasionally, and some retailers may never require to make entries in certain of the columns.

At the end of the month, or the quarter, according to the length of your trading period for VAT, all columns must be totalled. A retailer who wishes to simplify this addition should consider the purchase of a printing calculator. These are appreciably more expensive than an ordinary calculator, but they do give a print-out of your entries which you can use to compare with your VAT book.

The final total in Column 11 of the VAT book is the figure to be used for calculation of the output tax. This calculation will have to be in accordance with your Scheme leaflet, obtainable from your tax office; specimen calculations are given in Sections 18.7, 18.8, 18.9, 18.10, 18.11 and 18.12.

All calculations and records must be kept for six years, together with all documents relating thereto, unless a Customs & Excise official has authorised their destruction, permission for which must be sought well in advance.

VAT fractions

When output tax is calculated from Gross Daily Takings we have to use a VAT fraction. It is interesting to know how the fractions are arrived at. Here is a short explanation.

Standard-rate Goods – VAT Fraction $= \frac{3}{23}$

When we sell goods at standard rate, we add on 15 per cent VAT. The goods therefore sell at:

$$\text{Selling Price} + 15\% = 100\% + 15\% = 115\%$$

If we now want to find out how much VAT is included in the gross takings total for standard-rated goods it is not $\frac{15}{100}$, but $\frac{15}{115}$ ths of the total. $\frac{15}{115}$ cancels down to $\frac{3}{23}$ and that is why the VAT fraction for standard-rated goods is $\frac{3}{23}$.

Other positive-rated goods At present there are no goods sold at higher rates of VAT than the standard rate, but let us imagine that the Chancellor introduces a 25% rate. The calculation is:

$$\text{Selling Price} + 25\% = 100\% + 25\% = 125\%$$

The VAT element in this is now $\frac{25}{125}$ (not $\frac{25}{100}$) of the total $\frac{25}{125}$ cancels down to $\frac{1}{5}$, and that means the VAT fraction would be $\frac{1}{5}$th.

Adding VAT to Cost Price Totals

In certain Retailers Special Schemes the Output Tax is calculated by using the tax inclusive price of goods purchased for retailing. The simplest way to get this tax inclusive figure is to take the total of each positive rated column in the Input Records and add on the VAT at the correct rate. It would be a great waste of time to add back the Vat on each item, it is only necessary to add it to the final total. Since at the time of writing the Standard Rate is 15 per cent, all that is necessary is to increase the Cost Price column by 15 per cent.
(Note: In the schemes described below reference has been made to an imaginary 'higher rate' of 25%).

18.7 Retailers: Special Scheme A

This scheme, as explained in Fig. 18.3 is for traders who only supply goods or services (or both) at one positive rate of tax. This means that you need only keep records of the goods or services (a hiring, lease or rental of goods is deemed to be a service) supplied at this rate. If you also supply goods at zero-rate disregard these for the purpose of Scheme A.

Records. For Scheme A you must keep a full record of your daily gross takings for the supplies covered by the scheme, according to whether you use the Standard Method or the Optional Method (see Section 18.6). For this record you will use the Simplex Daily Takings page. If you are concerned with any special types of transactions, such as the sale of book tokens, make sure you deal with them correctly as shown in booklet 727, Sections 32-59, which your local VAT office will supply.

Calculation of VAT by Scheme A

Under this scheme the calculation is as follows:
Step 1. Find the *gross takings total* from your records by adding them up for the complete trading period. Suppose this comes to £23 756·00
Step 2. Multiply this figure by the VAT fraction for the rate of tax which applies to your goods and services. For standard-rate (15%) items the VAT fraction is $\frac{3}{23}$rds, for higher rate (25%) items it is one fifth. Let us imagine we are dealing with standard rate items. Then £23 756·00 $\times \frac{3}{23}$ = £3 098·61. To do this quickly and easily it is obviously best to use an electronic calculator.

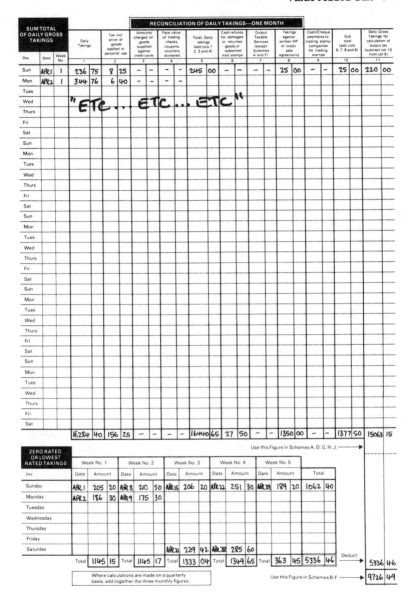

Fig. 18.7 *The Simplex method of calculating gross daily takings*

(Check: the best way to check this is to deduct the VAT from the gross takings total. This gives us £20 657·39. Now this must be the real selling price, and the VAT on this figure is 15%. If we find 15 per cent of £20 657·39 it should come to £3 098·61. On the calculator £20 657·39 × ·15 = £3 098·61. Our calculation of Output Tax is therefore correct.)

You should now be able to complete your VAT account, as shown in Fig. 18.6. A scheme leaflet about calculations is available free of charge from George Vyner Ltd.

18.8 Retailers: Special Scheme B

Scheme B, as explained in Fig. 18.3 is for retailers who supply goods at *only two* rates of tax. Services may also be included provided that they are sold at the higher rate of the two. There is a condition for the use of this Scheme, that the takings of the lower rated goods must not amount to more than one half (50 per cent) of the taxable turnover. Taxable turnover is defined as the total value, including VAT of all the supplies made under the scheme.

Traders who sell goods at standard rate and zero rate can use this scheme, and can include services if they are taxed at standard rate. So can traders who supply goods at standard rate and higher rate and they can include services if they are taxed at the higher rate.

The idea of the scheme is this. Some retailers cannot separate off their daily takings at the different rates and simply finish up with a total takings figure for the period. Let us suppose this figure is £44 000. How much of it is tax? Since this scheme is for people who only sell at two rates of tax, we can work out how much is tax by finding out from the input records how much of the takings was at the lower rate. Suppose the input records show that lower rate goods were bought worth £10 000. The retailer knows what profit margin he adds on—let us say 20 per cent. This means that the lower rate goods bought for £10 000 were sold for £12 000 + VAT. If zero rate tax applies they were sold for £12 000, but if the lower rate in this case was standard-rate, they would be sold for £12 000 + 15% = £12 000 + £1 800 = £13 800. Now if we take these figures from the grand total of £44 000 it means that the rest was the goods sold at the higher of his two rates. So a trader selling at zero rate and standard rate must have sold:

Zero Rate + Standard Rate = Total
£12 000 + £32 000 = £44 000

A trader selling at standard-rate and higher rate must have sold:

Standard Rate + Higher Rate = Total
£13 800 + £30 200 = £44 000

From this, by applying the correct VAT fractions, we can find out the Output Tax owed to Customs & Excise Department.

Calculation of VAT by Scheme B

Step 1. Find the gross takings total from your Simplex records by adding the daily takings together for the whole tax period.

Step 2. Find out the cost to you of the goods you bought at the lower of your two rates during the period. Add on your usual profit margin to this, and if your lower rate is the standard rate add 15 per cent tax as well.

Step 3. Take the total of Step 2 from the total of Step 1. The result is your estimated takings including VAT at the higher of your two rates.

Step 4. Now apply the proper VAT fraction to these totals. If your two rates are Zero and Standard Rate there will be no tax on the Zero Rate and $\frac{3}{23}$rds on the standard rate. If your two rates are standard and higher rate (25% imagined) there will be $\frac{3}{23}$rds of the standard rate total and $\frac{1}{5}$th of the higher rate total to account for.

Step 5. Now write up your VAT account as shown in Fig. 18.6. A scheme leaflet about the calculation is available free of charge from George Vyner Ltd.

18.9 Retailers: Special Scheme C

This scheme is for retailers in trades 8 201-8 239, whose taxable turnover is less than £50 000 per year. It cannot be used for services, which must be accounted for separately outside the Scheme. Since it bases the output VAT on the goods purchased for re-sale, it cannot be used by growers and manufacturers who are adding value to their products other than their profit margin.

The principle of the scheme is that Output Tax is calculated on the basis of input records, because for most trades what you sell is only what you buy with a profit margin added. The VAT authorities have laid down 5 bands of margins which are usual in the various trades, and the trader adds on the correct margin to his cost prices to find his selling prices. The VAT is then calculated on these selling prices.

Calculating VAT under Scheme C

Step 1. Add up the cost to you, including VAT, of all the things you buy to sell again at a *positive rate of tax.* You need a separate total for each positive rate you are dealing with.

Step 2. Add on the correct profit margin for your trade, which is given in the Scheme C leaflet issued by the VAT office. For example, at the time of writing, June 1982, Grocers add on 20 per cent and Jewellers 75 per cent.

Step 3. Now multiply this total (with the profit margin added on) by its correct VAT fraction ($\frac{3}{23}$ for standard rate; $\frac{1}{5}$ for higher rate). The result is the Output Tax due under the Scheme, for that class of goods. If you have both standard rate and higher rate goods add the two lots of output tax together to get your total tax due to Customs and Excise. You should now be able to complete your VAT account. A scheme leaflet about the calculation is available free of charge from George Vyner Ltd.

18.10 Retailers: Scheme D

Scheme D is for retailers whose turnover is less than £125 000 per year and who cannot conveniently distinguish sales at different rates of tax. They keep a record of daily gross takings either by the standard or the optional method, but the Output Tax on these takings is calculated from the input records. Because there must be a close link between what you buy and what you actually sell eventually, it is possible to calculate the output tax by working out the proportion of things bought at each rate of tax. Thus if one third of your purchases are standard rate presumably one third of your total takings will also be at standard rate, and by using the VAT fraction $\frac{1}{23}$ on that one third the Output Tax can be calculated.

One point about Scheme D is that it may result in an overpayment or underpayment of tax. For example, a retailer stocking up with Higher Rate goods which he intends to sell in the Christmas season, may find himself paying high output tax in the quarter concerned, when in fact sales of the highly taxed lines have barely started. For this reason there is a *Scheme Adjustment* annually. The calculation explained below, which is carried out in every tax period is repeated once a year with the whole year's figures. This will enable the retailer to discover whether he has overpaid tax or underpaid it. Any overpayment will be reclaimed at once out of the next VAT payment. Any under-payment must be accounted for.

As explained in Fig. 18.3 Scheme D cannot be used for manufacturing, or for farms and smallholdings etc., who raise stock or grow produce. It cannot be used for services either, since it depends upon finding Output Tax from the input records of goods bought for re-sale.

The step-by-step procedure for using Scheme D is quite long and to assist you the Scheme D leaflet obtainable from your local VAT office includes a worksheet at the back, which can be used to help you. The details are given in the next section. Once again an imaginary 'higher rate' of 25% has been used.

Calculating VAT under Scheme D

Step 1. Find the gross takings total for the tax period, using your Simplex VAT 'Reconciliation of Daily Takings' pages. Total (1).

Step 2. We are going to find out how much VAT output Tax we must pay on the total in Step 1, by finding how much the various types of goods cost us. We therefore need to find the cost, including VAT, of all the goods received for retailing at:

(a) the standard rate	= Total (2)
(b) the higher rate	= Total (3)
(c) the zero rate	= Total (4)

Grand Total = Total (5)

Step 3. The Output Tax payable is therefore as follows:

Tax on Standard Rate items $= \frac{(2)}{(5)} \times (1) \times \frac{1}{23}$

Tax on Higher Rate items $= \frac{(3)}{(5)} \times (1) \times \frac{1}{5}$

Total Output Tax is therefore found by adding these two answers together. It is hoped that the reader can follow the point of this calculation. The fraction of items bought at each rate—$\frac{(2)}{(5)}$ or $\frac{(3)}{(5)}$ respectively—gives us the fraction of total takings to be charged tax at that rate. For zero rated items there is no need to do a calculation, because the tax is zero. Once a year the '*Scheme Adjustment*' referred to above must also be made. You should now be able to complete your VAT Account. A scheme leaflet about the calculation is available free of charge from George Vyner Ltd.

18.11 Retailers: Special Scheme F

As explained in Fig. 18.3 Scheme F is a very straightforward scheme for retailers who can distinguish clearly their sales at each rate of tax. In such a case there is no problem at all in knowing the Output Tax to be accounted for.

Calculating VAT under Scheme F

Step 1. Keep separate daily gross takings records for supplies at each positive rate of tax.

Step 2. Multiply each total by the correct VAT fraction to find the Output Tax. You should now be able to complete your VAT Account. A scheme leaflet on this calculation is available free of charge from George Vyner Ltd.

18.12 Retailers: Special Scheme G

Scheme G is very similar to Scheme D, except that there is no limit of £125 000 turnover. Because the Scheme tends to understate the VAT payable, the final total has to be increased by one eighth ($\frac{1}{8}$) but for those who sell no zero rated goods at all, or whose zero rated goods are very small in number (less than 2 per cent of total sales) the uplift is reduced to one twelfth ($\frac{1}{12}$).

The rules for calculating output tax are a little complicated, and the best thing to do is to ask for a current scheme leaflet from your local VAT office. Not only does the cost (including VAT) of all goods received for retailing have to be used in the calculation but also the cost (including VAT) of the stock in hand at the start of the trading period. This leads to fairly complex rules in the calculation, which the leaflet makes clear. There is no Scheme Adjustment for Scheme G.

The scheme is very similar to Scheme D. Again a 25% Higher Rate has been used.

Calculating VAT under Scheme G

Step 1. Find the 'Gross Takings' total for the tax period (Total 1).

Step 2. Find the cost, including VAT, of goods *in stock* at the start of the period (but see paragraph 4 of the leaflet) and *received for retailing* during the tax period:

(a)	at the standard rate	= Total (2)
(b)	at the higher rate	= Total (3)
(c)	at the zero rate	= Total (4)
	Grand Total =	Total (5)

Step 3. The output tax is now calculated as follows:

Tax at the standard rate = $\frac{(2)}{(5)} \times (1) \times \frac{3}{23}$ but plus $\frac{1}{8}$ or $\frac{1}{12}$ as the case may be.

Tax at the higher rate = $\frac{(3)}{(5)} \times (1) \times \frac{1}{5}$ but plus $\frac{1}{8}$ or $\frac{1}{12}$ as the case may be.

Total output tax is found by adding these two answers together. Once again the Output Tax is found by taking the same proportion ($\frac{(2)}{(5)}$ or $\frac{(3)}{(5)}$ respectively) of the sales as the purchases at each tax rate bear to the total purchases, and applying the proper VAT fraction. You should now be able to complete your VAT Account. A scheme leaflet on this calculation is available free of charge from George Vyner Ltd.

18.13 Cautionary Note

It is almost impossible to describe these schemes fully without reproducing the whole 'Scheme Leaflet'. I have attempted—at the expense of some detail—to convey to the reader the general ideas behind the Schemes, which are in fact quite ingenious as ways of finding the tax payable. They are simple schemes, yet they do not read very easily, and the detail is often very important. Since a retailer who has decided upon one scheme has only to familiarise himself with that one scheme, he will soon get used to the complications of it. It must be said that the VAT offices are a mine of information about any particular point that appears difficult, and their generally helpful attitude is highly commendable. If this chapter helps you to select the appropriate scheme for you, it is unlikely that problems in that Scheme cannot be sorted out very easily by a quick call to your local VAT office.

18.14 Special Note: VAT on Capital Items

A special difficulty arises with VAT on capital items, except for the purchase of motor cars (not vans) on which VAT is not recoverable. Since the VAT element is not a long-term asset, but is only paid and refunded within three months, it must be recorded as a business expense for the current year in the Profit and Loss Account at the end of the year. If this is not done the profits will be overstated, and tax will be paid on the inflated profit figure.

The rules for this are as follows:

(a) Enter the purchase of the capital item (but not motor cars) in the VAT book in the ordinary way so that

(b) When entering the capital item in the weekly page put the figure in inclusive of VAT in either 'cash' or 'bank' column

(c) When carrying this capital item to the Summary of Capital Expenses at the back of the book enter the net value only in the Amount column, and enter the VAT alongside, as shown below.

(d) Now enter the £600 paid at the end of the year on the Profit and Loss Account, on the line below 'Customs and Excise VAT Payments" to read "VAT on capital items £600." This will reduce the profits you have made to the correct figure. The correct figure for the asset on the Balance Sheet is the 'Net Value'.

CAPITAL EXPENSES INCURRED DURING THE YEAR							
DATE	NATURE AND FULL DETAILS OF EXPENSE	INVOICE TOTAL		NET VALUE OF ASSET		VAT	
21·7·19..	PURCHASE OF MACHINE No XYZ 7184	4600	00	4000	00	600	00

Fig. 18.8 *VAT on capital items*

Unit Nineteen

The Simplex Licensees Account Book

19.1 Introduction

Some years ago George Vyner Ltd., were asked by a major brewery if they would devise a simple record book for licensees which would meet the special needs of the licensing trade. The result of this enquiry was the 'Simplex Licensees' Book, which incorporates both the ordinary financial records and the VAT records in one book. It follows exactly the same principles as the Simplex D Account Book and the VAT Record Book. Certain of the rulings have been altered to make them more appropriate to the licensees trade. Readers of Simplified Book-keeping for Small Businesses who are in this trade, or thinking of becoming managers or owners of a public house, should certainly obtain a copy of the Licensees Book and study it in conjunction with the present volume. If copies are not available at your local stationer write to George Vyner Ltd., at the address shown at the front of this book.

19.2 Layout of the Licensees Book

The layout of the licensees book follows the general pattern of the Simplex System but is adapted to meet the needs of the trade. The chief features of the book may be listed as follows:

    (a) The 53 weekly pages provided follow the usual patterns but the rulings have been adapted to assist the licensee to analyse his receipts under various headings, liquor, tobacco, catering etc.

    (b) The VAT input records are achieved in a special Invoice Register at the front of the book which gives room to record the invoices from suppliers and to draw up quarterly totals. These are then carried to a summary at the back of the book.

    (c) The VAT output records are extracted from the weekly pages (see (a) above) and carried to summaries at the back of the book and thence to VAT accounts for each quarterly period.

It is difficult to imagine a more simple and comprehensive system.

19.3 Special Note for Brewery Training Departments and College Lecturers

As a result of close liaison work between Mr. Keith Mayman of Bristol Polytechnic and leading brewers in the South West Area an educational package has been prepared for training prospective licensees. Full details may be obtained from George Vyner Ltd., at the address shown in the front of this book, and if necessary Mr. Mayman's services as lecturer can be arranged. Alternatively other education centres wishing to develop expertise in this field may staff this highly successful course using the package devised by Mr. Mayman, which has been extensively tested-out in the past year or two. It meets the needs of the trade in a very practical form, and includes a full set of exercises on the Weekly Page and Value Added Tax, and answer pages which permit students' work to be marked and appraised very easily.

The Simplex Everall Farm Account Book

20.1 Introduction
The Simplex Everall Farm Account Book is a convenient analysis book for farmers and smallholders which has been widely used for many years. It is in three sections, Receipts, Payments and Livestock.

20.2 The Receipts Section
This is an analysis of receipts under various headings, which enables the farmer to see what his receipts are over the course of the trading period in such areas as cattle, sheep, pigs, poultry, wool, potatoes etc. There are columns for VAT repayments, and other receipts of various kinds.

20.3 The Payments Section
Analysed in a similar way to the Receipts Section described above, the payments section permits the farmer to collect costs related to the care of particular animals, or incurred in raising various crops. At the end of the year this permits him to assess their relative profitability.

20.4 The Livestock Section
This section enables the farmer to keep a record month by month of changes in flocks, poultry etc., whether by births or deaths, purchase or sale.

Although the Farm Account Book does not at present incorporate a full Simplex system of accounts it is a very useful record to be compiled in association with a Simplex D Account Book for the financial results of an agricultural holding.

Unit Twenty-one

Discovering your Profit

21.1 Introduction

The man who undertakes the organization and risks of a business venture is entitled to some reward for his efforts. His reward may assume many forms, but the financial part is the profit he makes on the venture; in other words, it is the amount by which the receipts of the venture exceed the outgoings.

Profits are always worked out in two parts. The first part is called the *gross profit*, or total profit made. It is the profit on the trading activities of the firm, and hence the name *Trading Account* is applied to the section of the accounts where we find this gross profit. Some firms are not trading firms, so they do not have a Trading Account, or a gross profit. Instead they calculate all their profits in the *Profit and Loss Account*. This is the second half of the profit calculation with a trading firm. In the Profit and Loss Account we take all our overhead expenses and running expenses away from the gross profit, to which we also add any miscellaneous profits that are not trading profits, such as fees received, commission received, rent received, etc. This gives us the *net profit*, or 'clear' profit.

Calculating your profits at the end of the year is a process known as the 'preparation of final accounts'. In many small businesses this process is left entirely to professional accountants. We will assume that you, however, are reading this Unit because you wish to learn how to prepare your own final accounts. There are three parts to the exercise: we have to draw up

(*a*) the Trading Account, in which we find the gross profit,
(*b*) the Profit and Loss Account, in which we find the net profit, and
(*c*) the Balance Sheet, in which we list the assets and liabilities of the business.

From these final accounts you should be able to gauge the progress of your business and detect any weaknesses.

21.2 Drawing up the Trading Account

Users of the Simplex system can easily prepare a Trading Account at the end of the year, from the summary sheets which have been drawn up week by week. Before considering this in detail, we shall look at some very simple Trading Accounts which illustrate the underlying principles. Let us turn for a moment to Fig. 21.1.

Stock Valuation

Unfortunately the Trading Account shown in Fig. 21.1. is not very sensible, because in real life we rarely sell out completely, so there is always 'stock in hand' to worry about. Clearly we shall need to know how much of our stock remains unsold if we are going to work out the profits of the business. We shall have to count stock and then value it, and add up all the different items to give us a grand total which is the 'closing stock' figure. What value shall we place on the items? Shall we value them at cost price or at selling price? What about a shop-soiled item that will not fetch its original price?

Trading Account
(for year ending December 31st, 19..)

	£		£
Purchases	80	Sales	100
Gross Profit	20		
	——		——
	£100		£100

Fig. 21.1 *The simplest Trading Account possible: the cost price of the goods is set against the selling price, and the difference is the gross profit*

The answers to these problems are now laid down in an official Statement of Standard Accounting Practice from the accountancy bodies: *Stock is valued at the lower of cost, or net realisable value.* If an item will sell above cost price you must value it at cost price; if it is shop-soiled or in some way unsatisfactory so that you will lose money on it, you must value it at net realisable value.

When we have valued our stock we can draw up a slightly more realistic Trading Account by including opening- and closing-stock figures, as shown in Fig. 21.2.

Trading Account
(for year ending December 31st, 19..)

	£		£
Opening Stock	15	Sales	100
Purchases	80		
	——		
	95		
less Closing Stock	27		
	——		
	68		
Gross Profit	32		
	——		——
	£100		£100

Fig. 21.2 *A slightly more realistic Trading Account*

According to Fig. 21.2 the profit has now increased to £32. This is because some of the goods purchased have not been sold (£27 worth in fact) but we have sold the rest of the £80 worth, and also £15 worth that were in hand at the start of the year. We have thus sold £15 + (£80 − £27) = £68 worth of goods for £100, giving a profit of £32.

Note that if you tried to tell the inspector of taxes that your profit was only £20, as revealed in Fig. 21.1, he would doubtless remind you that unsold stock has to be taken into account before you can find your true profit.

LAST YEAR		TRADING ACCOUNT for year ending 31ST DECEMBER 19..	19...		LAST YEAR			19..	
5420	90	Opening Stock at 1·1·19...	7295	45	67259	80	Sales or Work completed	98250	50
45525	60	Purchases during year	62355	00	1011	20	Value of goods taken for own consumption	1249	50
50946	50		69650	45	68271	00	TOTAL TURNOVER	99500	00
7295	45	Less Closing Stock at 31 DEC. Total	11214	60					
43651	05	COST OF SALES Total	58435	85					
24619	95	Gross Profit (Carried to Profit & Loss Account)	41064	15					
68271	00	TOTAL	99500	00	68271	00	TOTAL	99500	00

Fig. 21.3 *A Trading Account from the Simplex account book*

Notes:

(a) A Trading Account always indicates by a date at the top the period which it covers in the lifetime of the business.

(b) The goods taken for own consumption are added at selling price to the 'Sales' figure (see improved presentation below).

(c) The gross profit figure of £41 064.15 is carried to the Profit and Loss Account.

(d) The previous year's figures, for comparison purposes, are given alongside those of the current year. This meets the requirement of the Companies Act 1985. It is not strictly necessary for small businesses which are not trading as companies.

The only difference between the Trading Account which appears in Fig. 21.2 and the Simplex Trading Account shown in Fig. 21.3 is that the latter includes the value of goods taken for own consumption. The Simplex book carries an instruction that any goods taken for own consumption should be paid for at selling price and (as in Fig. 21.3) their value is to be added to the 'Sales' figure. In a legal decision in the case of 'Sharkey v Wernher' it was held that where a person takes goods from Stock for own consumption this must be treated as a transfer at current market value.

Ignoring this for the moment, note that the figures used in the Trading Account are the annual totals, taken from the 'Weekly Summary of Payments for Goods Purchased' and the 'Weekly Summary of Takings'. These summaries, carefully built up over the year, supply the figures from which the Gross Profit may be calculated.

Returning to the ruling in 'Sharkey *v* Wernher', had this decision not been made the trader taking goods for his own consumption would not have taken them at selling price but at cost price. In the first place, it is well recognised in law that a 'sale' involves the transfer of property from one person to another, and clearly there has been no such transfer in this case. Secondly, it is well recognised in accounting that a person cannot make profits on himself. It is therefore most unfair for the Inland Revenue to demand tax on profits that have never been made. The House of Lords decision was made 'per incuriam' which means that the points were not properly put to their lordships, so that they were unaware of some aspects of the point being decided. The fact that the Inland Revenue themselves, in the case of hotel and restaurant owners, allow goods taken for "own consumption" to be on the basis of disallowing cost shows how weak the rule is. Also the Customs and Excise Authorities, in the VAT regulations for retailers (Notice No. 727, Paragraph 34) allows goods taken for own consumption to be deducted at cost price.

The effect of treating the goods as taken for own consumption at cost price is illustrated in Fig. 21.4 and explained in the notes below it. Traders who feel aggrieved at the absurdity of the application of the Sharkey *v* Wernher rule to them may like to know that the Inspectors' instructions do say that they should 'take a reasonably broad view in applying this principle'. This means that 'Inspectors should not seek to make adjustments to computations of profit where the addition to the profit is 'trivial'.' It is not clear what 'trivial' means, but this is at least some concession on a matter which really needs to be re-examined at the highest level.

LAST YEAR			TRADING ACCOUNT for year ending 31ST DECEMBER 19..	19..		LAST YEAR		Sales or Work completed	19..	
5420	90		Opening Stock at 1·1·19..	7295	45	67259	80	Sales or Work completed	98250	50
45525	60		Purchases during year 62355·00							
50946 50			Less value of goods							
- 596 80			taken for own use 737·20	61617	80					
50349	90		Less	68913	25					
7295	45		Closing Stock at 31ST DEC. Total	112114	60					
43054	45		Total	57698	65					
			Gross Profit (Carried to Profit &							
24205	35		Loss Account)	40551	85					
67259	80		TOTAL	98250	50	67259	80	TOTAL	98250	50

Fig. 21.4 *An improved Trading Account: the value of goods taken for own consumption is deducted from the Purchases figure*

Notes:

(*a*) The item 'Goods taken for own consumption' has been valued at *cost* price, not at selling price.

(b) It has been deducted from Purchases instead of being added to Sales.

The gross profit figure has fallen by £512·30 which is the profit margin on these goods. The result is a possible tax saving of about £150, which, but for the rule in Sharkey v Wernher, could be saved by the trader.

We have now discovered the true gross profit of the business, and have completed the first part of our 'final accounts'.

21.3 Drawing up the Profit and Loss Account

The Profit and Loss Account is opened with the entry of the gross profit, transferred from the Profit and Loss Account. To this gross profit are added any miscellaneous receipts which have been collected in the columns of the 'Summary of Other Receipts'? VAT refunds will also be added if the trader has received any.

The expenses to be charged against the profits are listed on the left-hand side of the Profit and Loss Account. They are the totals carried from the 'Summary of Payments for Expenses' pages. The grand total of these expenses when deducted from the profits available, as shown in Fig. 21.5, reveals the net profit.

The net profit is the clear profit made by the business. It is the profit figure on which tax is calculated, and forms the starting point for the inspector of taxes in assessing the tax payable. This is discussed in Unit 22.

PROFIT AND LOSS ACCOUNT for year ending 31ST DECEMBER 19..										
LAST YEAR			**19..**		**LAST YEAR**				**19..**	
1870	50	Rent and Rates	2950	00			Gross Profit (brought down from			
864	00	Light and Heat	1464	00	24619	95	Trading Account)		41064	15
55	26	Carriage and Postages	47	56						
85	30	Paper	147	70	4265	50	Miscellaneous Receipts		2042	95
456	50	Motor Expenses	952	05						
12	44	Travelling	37	24	=	=	Customs & Excise VAT Repayments		=	=
748	00	Cleaning	1248	00	1000	=	ENTERPRISE ALLOWANCE		1080	—
136	20	Printing and Stationery	272	00			(IF ANY)			
306	72	Telephone	495	50						
152	80	Repairs and Renewals	276	00						
46	28	Insurance (Business)	134	00						
232	50	Advertising	468	00						
4268	50	Wages (gross)	7259	00						
232	00	Nat. Ins. Contributions	386	00						
12	25	Bank Charges	27	50						
580	75	Sundries	1237	50						
240	00	Depreciation (Fixtures & Fittings)	480	00						
960	00	—do— (Motor Car)	1240	00						
3384	20	Customs & Excise VAT Payments	5725	00						
127	80	VAT on Capital Items	238	00						
14772	00	Total	24984	05						
15113	45	Net Profit During Year	19203	05						
29885	45	TOTAL	44187	10	29885	45	TOTAL		44187	10

Fig. 21.5 *Finding the net profit in the Profit and Loss Account*

21.4 The Balance Sheet of the Business

A Balance Sheet may be described as a 'snapshot' picture of the affairs of the business, at a given moment in time. It is only true for that particular moment, which is shown by the date which is always written at the top. Strictly speaking even the time ought to be stated, but we usually take for granted that the Balance Sheet applies to the close of business on the date shown.

A tremendous amount of information can be gathered from a Balance Sheet by the astute businessman, and the reader will find in Section 23.6 of this book a guide to interpreting the evidence displayed. A few introductory points may be mentioned here.

(a) Marshalling the Assets

It is a principle of modern accounting that the accounts should be arranged in such a way that anyone (provided he has some basic understanding of the subject) will be able to appreciate immediately the important aspects of the business, and be able to assess the firm's true position. In former times accounts were sometimes drawn up deliberately in such a way as to hide the true state of affairs from interested parties. This was particularly undesirable with limited companies, since innocent shareholders, unable to discover weaknesses in the business until too late, were often left with worthless shares on their hands. Today the Companies Act 1985 requires auditors to report whether, in their opinion, the accounts do give a 'true and fair view' of the affairs of the company.

BALANCE SHEET AS AT 31ST DEC. 19..

Liabilities

LAST YEAR		CAPITAL ACCOUNT			19..	
32125	10	Balance at 1ST JANUARY			37238	55
15113	45	Add Net Profit during year	19203	05		
–	–	Extra Capital Contributed	1500	00		
15113	45	Total	20703	05		
10000	00	Less Drawings & Income Tax	12285	00	8418	05
37238	55	LONG TERM LIABILITIES			45656	60
19000	00	Mortgage	17500	00		
3112	45	Loan	2500	00	20000	00
		CURRENT LIABILITIES				
4264	50	Sundry Creditors	2350	50		
327	50	Accrued Charges	217	50		
–	–	Bank Overdraft	–	–	2568	00
63943	00				68224	60

Assets

LAST YEAR		FIXED ASSETS	At Cost		Less Depreciation		19..	
1000	00	Goodwill					1000	00
42000	00	Premises					42000	00
3880	00	Fixtures & Fittings	6000	00	2600	00	3400	00
4560	00	Motor Vehicles	5800	00	2480	00	3320	00
51440	00	CURRENT ASSETS			Total		49720	00
7295	45	Stock in Trade			11214	60		
2865	50	Sundry Debtors			3400	00		
2146	00	Cash at Bank			3526	00		
84	00	Cash in Hand			124	00		
112	05	Payments in Advance			240	00	18504	60
63943	00						68224	60

Fig. 21.6 *The Simplex Balance Sheet*

One of the ways in which a clear picture can be presented is to divide up the assets into separate classes. There are about four types of asset, but here we shall only consider the two chief types: *current assets* and *fixed assets*

Current Assets. Current assets, sometimes called *circulating assets*, are assets which are continually being turned over. The word 'current', like the French word *courant*, means 'running'. Fig. 21.7 illustrates the way in which stock which has been manufactured or purchased for resale is marketed and sold, either for cash or on credit terms. The cash received (or eventually received) is then used to purchase further stock for resale.

These current assets may be seen listed in the Balance Sheet of Fig. 21.6; the most liquid assets 'Cash in hand' and 'Payments in Advance' being placed at the bottom of the list below the more permanent items. Payments in advance is so liquid you have actually spent it.

Fixed Assets. Fixed assets are assets which are not 'turned over' and sold at a profit, but are 'fixed' in the business and retained for a very long period. They are often called *capital assets*, since they form part of the permanent capital equipment in use. The longest-lasting item is land, which may be said to be eternal. Fixtures are expected to last for several years, while assets like motor vehicles are written off after only a few years.

All assets are obtained in order to carry on the affairs of the business, but fixed assets serve their purpose for many years, and may be defined as *assets which permanently increase the profit-making capacity of the business*.

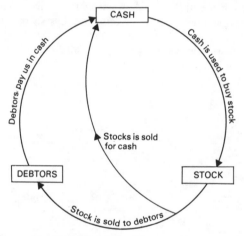

Fig. 21.7 *'Circulating' or current assets*

(b) Marshalling the Liabilities

Just as the separation of current assets from fixed assets on the Balance Sheet is helpful in presenting a simple picture to the businessman, so is a clear division of the liabilities. The liabilities of any business are the funds it owes. The people to whom these funds are owed are the creditors of the business, and they may be listed under three headings:

(i) *Short-term creditors* who may expect to be paid almost at once. The funds owed to these people are called *current liabilities*. The commonest balance-sheet items of this sort are 'sundry creditors' and bank overdrafts.

(ii) *Long-term creditors*. These will usually have made a special contract with the owner of the business, and their repayment terms will be specified in that contract. The funds owed to these creditors are known as *long-term liabilities*. Examples are mortgages and personal loans.

(iii) *The owner himself.* The owner of a business expects eventually to be repaid the capital he originally contributed, plus any profits retained in the business over the course of the years. The amounts owing to the owner are contained in his Capital Account. By convention it is usual to display on the Balance Sheet the capital at the start of the trading period, adding the net profit after deducting drawings (as shown in Fig. 21.6). This enables anyone studying the Balance Sheet to see the profits earned in the trading period.

In the example shown in Fig. 21.6 there are no long-term liabilities, and you should remember that both the drawings and the sums paid to the Inland Revenue for the owner's *personal* tax liability have to be deducted from the capital.

Remember also that if VAT liabilities to the Customs & Excise exist, they should be included under 'Accrued Charges' as a current liability; any VAT refunds owed to you by the Customs & Excise should be included under 'Payments in Advance' as a current asset.

With this final clear picture of your business you have completed your set of Final Accounts, which may now be submitted to the inspector of taxes as a true record of your profits for the year.

21.5 Do You Understand Your Capital?

Many businessmen do not really understand what capital is, and consequently find it difficult to prepare a Balance Sheet. Since a well prepared Balance Sheet such as Fig. 21.6 makes it very easy to understand 'Capital' this is an appropriate moment to discuss the matter.

First of all 'capital' is not money (and neither is profit). Because most businesses start with the proprietor bringing in some capital in cash form, it is a popular misconception that 'capital' is another word for 'money'. It is not.

Capital is the liability that the business has to the owner(s) of the business.

Thus, on the first day when a business starts up, the owner bringing in £1 000 as his capital, the Balance Sheet reads:

Balance Sheet
(AS AT JANUARY 1st 19..)

Liabilities	£	Assets	£
Capital	1 000·00	Cash	1 000·00

The capital is what the business owes to the owner of the business.

Suppose, on that first day, the new businessman buys a second hand car for £400·00 and sells it for £500. By the end of the day the situation is as follows:

Balance Sheet
(AS AT 5pm, JANUARY 1st 19. .)

Liabilities	£	Assets	£
Capital at start	1 000·00	Cash	1 100·00
Add Net Profit	100·00		
	£1 100·00		£1 100·00

The cash is an asset—in the cash box. The capital, and the profit are not money at all. They are what the business owes to the owner of the business—a liability. The business now owes him his original capital + £100 profit on the car.

If we now return to consider Fig. 21.6 the reader will note that on the assets side there are now many assets, Premises, Fixtures, Motor Vehicles etc., etc., and some money £10·08. How have these assets been obtained. If we look across to the liabilities side we can see that the creditors provided £661·26 of the assets (chiefly by supplying goods without payment as yet). There were no loans, but if there had been the money provided by the Bank, or the Building Society would have helped to purchase the assets. In this particular case the vast majority of the assets were provided by the proprietor, either as the original capital many years ago, or as profits ploughed back over the years. The business now owes the proprietor £26 570·03 which he has provided.

To find the capital of any firm the rule is

(*a*) find the total assets.

(*b*) Take away from this total the *external* liabilities (to the creditors, or accrued charges, or to those who made loans).

(*c*) The remainder is the capital, which we might call the *internal* liabilities, what the business owes *within the firm*—to the proprietor.

21.6 Adjustments in Final Accounts

One of the most difficult problems met by the owners of small businesses who are keeping their own accounts is the question of 'adjustments'. For many small businesses the Inland Revenue department disregards adjustments altogether and allows the accounts to be kept on a 'Receipts and Payments' basis. This means that the moneys actually received during the trading period are counted in as income as far as profits are concerned, while the payments actually made during the year are allowed as expenses against the profits earned. Strictly speaking this is not correct, for I might pay out money this year (for example for a stock of advertising brochures) which I do not intend to give away until next year. Strictly speaking this expense should be deducted from next year's profits, not this year's and I ought to do an adjustment for it.

Adjustment No. 1: Payments in Advance

Let us take an example to illustrate the adjustment. In Fig. 21.5 there is an entry for Advertising £468·00 in the Profit and Loss Account. This is my payment for advertising brochures delivered to the houses in the town every four weeks, giving details of Special Offers etc. In fact the total of my advertising column in the summary of expenses totalled £508·46, but it included an amount I had just paid on December 30th for the January leaflets which the printer sent round on that date. The cheque was for £40·46.

The adjustment looks like this:

	£
Total of advertising column	= 508·46
Deduct item for January	= 40·46
	£468·00

Therefore the amount I must enter in the Profit and Loss Account is £468·00 for the year, and the £40·46 must be carried forward to the next year. As I am going to carry it forward it must appear on the Balance Sheet. Is it an asset or liability? Clearly it is an asset, for I have this stock of brochures ready to send out, which I have paid for in advance.

The item appears on the assets side of the Balance Sheet.

Current Assets: Payments in Advance £40·46

The effect of the adjustment in this case is to reduce the amount written off the Profit and Loss Account—the balance being carried forward as an asset for use next year.

Adjustment No. 2: Accrued Charges

Of course adjustments might be necessary in the opposite direction. In Fig. 21.5 again there is an entry for Light and Heat £1 464·00. As a matter of fact, the total of my Light and Heat column in the Summary of Expenses in my Simplex D Account Book shows that I have paid £1 246·50 in the year, but a large electricity bill for £217·50 has just come in, although I have not yet paid it. Clearly the adjustment required is as follows:

	£
Total of Light and Heat column	= 1246·50
Add electricity bill due	= 217·50
	£1464·00

I must now enter the figure of £1 464·00 in my Profit and Loss Account —since that is the true loss for the year, and carry the overdue bill into the Balance Sheet as a current liability—Accrued Charges £217·50.

Keeping accounts in this way—using adjustments—is called keeping accounts on an 'accruals basis'. This means that the Trading Account, and the

Profit and Loss Account, are adjusted so that they include every penny of loss suffered during the year, and every penny of profit earned in the year, but they do not include anything that applies to the next trading period or the previous trading period. Such accounts are more accurate than the simpler accounts kept on a 'receipts and payments' basis.

A full description of adjustments is not possible here, but those who wish to pursue the matter further should purchase a copy of '*Success in Principles of Accounting*' by Geoffrey Whitehead (published by John Murray Ltd.). This book also has a complete answer book to help students check their work.

21.7 The Simplex System and Partnerships

Some points about the general nature of partnerships will be found in Unit Twenty-four. Here we are only dealing with the book-keeping arrangements.

The Simplex system is entirely adequate for keeping the records of partnership businesses but the 'final accounts' pages at the back of the book are not appropriate. It has not been possible to include sufficient pages to provide a full description of partnership accounts in the Simplex D book and for this reason George Vyner Ltd., offer free of charge 'Pages for the Final Accounts of Partnerships'. These will be sent gratis to anyone who operates as a partnership and wishes to submit a suitable set of Final Accounts to the Inland Revenue. The package consists of two pages each having on one side a Trading Account, Profit and Loss Account and **Appropriation of Profit and Loss Account,** while the other side has the **Current Accounts of the Partners** and a Balance Sheet. Also provided is an explanatory leaflet. One of the copies should be sent to the Inland Revenue inspector, the other should be kept for reference.

Partnership Accounts. A full set of Partnership Accounts requires:
- (*a*) A Trading Account
- (*b*) A Profit and Loss Account
- (*c*) An Appropriation Section of the Profit and Loss Account, in which the partnership profits are appropriated in the way agreed
- (*d*) A Current Account for each partner
- (*e*) A Balance Sheet.

Parts (*a*) and (*b*) are exactly the same as for the sole trader and are not repeated here, but parts (*c*), (*d*) and (*e*) are illustrated and explained below.

The Appropriation Account

The word 'appropriate' means 'allocate to a particular use'. When the Net Profit has been found in the Profit and Loss Account it has to be allocated to the partners in the way that they have agreed, and this is illustrated in Fig. 21.8.

APPROPRIATION ACCOUNT for year ending 31st December 19..								
Last Year			This Year		Last Year		This Year	
250	00	Goodwill (written off)	250	00	6458	00	Net Profit (brought down from	8200	58
1000	00	Salary (Mr. A)	1000	00			Profit and Loss		
300	00	Interest on Capital (Mr. A)	300	00			Account)		
1800	00	" " " (Mr. B)	1800	00					
1036	00	Share of residue (Mr. A) - ⅓	1616	86					
2072	00	" " " (Mr. B) - ⅔	3233	72					
6458	00	TOTAL	8200	58	6458	00	TOTAL	8200	58

Fig. 21.8 *The Appropriation of profits in a partnership business*

Notes:

(i) First the partners decide to reduce Goodwill on the Balance Sheet by £250·00. Remember writing off goodwill in this way has to be done out of profit, it cannot be charged to Profit and Loss Account as a business expense.

(ii) Mr. A. (the younger partner) is given his agreed salary, which reflects the fact that he is doing a good deal of the physical work of the partnership.

(iii) Each partner is then given interest on his capital at the agreed rate (here we are imagining 10 per cent). Note that Mr. B. the senior partner, has much more capital in the business than Mr. A. If it is decided to do so partners can give interest on the balance left in Current Accounts at the start of the year, and can *charge* interest on overdrawn Current Accounts at the start of the year and also interest on drawings made during the course of the year. They then charge the agreed rate pro rata for the number of months to run until the end of the year, from the time of the drawing.

(iv) The residue of the profit is shared up one third to Mr. A; two thirds to Mr. B.

(v) Each of the sums appropriated to the partners is taken to the partners' Current Accounts, as shown below.

The Capital Accounts of Partners

It is usual for the Capital of partners to remain fixed during the years of the partnership unless a firm arrangement to increase capital in some agreed way is made. This would be a fairly rare event. This 'fixed' nature of partnership capital means that at the end of the year we do not (as with sole traders) add on profits and take away drawings, with the capital that results changing year by year. As shown in the Partnership Balance Sheet (see Fig. 21.10) Capital Accounts remain unchanged. Instead the fluctuations connected with profit-making and drawings are carried in a Current Account as shown in Fig. 21.9.

The Current Accounts of Partners

The Current Accounts of partners must not be confused with the Bank Account, which is a Current Account at the bank. The name is the same, because like a Bank Account, the partners' Current Accounts are credited with any appropriations due to the partner and debited with any amounts drawn out by the partner (Drawings).

The use of the Current Account is made clear in Fig. 21.9, and explained in the notes below it. The final total on the Current Account of each partner will then appear on the Balance Sheet (Fig. 21.10).

THE CURRENT ACCOUNT OF PARTNERS

PARTNERS NAME: Mr. A

19__			£		19__			£	
Dec. 31	Drawings for year		2500	00	Jan. 1	Balance	b/fwd	186	00
" 31	Balance	c/fwd	602	86	Dec. 31	Salary		1000	00
					" 31	Interest on Capital		300	00
					" 31	Share of Residue		1616	86
		£	3102	86			£	3102	86
					Jan. 1	Balance	b/fwd	602	86

PARTNERS NAME: Mr. B

19__			£		19__			£	
Jan. 1	Balance	b/fwd	480	00	Dec. 31	Interest on Capital		1800	00
Dec. 31	Drawings for year		3500	00	" 31	Share of Residue		3233	72
" 31	Balance	c/fwd	1053	72					
		£	5033	72			£	5033	72
					Jan. 1	Balance	b/fwd	1053	72

Fig. 21.9 *The Current Accounts of the Partners*

Notes:

(i) Notice that at the start of a year the Current Account can have either a credit balance or a debit balance. Mr. A. had a credit balance on January 1st. This means that the business besides owing him his capital also owed him £186·00 on his Current Account. Mr. B.—on the contrary—had drawn out so much drawings in the previous year that he was in debt to the business for £480·00.

(ii) The various appropriations of profit are carried from the appropriation account to the credit side of the partners' Current Accounts. Mr. A. has his salary, interest on capital and one third share of the residue of the profit. Mr. B. of course was not given a salary.

(iii) The total of drawings for the year is debited to the account since the partners have already had this money in expectation of profits made. In both cases the total drawn is less than the total earned so that both accounts finish up with credit balances. This means that the business owes both partners a balance of profits earned, which they can draw out if they wish. In the meantime these balances must appear on the Balance Sheet.

The Balance Sheet

The chief difference between the Balance Sheet of a partnership and that of a sole trader is that the capital of the partners remains fixed, as explained above. The two capitals are shown in Fig. 21.10 below. The Current Accounts, which have been shown in Fig. 21.9 appear also on the Balance Sheet, and if they are both credit balances appear as liabilities. Where a partner has drawn more in Drawings than he earned in profits the debit balance would appear on the assets side; the partner would then be temporarily a debtor of the business for that amount.

The rest of the Balance Sheet is exactly the same as the sole trader's Balance Sheet.

BALANCE SHEET of a PARTNERSHIP

Liabilities

Last Year		Liabilities			This Year	
		CAPITAL ACCOUNT				
3000	00	Mr. A.	3000	00		
18000	00	Mr. B.	18000	00	21000	00
		CURRENT ACCOUNTS				
186	00	Mr. A.	602	86		
-	-	Mr. B.	1053	72	1656	58
21186	00				22656	58
		LONG TERM LIABILITIES				
15800	00	Mortgage			15000	00
		CURRENT LIABILITIES				
6763	00	Sundry Creditors	4736	02		
66	00	Accrued Charges	54	00	4790	02
43815	00	TOTAL			42446	60

Assets

Last Year		Assets				This Year	
		FIXED ASSETS					
1250	00	Goodwill	£1250 - £250			1000	00
25000	00	Premises				25000	00
2400	00	Fixtures	£2400 - £400			2000	00
		Motor Vehicles		3850	00		
3850	00	Loss Depreciation		770	00	3080	00
32500	00					31080	00
		CURRENT ASSETS					
4200	00	Stock in Trade		4500	00		
2950	00	Sundry Debtors		2750	00		
3500	00	Cash at Bank		3850	00		
185	00	Cash in Hand		225	00		
480	00	Payments in Advance		41	60	11366	60
43815	00	TOTAL				42446	60

Fig. 21.10 *A partnership Balance Sheet*

21.8 Exercises in the Preparation of Final Accounts

1. Using the figures given below for Tom Price's business taken from the summary pages of his Simplex Account book draw up the Trading Account and Profit and Loss Account for the year ending December 31st, 19. . and the Balance Sheet as at that date.

(Supplies of Final Accounts paper can be obtained from George Vyner Ltd., at the address given at the front of this book.)

Trading Account: Opening Stock £1 200·00; Purchases £26 000·00; Sales £42 000·00; Closing Stock £1 450·00; Goods taken for own consumption £250·00.

Profit and Loss Account: Miscellaneous Receipts £350·00; Customs and Excise Repayments £148·50; Rent and Rates £682·00; Light and Heat £420·00; Carriage and Postages £186·00; Paper £124·00; Motor Expenses £372·00; Travelling £56·00; Cleaning £284·00; Printing and Stationery £130·00; Telephone £285·00; Repairs and renewals £176·00; Insurance £125·00; Advertising £230·00; Wages £2 756·00; National Insurance Contributions £525·00; Bank Charges £60·00; Sundries £124·00; Depreciation (fixtures) £250·00; Depreciation (Motor Car) £500·00.

Balance Sheet: Premises £12 000·00; Fixtures £750·00; Motor Vehicles £950·00; Debtors £24·85; Cash at Bank £796·50; Cash in Hand £23·15; Capital at Start £8 008·00; Drawings during year £1 865·00; Creditors £138·00.

2. Using the figures given below for Brian Wood's business taken from the summary pages of his Simplex Account book draw up the Trading Account and Profit and Loss Account for the year ending December 31st, 19. . and the Balance Sheet as at that date.

The details are:

Trading Account: Opening Stock £1 350·00; Purchases £27 550·00; Sales £37 700; Closing Stock £1 850·00; Goods taken for own consumption £1 250·00.

Profit and Loss Account: Miscellaneous Receipts £250·00; Customs and Excise repayments £249·00; Rent and Rates £600·00; Light and Heat £501·50; Carriage and Postages £176·00; Paper £84·00; Motor Expenses £422·00; Travelling £50·00; Cleaning £300·00; Printing and Stationery £120·00; Telephone £145·00; Repairs and renewals £166·00; Insurance £95·00; Advertising £190·00; Wages £3 000·00; National Insurance Contributions £531·00; Bank Charges £10·00; Sundries £130·00; Depreciation (Fixtures) £200·00; Depreciation (Motor Car) £556·00.

Balance Sheet: Premises £10 000·00; Fixtures £1 000·00; Motor Vehicles £1 950·00; Debtors £525·50; Cash at Bank £850·35; Cash in Hand £85·00; Capital at Start £12 865·35; Drawings during year £2 500·00; Creditors £773·00.

3. Using the figures given below, and taking into account the adjustments given at the end of the question, draw up the Trading Account and Profit and Loss Account of the business of A. Fashionable and her Balance Sheet as at 31st December, 19. ..

Trading Account: Opening Stock £1 550·00; Purchases £25 250·00; Sales £39 750·00; Goods taken for own consumption £725·00.

Profit and Loss Account: Miscellaneous Receipts £725·00; Rent and Rates £450·00; Light and Heat £386·00; Carriage and Postages £275·00; Paper £284·60; Motor Expenses £725·55; Travelling £178·50; Cleaning £728·50;

Printing and Stationery £165·50; Telephone Expenses £184·00; Repairs and Renewals £1 318·00; Insurance £258·00; Advertising £425·00; Wages £4 728·50; National Insurance Contributions £482·50; Bank Charges £42·60; Sundries £427·50.

Balance Sheet: Premises £20 000·00; Fixtures £1 800·00; Motor Vehicles £2 000·00; Debtors £147·50; Cash at Bank £1 585·65; Cash in Hand £13·72; Capital at start £25 560·00; Drawings £3 500·00; Creditors £146·62.

The Adjustments are as follows:

(a) Closing Stock is found at stocktaking to be £1 750·00.

(b) You are asked to depreciate fixtures by £360·00 and motor vehicles by £500·00.

(c) A bill for outstanding Light and Heat is due (£14·00) and is to be included in the sums paid under this expense and carried forward as an accrued charge.

4. Using the figures given below, and taking into account the adjustments given at the end of the question, draw up the Trading Account and Profit and Loss Account of Julia Browne's business and her Balance Sheet at 31st December, 19...

Trading Account: Opening Stock £1 470·00; Purchases £31 350·00; Sales £49 840·00; Goods taken for own consumption £285·00.

Profit and Loss Account: Miscellaneous Receipts £262·50; Rent and Rates £1 400·00; Light and Heat £478·00; Carriage and Postages £138·75; Paper £186·50; Motor Expenses £824·65; Travelling £290·00; Cleaning £485·00; Printing and Stationery £378·50; Telephone Expenses £295·65; Repairs and Renewals £1 460·00; Insurance £148·00; Advertising £869·70; Wages £5 358·60; National Insurance Contributions £428·70; Bank Charges £38·50; Sundries £217·00.

Balance Sheet: Premises £18 000·00; Fixtures £3 600; Motor Vehicles £1 800; Debtors £155·50; Cash at Bank £1 725·60; Cash in Hand £23·30; Capital at Start £23 438·95; Drawings £4 000·00; Creditors £1 295·50.

The Adjustments are as follows:

(a) Closing Stock is found at stocktaking to be £1 650·00.

(b) You are asked to depreciate fixtures by 10% and motor vehicles by 20%.

(c) A bill for outstanding Motor Expenses is due (£48·50) and is to be included in the sums paid under this expense and carried forward as an accrued charge.

5. The following trial balance was extracted from the books of the partnership of Smith and Jones at December 31st 19..., after the profit for the year had been ascertained:

	Dr.	Cr.
Capital Accounts (January 1st, 19..):		
Smith		14 000·00
Jones		5 000·00
Current Accounts (January 1st, 19..):		
Smith		1 000·00
Jones	800·00	
Drawings during year:		
Smith	2 800·00	
Jones	1 600·00	
Profit for year		9 300·00
Cash in Hand	125·00	
Balance at Bank	1 750·00	
Goodwill	500·00	
Furniture and Fittings	1 500·00	
Sundry Debtors and Creditors	635·00	285·50
Rend due to landlord		200·00
Stock	4 950·00	
Premises	15 000·00	
Insurance Prepaid	125·50	
	£29 785·50	£29 785·50

You are required to draw up the Balance Sheet of the partnership as at December 31st, 19.., having regard to the following notes:

(a) Goodwill is to be written down to zero this year.

(b) Jones is to have a salary of £1 500 for his extra activity as a junior partner.

(c) Interest on capital at 10 per cent is to be allocated to both partners (No interest will be given or charged on Current Accounts).

(d) The residue of profit after making these arrangements is to be shared two thirds to Smith and one third to Jones.

(e) In preparing the Balance Sheet, you are to group the assets and liabilities so that the totals can be clearly seen of (i) the fixed assets, (ii) the current assets, and (iii) the current liabilities.

6. Brewer and Stillman conduct a merchanting business in partnership on the following terms:

(a) Interest is to be allowed on partners' Capital Accounts at 10 per cent per annum.

(b) Stillman is to be credited with a partnership salary of £2 000·00 per annum.

(c) The balance of profit in any year is to be shared by the partners in the ratio $\frac{3}{4}$ to Brewer $\frac{1}{4}$ to Stillman.

After preparing their Trading and Profit and Loss Account for the year ended March 31st, 19.., but before making any provision for interest on capital or for partnership salary, the following balances remained on the books:

	Dr.	Cr.
Capital Accounts:		
Brewer (as on April 1st previous year)		15 000·00
Stillman (as on April 1st previous year)		5 000·00
Current Accounts:		
Brewer (as on April 1st previous year)		500·00
Stillman (as on April 1st previous year)	1 000·00	
Drawings Accounts:		
Brewer	3 850·00	
Stillman	2 500·00	
Profit and Loss Account—Net Profit for year		8 650·00
Stock at end of year	8 450·00	
Goodwill Account	1 000·00	
Plant and Machinery, at cost	7 700·00	
Plant and Machinery, depreciation		1 700·00
Fixtures and Fittings, at cost	9 250·00	
Fixtures and Fittings, Depreciation		1 250·00
Trade Debtors and Creditors	942·00	825·75
Loan from H. Smith		3 000·00
Rent accrued due at March 31st, 19. .		200·00
Insurance unexpired at March 31st, 19. .	258·50	
Cash at Bank, Current Account	1 175·25	
	£36 125·75	£36 125·75

It is agreed by the partners to reduce the book value of goodwill by writing off £250·00 at March 31st, 19. . (to be charged to the Appropriation section of the Profit and Loss Account).

You are asked to prepare the Appropriation section of the firm's Profit and Loss Account and the partners' Current Accounts for the year ended March 31st, 19. ., together with the Balance Sheet as on that date.

Unit Twenty-two

Income Tax and the Small Business

22.1 The British Tax System

Taxation is a system adopted by governments to finance their activities. These days, especially in Britain, government agencies perform such a wide variety of activities that enormous sums have to be collected to finance the nation's defence, education, social security and medical services. Whether or not you personally support such programmes, you have to keep within a framework of taxation laws which are imposed by the government and will be enforced against you if you infringe them. This body of rules is being constantly changed and revised, from year to year. Penalties for breaches of the tax laws can be severe, but are usually reduced where full and frank admissions of misconduct are made. The best rule is to keep accurate and honest records, and thus pay your fair contribution to the needs of the nation. Genuine grievances can usually be adequately aired through trade associations, or your Member of Parliament.

The British tax system operates through a series of rules called 'Schedules', each of which deals with a particular type of income. Schedule D is the one that affects most businessmen, and has actually seven 'cases' or subdivisions of income. Case I covers profits which are the result of a trade or business; Case II, covering professional businesses, relates to doctors, accountants, etc.

Taxable Persons. Every person earning income, either from employment or through business activities, is liable to pay tax on that income. Certain 'allowances' may be obtained. For example 'personal allowance' is given to single people (£2 335) and to married couples (£3 655); these figures vary from year to year. Other allowances are given for certain children, for dependent relatives, for married women who are earning, etc. Where a firm is operated as a partnership or sole-trading enterprise, the profits of the firm are reduced by the personal allowances mentioned, and tax is only paid on the remaining 'table income'.

Limited companies are, however, separate legal personalities, quite independent of the individuals who form the company, and are taxed on the full profits agreed to have been earned. The present rate of 'Corporation Tax' (tax on companies) is 52% on large companies and 40% on companies making less than £90 000 profit.

22.2 Tax Avoidance

While accepting the statutory requirement to keep honest records and pay your fair contribution to the nation's finances, it should be stated that the courts have held that the taxpayer is entitled to take any legal means to avoid paying tax. If the Chancellor imposes a heavy tax on tobacco, I am free to avoid it by giving up smoking. If he taxes certain business activities, it is quite permissible for me to change my arrangements so that I can legally avoid the tax. It is for the Chancellor to devise a tax system which is free of loopholes. What you, as a businessman, may not do is to avoid taxation by illegal means, such as making fraudulent declarations.

A word of warning here. It is clearly undesirable for a taxpayer to rewrite his whole year's records, since the rewriting of records is usually associated with some sort of fraudulent practice. It might be thought that no one could ever know whether records have been rewritten, but in fact most editions of account books have coded markings which indicate when they were printed. A taxpayer who submits his accounts, purporting to start in March, in a book that only rolled off the presses in August, is clearly suspect. He may not in fact be guilty of a deceitful practice, for he may genuinely have fallen behind with his records through no fault of his own. Even so, it will be difficult for him to establish that his records were *efficiently* kept after such a long delay.

22.3 The Adjustment of Profits

Whatever profit you arrive at in your accounts, it is almost certain that the inspector of taxes will adjust it in the light of the tax laws as they stand at the time of assessment. For example, he will add back any expenses which you have deducted if these are disallowed by law. He may also deduct any income you have included which is not taxable, such as dividends which have already paid tax at source.

In adjusting your profit the inspector will be guided by certain rules, including those listed below which have been laid down by the courts over the years.

(*a*) Expenditure which is allowable as a charge against the profits (deductible expenditure) must have been *wholly and necessarily incurred in the earning of the profit*. Thus a telephone call to book accommodation at a trade fair would be deductible, but a call to book your annual holiday would not.

(*b*) Expenditure which is of a capital nature is not deductible, and depreciation often charged by businessmen in their accounts is not deductible. Instead, capital allowances are deductible, and these vary from year to year as the various Finance Acts of recent years have ordered.

(*c*) Personal expenditure relating to the proprietor's own pocket, his domestic establishment, etc., is to be treated as drawings. It is not allowable as a business expense.

(*d*) All profits arising from the trade or profession are taxable, including casual earnings and rents receivable. Capital profits may be taxed under the Capital Gains regulations.

22.4 Keeping Up-to-Date on Tax Matters

Unfortunately tax changes occur every year and it is quite impossible for a book of this type to explain the tax system fully or keep its readers up-to-date about changes. There are special publications which cover this ground for the small business. Perhaps the best is *Taxation Simplified*. Subscribers to this publication receive a revised booklet within a few weeks of the Budget, and another later in the year when the Finance Act has been passed by Parliament. Thus the reader is kept aware of the latest changes in taxation and is provided with a mine of information about tax matters. The addresss of the publishers will be found in the Foreword at the front of this book.

Another useful publication is the 'Money Which' Tax Saving Guide, which is issued annually and has a great deal of useful information on such things as "How to check an assessment". 'Money Which' is obtainable from the Consumer Association at the address shown in the front of this book.

22.5 What Happens if you Delay your Tax Return

It is always instructive to spend a few hours in the public gallery of the bankruptcy court. You will soon discover that the Department of Inland Revenue is the chief creditor in many of the cases being heard, and that bankruptcy often results from a procedure which the Department adopts to deal with taxpayers whose returns are late in arrival, or whom they suspect of fraudulent practices.

Let us consider the owner of a small business, perhaps a grocer, who delays sending in his accounts because he is very busy and cannot find the time to complete them. The Inland Revenue authorities have the records of the entire nation to refer to, and consequently know that grocery businesses of this size and situation normally earn between £7 000 and £12 000. They will therefore send him an assessment, without any calculations at all, near the upper end of the scale. They do not expect him to pay it, but they do expect him to wake up and take an interest. If he pays it without a murmer they conclude that they guessed too low, and next year they will send him a much bigger assessment. If he pays that, an even bigger one will follow the next year.

It follows that one should always respond to such an assessment by writing a letter of apology and enclosing one's true profit figures. The inspector of taxes will accept your apology gracefully and establish your true tax assessment without delay. This is payable in two parts for sole traders and partnerships, on January 1st and July 1st of the year following. For companies it is payable in one lump on January 1st of the following year.

Suppose now that his book-keeping records reveal that our grocer is making a net profit of £3 400 per year. According to the statistics available the average business of this type earns much more, says £8 800 per year. Clearly there is something suspicious here, and the inspector of taxes will proceed to investigate the accounts rigorously. He may call the trader in and discuss the situation. Either the trader can produce some acceptable reason for his depressed profit, or he may admit that his records are not accurate. If he refuses to admit any such thing, a confrontation is inevitable and he will be assessed at a much higher figure. If he wishes to appeal he is going to have to prove his case to the satisfaction of the Commissioners of Inland Revenue.

These examples illustrate that it is highly desirable *(a)* to keep an honest set of accounts in a regular way, week by week throughout the year, and *(b)* to complete and render one's tax returns promptly. Any disagreement should be settled by a visit to the tax office.

The inspector of taxes is always reasonable and always available. Very few tax problems arise in the small business which cannot be solved by keeping accounts systematically with the aid of a Simplex book, a copy of *Income Tax Simplified* and an occasional visit to the tax office.

22.6 Capital Transfer Tax

When death duties were replaced by Capital Transfer Tax in 1975 considerable apprehension was felt by the owners of small businesses about the new system of taxation. Some of the more worrying aspects were reduced by subsequent legislation and the whole scene is subject to almost annual review. It is also a rather complex and technical body of law which cannot possibly be dealt with fully in the present volume.

As far as small businesses are concerned, from 26.10.1977 only 50% of the value will be charged to the tax when a business passes either by gift or at death. There is a lower limit for individuals of £64 000, so that at present (June 1984) with the 50% rule referred to above a trader whose business is transferred at death or during his/her lifetime would get exemption up to £128 000 in some cases. Once again the rules are complex and cannot be covered in a book of this sort. Inflation means that many businesses would come into higher value brackets than £100 000 and consequently be caught by the tax.

It follows that businessmen/women with chargeable property around these figures would do well to look at **capital transfer tax mitigation schemes.** These seek to keep the tax to as low a level as possible, and to provide, through life assurance policies, sums which will become available in the event of death to meet the Capital Transfer Tax liability. The subject, like 'Pension Planning' (see below), is one where reliable advice from a consultant is invaluable. Such advice for those interested may be obtained from James Lemon, FLIA whose address is given in the foreword of this book.

22.7 Pension Planning

In recent years the extension of earnings related pension schemes to all employees through the National Insurance Scheme has left the self-employed in an anomalous position in that they only qualify for the smaller 'State' pension. This unsatisfactory situation has been resolved by making it possible for self-employed people to provide adequate pensions for themselves if they choose to do so, the premiums payable being subject to tax relief at the highest rate paid by the applicant. If such pensions are provided for controlling directors of private limited companies the rate of relief is the same rate as Corporation Tax.

In order to obtain the tax free concessions the contributions have to be made through an approved body such as a Life Assurance Company. The tax advantages are as follows:

(a) Contributions to the plan are deductible from the earned income of the plan holder for tax purposes. They attract relief at the highest rate of tax paid, excluding the investment income surcharge.

(b) Contributions to such plans accumulate free of all U.K. taxes except Development Land Tax and even this tax is rarely incurred.

(c) Part of the annuity is permitted to be commuted into a tax-free lump sum on retirement (similar to many pension schemes for employees).

(d) Finally the annuity payable to the insured, or to his widow or dependents, is treated as earned income when it is received, and consequently is taxed more favourably.

(e) Death benefits payable to the estates of deceased pensioners arising under a Pension Plan can be so arranged as to be free from Capital Transfer Tax.

Of particular interest here is the effect of compound interest on the size of the pension. Never was it truer to say that it pays to start building your pension while you are young. It is almost impossible to catch up later. For a young man electing to subscribe to a pension/retirement contract, or indeed to a fund for early retirement and taking advantage of tax relief based on relevant earnings, I will give you three illustrations assuming annual premiums of £1000, to a selected retirement age of 65.

Age next birthday	Estimated Pension per annum
20	£206 833
25	£114 225
30	£63 031

This illustrates the significance and the advantages of starting early when planning for ones retirement. A person starting at 50 would only receive a pension of £5 368, though even that is an extremely good, tax-efficient investment.

How to Control Your Business

23.1 Introduction

When a business has been running for some time it becomes possible to compare the current trading period with earlier periods. Such comparisons are almost always interesting, especially if attention is paid to *relative* changes rather than *absolute* changes. For example, a manager who tells you that sales have increased by £100 per week is giving you the actual figure of the increase, i.e. the absolute change that has taken place. It sounds very impressive, but you should inquire what relative change the increase represents, i.e. what percentage change. If sales have been running at £10 000 per week, the £100 increase is only a 1 per cent change and no one would think it miraculous. The success of an advertising campaign or similar activity is always best judged in percentage terms.

Even if the business has only been running for a short time, it is possible to compare it with similar businesses; statistics are usually available from trade associations and similar bodies which analyse the activities of enterprises in their particular field. It is also possible, if a certain amount of planning is undertaken, to make estimates of future performance in selling, expenditure, cash turnover and so on. These budgets may then be compared with actual performance as the weeks go by. This is the system known as *budgetary control*.

The most useful control figures which can be derived from the final accounts are as follows:

(a) *From the Trading Account*

    (i) the gross-profit percentage
    (ii) the rate of stock turnover

(b) *From the Profit and Loss Account*

    (i) the net-profit percentage
    (ii) the expense ratios

(c) *From the Balance Sheet*

    (i) the working-capital ratio
    (ii) the acid-test ratio
    (iii) the debtors-to-sales ratio
    (iv) the return on capital invested

As we consider these control figures we shall learn the meaning of several technical terms, such as 'turnover', 'average stock', 'fixed capital', 'floating capital', 'working capital', 'liquid capital', 'overtrading', 'insolvency', 'opportunity cost' and other useful pieces of account vocabulary. The more important control figures are listed in Fig. 23.1 and Fig. 23.2 along with the methods of calculation and the uses to which they may be put.

Background figure	Formula	Ratios derived (see Fig. 21.2)
Turnover	Total sales — Returns by customers	Gross-profit percentage Net-profit percentage Expense ratios Debtors-to-sales ratio
Average stock at cost price	$\dfrac{\text{Opening stock at start of year} + \text{Closing stock at end of year}}{2}$	Rate of stock turnover
Average stock at selling price	$\dfrac{\left\{\begin{array}{l}\text{Opening stock}\\+ \text{profit margin}\end{array}\right\} + \left\{\begin{array}{l}\text{Closing stock}\\+ \text{margin}\end{array}\right\}}{2}$	Rate of stock turnover
Working capital	Current assets — Current liabilities	Working-capital ratio
Liquid capital	$\left\{\begin{array}{l}\text{Current} - \text{Stock}\\\text{assets}\end{array}\right\} - \begin{array}{l}\text{Current}\\\text{liabilities}\end{array}$	Acid-test ratio (Liquidity ratio)
Capital invested	*For ordinary firms:* Capital at start of year *For companies:* $\begin{array}{l}\text{Capital at start}\\\text{of year}\end{array} + \begin{array}{l}\text{Profits}\\\text{ploughed back}\end{array}$	Return on capital invested
Opportunity cost	The earnings you could expect in some other form of employment	Return on capital invested

Fig. 23.1 *Background figures required to calculate control ratios*

Before preparing any control figures it is essential to have a set of 'final accounts' in good style, prepared in the way suggested throughout this book. It is not easy to analyse the affairs of a business whose accounts have been prepared poorly: first you must rearrange the accounts in good style, then most of the control figures may be readily determined.

23.2 Controlling Trading—a Trading Account for Analysis

Let us consider the Trading Account shown in Fig. 23.3. We will assume that the gross profit in the previous year was £13 700 on sales of £32 000, so both the turnover and the profit have increased.

The points to consider in analysing the results shown by a Trading Account are, first, the gross profit expressed as a percentage of turnover and, secondly, the rate of stock turnover.

Control ratio	Formula	Purpose	Remarks
Gross-profit percentage	$\dfrac{\text{Gross profit}}{\text{Turnover}} \times 100$	To check on trading profitability and detect trouble in trading areas	Commonly in range 25–40%
Rate of stock turnover	*either* $\dfrac{\text{Cost of stock sold}}{\substack{\text{Average stock at}\\\text{cost price}}}$ *or* $\dfrac{\text{Turnover}}{\substack{\text{Average stock at}\\\text{selling price}}}$	To detect rapidity of turnover with a view to increasing profitability	Varies with product; e.g. 360 for newspapers, 1 or 2 for grand pianos
Net-profit percentage	$\dfrac{\text{Net profit}}{\text{Turnover}} \times 100$	To check on overall profitability	Commonly about 10–12%; lower for groceries etc.
Expense ratios	$\dfrac{\text{Expense item}}{\text{Turnover}} \times 100$	To detect areas where expenses are rising, with a view to control	Useful in diagnosing possible inefficiency
Working-capital ratio	$\dfrac{\text{Current assets}}{\text{Current liabilities}}$	To detect risk of failing to meet current liabilities	Should be about 2:1
Acid-test (or liquidity) ratio	$\dfrac{\text{Current assets} - \text{Stock}}{\text{Current liabilities}}$	To detect really serious trouble in being able to meet current liabilities	Should be about 1:1
Debtors-to-sales ratio	$\dfrac{\text{Debtors}}{\text{Sales}} \times 12$	To discover the average credit period in months	Normally about one month, i.e. 30 days' credit
Return on capital invested	$\dfrac{\substack{\text{Net profit} -\\\text{Opportunity Cost}}}{\text{Capital at start}} \times 100$	To discover whether being in business is worth while	Should be at least 10%

Fig. 23.2 *Control ratios to help you evaluate and control your business*

23.3 The Gross-profit Percentage on Turnover

The gross-profit percentage on turnover is found by the formula

$$\frac{\text{Gross profit}}{\text{Turnover}} \times 100$$

Turnover is the net sales of the business, i.e. the sales less returns inwards.

In Fig. 23.3 the percentage is $\dfrac{£16\,500}{£42\,000} \times 100$

$$= \frac{275}{7}$$

$$= 39 \cdot 3\%$$

Sunshine Boutique (*E. Rawlinson*)
Trading Account
(for year ending December 31st 19..)

19..		£	19..		£
Dec. 31 Opening Stock		2 564	Dec. 31 Sales		42 240
Purchases	29 860		*less* Returns		
less Returns			(if any)		240
(if any)	424				
			Net Turnover		42 000
		29 436			
Total Stock					
Available	32 000				
less Closing Stock	6 500				
Cost of Stock Sold	25 500				
Gross Profit	16 500				
		£42 000			£42 000

Fig. 23.3 *A Trading Account to be appraised*

Constancy of the Gross-profit Percentage

One of the interesting things about the gross-profit percentage is that *it will tend to be constant*, i.e. the same from year to year, if business trends are steady. For example, supposing business doubled in the following year. Sales would be twice as great and purchases would be twice as great; profits ought therefore to double as well. When we come to work out the gross-profit percentage we find that

$$\frac{\text{Gross profit}}{\text{Turnover}} \times 100$$
$$= \frac{\pounds33\ 000}{\pounds84\ 000} \times 100$$
$$= 39\cdot3\% \text{ as before}$$

So the percentage tends to remain the same even if everything has doubled. The usefulness of the gross-profit percentage is that it shows the *relative* profitability of the business, this year compared with the previous year. If business conditions are steady the gross-profit percentage will be steady too.

Returning to Fig. 23.3, it is possible to compare this figure of 39·3 per cent with last year's gross-profit percentage. Last year the figures were gross profit £13 700 and sales £32 000.

$$\therefore \frac{\text{Gross profit}}{\text{Turnover}} = \frac{\pounds13\ 700}{\pounds32\ 000} \times 100$$
$$= 42\cdot8\%$$

Clearly the gross-profit percentage has fallen from 42·8 per cent to 39·3 per cent. This is a significant fall and, although it may have occurred for perfectly good reasons, it certainly detracts to some extent from the apparent performance of the business. Let us examine the possible causes of a decline in gross-profit percentage.

Causes of a Decline in Gross-profit Percentage

(a) **Cash losses.** If the manager takes money out of the till before cashing up the daily takings, the 'Sales' figure will be reduced; this in turn will reduce the gross profit, and hence the gross-profit percentage. It would be unwise, on this evidence alone, to accuse the manager of theft, but if his way of life suggests that he is living beyond his earnings it may be necessary to take some corrective action. If the manager is not at fault it may be that someone else is the culprit. Where there are several cash registers it is possible for staff to steal money by incorrect ringing up of receipts. A trader should be suspicious if a till has been deliberately placed so that the customer cannot see the amount being rung. Modern tills do much to overcome this type of theft by keeping an automatic record of each sum as it is rung up. The practice of giving customers till receipts for every purchase also reduces the chances of embezzlement.

(b) **Stock losses.** If the takings are being properly recorded, the cause of a fall in gross-profit percentage may be theft of stock. Regular losses of small quantities of stock by theft will reduce the stock in hand at the end of the trading period. This will increase the 'Cost of Stock Sold' and reduce the gross profit and hence the gross-profit percentage. The two common forms of theft are *passing out* (deliberate handing over by staff of stock without payment to friends or accomplices) and *shoplifting*. Shoplifting is believed to cost at least £10 million each year to shops in the United Kingdom. The provision of store detectives, two-way mirrors and other devices helps reduce this activity—especially when it leads to a successful prosecution.

Other forms of stock losses include *breakages* in departments where fragile goods are sold. Some assistants are naturally clumsy and should be transferred from departments where this is a disadvantage. Skylarking and tomfoolery should be discouraged and action taken against offenders. The *spoiling* of perishable commodities usually indicates bad buying. Poor storage may lead to stock losses due to evaporation, blowing away of powdery commodities like meal and flour, and the contamination of foods by other substances or by insects.

(c) **Clearance items.** Sometimes stock has to be disposed of at reduced prices because it is shop-soiled, or selling too slowly. This is another indication of bad buying. Some buyers may be out of touch with what is fashionable and readily saleable. Products which for some reason do not achieve expected sales figures may have to be marked down, thus reducing the gross profit and the gross-profit percentage. An appraisal of such 'clearance items' may reveal that a particular buyer is responsible for a high proportion of them, and the remedy is then fairly obvious.

(*d*) **Increased purchase prices.** Fluctuations in world prices of raw materials often result in higher purchase prices for goods. Increased purchase prices should be passed on to the consumer as increased selling prices. Sometimes this is not possible because of competition, and the result is falling profit margins and a lower gross-profit percentage. At least a businessman who is aware of these falling profit margins can be ready, when circumstances are less competitive, to recoup past losses. He may also vary his mixture of goods to include more items where competition is less fierce, reducing those where his rivals are particularly efficient and are able to undercut him.

(*e*) **Incorrect stock valuation.** An overvalued stock overstates the profit and gives an artificially high percentage of gross profit. As this stock then becomes the 'Opening Stock' of the next period, it will artificially inflate the 'Cost of Stock Sold' and lower the percentage of gross profit in the following year. The consequent difference between the two successive years is a symptom of bad stock-taking rather than of bad management. Undervalued stock understates the profit this year and overstates it next year.

Securing a Rise in Gross-profit Percentage

Whilst a fall in gross-profit percentage signals that something is wrong with our business we must always seek wherever possible to *raise* the gross-profit percentage. The chief ways to achieve this are by better buying—buying what the customer wants so that slow-moving 'shelf-warmers' and other clearance items are avoided; the protection of stock both from inherent vices (decay, dessication, fading of material, etc) and protecting stock from theft, accidental damage, etc. Careful supervision of staff, stock levels, cash handling and use of materials may do much to assist the gross-profit percentage.

23.4 The Rate of Stock Turnover

The rate of stock turnover (also called rate of stockturn) is a figure which can be calculated to show how many times the stock turns over in a year. It is significant because every time the stock turns over it yields a profit, so a rapid turnover will increase the total profit earned in the year. Turnover must be rapid with some merchandise; perishable foods and newspapers, for example, should turn over every day if possible. At least one chain of supermarkets throws away all cut meat products unsold at the end of the day. Overstocking in such circumstances can be very expensive.

Two formulas are available for finding the rate of stock turnover. The easier to use is

$$\text{Rate of stock turnover} = \frac{\text{Cost of stock sold}}{\text{Average stock at cost price}}$$

The other is

$$\text{Rate of stock turnover} = \frac{\text{Turnover}}{\text{Average stock at selling price}}$$

Applying the first formula to the Trading Account in Fig. 23.3, we have

$$\text{Rate of stock turnover} = \frac{\text{Cost of stock sold}}{\text{Average stock at cost price}}$$

$$= \frac{25\,500}{(2\,564 + 6\,500) \div 2}$$

$$= \frac{25\,500}{4\,532}$$

$$= 5 \cdot 6 \text{ times}$$

Is this a satisfactory rate of turnover? The answer depends on what the product is. It would be satisfactory for grand pianos but quite inadequate for groceries. It would perhaps do well enough for antiques, but not for sweets or tobacco.

The rate of stock turnover tells us how many times the stock turns over in a year. If we divide the 52 weeks of the year by the rate of stock turnover we find how long the average item is in stock. In the example above it is clearly $52 \div 5 \cdot 6 = 9 \cdot 3$ weeks. Rather too long for bread or bacon, but perfectly satisfactory for furniture or ironmongery.

Improving the Rate of Stock Turnover

Since the point of turnover is the point at which profit is made, it follows that all businesses should try to improve the rate of stock turnover. In implementing any plans to effect such an improvement we must watch the situation carefully, for the policy may prove to be less profitable than we hoped. Many firms have gone in for unlimited expansion of turnover only to find that they have saturated the market, or increased costs to the point where profitability of the enterprise declined. Expansion achieved by offering bonus schemes to salesmen will be marginally less profitable. This means that the extra business (the marginal sales) will contribute less to profit than the earlier sales did.

The rate of stock turnover may be increased by:

(a) Extending opening hours, within the limits set by law.

(b) Improving goodwill by courtesy, efficiency, honesty and service.

(c) Advertising selectively in local and national newspapers.

(d) Tightening stock control. This attempts to reduce 'average stock' by eliminating slow-moving items. It may conflict with (b) above, since customers who know that you are likely to have the less common items in stock may call more frequently; but in general reduction of average stock is a desirable thing since it reduces the capital tied up in stock and releases space on shelves and counters for more saleable items.

23.5 Controlling Expenses—the Profit and Loss Account

The gross profit is carried forward to the Profit and Loss Account where other profits are added to it and losses are deducted. The resulting net profit can be used as the basis for a *net-profit percentage*, which is found by the formula

$$\text{Net-profit percentage} = \frac{\text{Net profit}}{\text{Turnover}} \times 100$$

Once again there is a tendency (though it is less clear cut than with gross-profit percentage) for this to be constant from year to year. If it is not we should seek for an explanation. For example, in Fig. 23.3 the gross profit to be carried forward is £16 500.

Sunshine Boutique (E. Rawlinson)
Profit and Loss Account
(for year ending December 31st 19..)

19..		£	19..		£
Dec. 31	Wages	5 500	Dec. 31	Gross Profit	16 500
	Salaries	1 500		Discount Received	750
	Administration			Commissions	
	Expenses	420		Earned	1 550
	Light and Heat	680			
	Rent and Rates	1 650			18 800
	Insurance	450			
	Advertising	1 240			
	Carriage Out	100			
		11 540			
	Net Profit	7 260			
		£18 800			£18 800

Fig. 23.4 *A Profit and Loss Account to be appraised*

The Profit and Loss Account may be imagined to be as shown in Fig. 23.4. Calculating the net-profit percentage, we have

$$\text{Net-profit percentage} = \frac{\text{Net profit}}{\text{Turnover}} \times 100$$

$$= \frac{7\,260}{42\,000} \times 100$$

$$= 17 \cdot 3\%$$

Analysing the Net-Profit Percentage

The net-profit percentage will never be as constant as the gross-profit percentage, for many of the expenses do not vary with turnover. For example, rent and rates are not linked to turnover, nor are administration expenses and insurance. The chief advantage of the ratio is that it enables us to compare one trading period with another. Let us imagine that last year the net-profit percentage of Sunshine Boutique was 20 per cent. Evidently there has been a fall of 2·7 per cent over the past twelve months. What can have been the cause of this decline? If the *gross*-profit percentage has remained constant we may assume that the reason has nothing to do with the trading activities of the firm. There can only be two explanations:

(*a*) The expenses have increased for some reason.

(*b*) The 'other profits' may have declined for some reason.

(*a*) Increasing Expenses

A useful method of diagnosis here is to prepare *expense ratios*. Expense ratios enable the accountant to compare every expense with its counterpart from the previous year to see which, if any, has risen abnormally. The formula is

$$\text{Expense ratio} = \frac{\text{Expense item}}{\text{Turnover}} \times 100$$

By way of example, let us apply the formula to the salaries paid by Sunshine Boutique.

$$\text{Salaries ratio} = \frac{1\,500}{42\,000} \times 100$$

$$= 3 \cdot 57\%$$

Suppose that last year the salaries were £1000 and turnover was £32 000. Then

$$\text{Salaries ratio (previous year)} = \frac{1\,000}{32\,000} \times 100$$

$$= 3 \cdot 13\%$$

There has been quite a large increase in the salaries figure relative to the volume of trade done, and this seems to indicate some inefficiency somewhere.

(*b*) Falling 'Other Profits'

If the decline in net-profit percentage cannot be attributed to an increase in expenses, it may have been caused by a decrease in 'other profits' such as commission received or rent received. Perhaps a sub-tenant has been given notice to quit because his share of the building was required for expansion. In such a case there is nothing we can do about the lost rent. Perhaps commission previously earned has not been forthcoming for some reason. Here we can do something: we must determine that this type of earnings is pursued more vigorously in the following year.

Regular analysis of changes in the gross-profit percentage and net-profit percentage between successive trading periods is extremely useful in revealing the trends (both favourable and unfavourable) that are taking place in the business. Many firms prepare quarterly *interim* final accounts so that they can check the profitability of their enterprises at three-monthly intervals.

23.6 The Condition of a Business—a Balance Sheet for Interpretation

Fig. 23.5 shows the Balance Sheet of Sunshine Boutique as a basis for discussion. The reader will recall that it is a 'snapshot' of the affairs of the business at a moment in time.

Sunshine Boutique (E. Rawlinson)
Balance Sheet
(as at December 31st 19..)

Capital		£	Fixed Assets		£
At Start		58 080	Goodwill		14 000
add Net Profit	7 260		Land and Buildings		28 000
less Drawings	3 600		Fixtures and Fittings		3 600
	——	3 660	Motor Vehicles		1 000
		61 740			46 600
Long-term Liabilities			*Current Assets*		
Mortgage		15 000	Stock	32 540	
Current Liabilities			Debtors	2 240	
Creditors	12 350		Cash at Bank	7 800	
Wages Due	150		Cash in Hand	60	
	——	12 500		——	42 640
		£89 240			£89 240

Fig. 23.5 *A Balance Sheet to be appraised*

We have already met in Unit 21 the main terms used in drawing up a Balance Sheet, including Fixed Assets, Current Assets, Capital, Long-term Liabilities and Current Liabilities. We now have to extend our vocabulary with a further array of book-keeping terms, many of which are simply alternative phrases for those with which you are already familiar. The others extend your knowledge and increase your ability to appraise a Balance Sheet.

In appraising a Balance Sheet we want to know as a matter of course the total value of the business, and who 'owns' it. To say that it all belongs to the proprietor(s) or to the shareholders would be too simple a view. Let us now consider the question in relation to the ownership of Sunshine Boutique.

(a) The 'Capital Employed'
In the Balance Sheet of Sunshine Boutique (Fig. 23.5), the owner's capital at start is given as £58 080; yet the business is worth £89 240, as the total of the Balance Sheet shows. It follows that the capital employed in this business is greater than £58 080, and must have been provided in some other way than by the original contribution of the proprietor, E. Rawlinson. It is easy to see where these extra funds came from. A mortgage provided £15 000, creditors supplied goods worth

£12 350 without payment, employees are waiting for their wages and to this small extent are providing funds for the business, while £3 660 was ploughed back out of profits over the year. The capital employed in this business has therefore been provided in five different ways.

There are various ways of defining capital employed, but the one in commonest use is to take the figure of long term capital used—which implies the Capital of the proprietor, plus profits retained in the business, and the long-term liabilities. With a company it would be useful to take the capital contributed by the shareholders, plus the reserves, plus the debentures and any long-term loans. In this particular case we have:

$$\text{Capital employed} = £61\ 740 + £15\ 000$$
$$= £76\ 740$$

(b) Fixed Capital and Circulating Capital

The 'capital employed' above is being used to provide two classes of asset: fixed assets and current assets. Capital used to provide fixed assets is called *fixed capital*, and that used to provide current assets is called *circulating capital* or *floating capital*. In other words, fixed capital is tied up in fixed assets, which are in permanent use in the business and form the framework for running its affairs, while circulating (or floating) capital is tied up in current assets, which are in the process of turning over, or circulating, in the manner shown in Fig. 21.7.

For Sunshine Boutique the figures are

$$\text{Fixed capital} = \text{Total of fixed assets} = £46\ 600$$
$$\text{Circulating capital} = \text{Total of current assets} = £42\ 640$$

(c) Liquid Capital

'Liquid' capital is the name given to capital tied up in liquid assets, which may be described as cash and 'near-cash' items. Liquid assets are cash in hand, cash at the bank, debtors (who have a legal obligation to pay) and any investments which are readily marketable. The best definition is:

$$\text{Liquid capital} = \text{Current assets} - \text{Stock}$$

For Sunshine Boutique the current-assets total is £42 640, including £32 540 worth of stock. Hence

$$\text{Liquid capital} = £42\ 640 - £32\ 540$$
$$= £10\ 100$$

(d) Working Capital

The most important guiding figure when appraising a Balance Sheet is the 'working' capital. This is that portion of the capital employed which is not tied up in fixed assets (fixed capital) but is available to 'work' the business; in other words, it is available to *meet revenue expenditure*. The figure is found by the formula

$$\text{Working capital} = \text{Current assets} - \text{Current liabilities}$$

Applying this formula to Sunshine Boutique, which has current assets of £42 640 and current liabilities of £12 500,

$$\text{Working Capital} = £42\,640 - £12\,500$$
$$= £30\,140$$

(e) Working-Capital Ratio and Acid-Test (or Liquidity) Ratio

The *working-capital ratio* is an important figure which tells us the ratio between the saleable part of a firm's assets and its current liabilities. It is defined by the formula

$$\text{Working-capital ratio} = \frac{\text{Current assets}}{\text{Current liabilities}}$$

The figure for Sunshine Boutique is

$$\text{Working-capital ratio} = \frac{£42\,640}{£12\,500}$$

$$= \frac{3 \cdot 4}{1}$$

As a general rule it is agreed that 2:1 is a satisfactory working-capital ratio, so Sunshine's result appears to be quite good. However, we shall now apply a more crucial test.

The *acid-test ratio* (or liquidity ratio) tells us the ratio between a firm's readily available cash or near-cash assets (i.e. its liquid assets) and its current liabilities (due for payment in one month). It is defined by the formula

$$\text{Acid-test ratio} = \frac{\text{Liquid assets}}{\text{Current liabilities}}$$

For Sunshine Boutique the figure is

$$\frac{\text{Liquid assets}}{\text{Current liabilities}} = \frac{\text{Current assets} - \text{Stock}}{\text{Current liabilities}}$$

$$= \frac{£42\,640 - £32\,540}{£12\,500}$$

$$= \frac{0 \cdot 8}{1}$$

The acid-test ratio should never be less than 1:1, except in a temporary situation which the management has anticipated and for which suitable provision (e.g. an overdraft) has been made. Sunshine Boutique is clearly too short of liquid capital; it could not meet its short-term liabilities and would need to borrow to pay them.

To the investor considering the purchase of shares, the acid-test ratio offers a particularly valuable means of comparing the liquidity position of one firm with another.

(f) Debtors-to-Sales Ratio

The chief cause of illiquidity in any firm is the failure of debtors to pay promptly for goods supplied. If you allow debtors to become slip-shod over payments, your volume of debtors will increase and bad-debt losses will be suffered. The *debtors-to-sales ratio* will assist in evaluating your debtors' position. Its formula is

$$\frac{\text{Debtors}}{\text{Sales}} \times 12 = \text{Average debt (in months)}$$

Applying this ratio to Sunshine Boutique, we find that the average debt is

$$\frac{\text{Debtors}}{\text{Sales}} \times 12 = \frac{2\,240}{42\,000} \times 12$$
$$= 0\cdot64 \text{ months}$$

This is less than a month, and is therefore very satisfactory.

Where debts exceed on average one month, it is clear that some debtors must be breaking that rule of good business which says that an honest trader settles his debts monthly. The stages for ensuring good control of debtors are as follows:

(i) Appraise the individual debts, and decide which debtors are the problem cases.

(ii) See the debtor personally or write to him, pointing out the bad habits that have developed and threatening to cut off credit if the debt is not paid.

(iii) For really bad cases of intentional non-payment you have two courses of action: you can sue the debtor or you can sell the bad debt to a 'debt factor'. If you decide to sell the debt you will receive perhaps 50 per cent of the amount owed—but half a loaf is better than no bread.

(g) Return on Capital Invested

The last of the important figures used in the appraisal of a Balance Sheet is the *return on capital invested*. It is given by the formula

$$\text{Return on capital invested} = \frac{\text{Net profit} - \text{Opportunity cost}}{\text{Capital invested at start}} \times 100$$

To understand this ratio you will have to think about your business very clearly for a few minutes. You are working in this business to earn a living, and by doing so you surrender the chance of earning money in some other occupation. You could, for example, seek employment as manager in a similar enterprise, working for someone else. You might even take a totally different kind of job, as a clerk, teacher, bus driver, TV personality—the list is endless. By being in business you lose all these other opportunities which otherwise would be open to you. The *opportunity cost* of your present business is the best of the lost opportunities you decide not to take up.

Suppose you are making a clear £100 a week out of your present business, but could earn £90 a week as a manager for someone else. All the business is really paying you is £10 a week. Suppose your wife is helping in the business too, and she could earn £50 a week as a copy typist. You are actually worse off by being in business. Of course there is more to job-satisfaction than mere monetary reward, and it may well be that you chose your present occupation because you personally place a high value on the independence, for example, or service to the community which it affords. The 'return on capital invested' is a ratio which enables you to see what extra monetary satisfactions you get from your business. You must add this monetary satisfaction to the non-monetary ones, and then decide whether the whole enterprise is worth while.

Let us assume that E. Rawlinson, the proprietor of Sunshine Boutique, could earn £4 500 a year in another employment. We can calculate his return on capital invested as follows:

$$\text{Return on capital invested} = \frac{\text{Net profit} - \text{Opportunity cost}}{\text{Capital invested at start}} \times 100$$

$$= \frac{£7\,260 - £4\,500}{£58\,080} \times 100$$

$$= \frac{£2\,760}{£58\,080} \times 100$$

$$= 4.75\%$$

Usually a return of about 10 per cent is regarded as a worth while figure. A return of 20 per cent is much more satisfactory, and a proprietor only able to earn about 5 per cent could invest his capital more fruitfully in a Building Society. However, we should bear in mind the industrialist who, faced with the stricture that he was only in business to make a profit, rebuked his critic with the remark 'Not at all; I am in business to make shoes.' Such a man will not be too worried about a low return on capital invested.

23.7 Exercises in the Control of Business

1. Swish-shops Ltd., has four branches, each selling the same classes of goods in very similar areas. The following results are achieved:

Branch	Quarterly Turnover	Gross Profit	Selling Expenses	Net Profit
	£	£	£	£
(a) Seatown	42 000	15 000	10 200	?
(b) Riverton	38 000	17 200	8 800	?
(c) Marshville	26 000	8 500	3 250	?
(d) Markton	68 000	19 000	12 000	?

Find the Gross-Profit Percentage for each branch (correct to one decimal place). Find the Net-Profit Percentage for each branch (correct to one decimal place). Hence conclude: (*a*) which branch is making the best efforts; (*b*) which branch is making the worst efforts.

Give some reasons why they might be successful or unsuccessful in each case.

2. Newsagents Ltd., has five branches, each selling the same classes of goods in very similar areas. The following results are achieved:

Branch	Monthly Turnover	Gross Profit	Selling Expenses	Net Profit
	£	£	£	£
A	8 250	4 000	1 500	?
B	7 700	3 800	1 850	?
C	9 500	6 200	2 600	?
D	6 500	4 800	1 800	?
E	13 250	4 750.	1 350	?

Find the Gross-Profit Percentage for each branch (correct to one decimal place). Find the Net-Profit Percentage for each branch (correct to one decimal place). Hence conclude: (*a*) which branch is making the best efforts; (*b*) which branch is making the worst efforts.

Give some reasons why they might be successful or unsuccessful in each case.

3. Fill in the missing parts of the following table.

	Opening Stock	Closing Stock	Average Stock	Mark-up	Rate of Turnover	Sales Figure	Gross Profit
Mr. Smith	£2 000	£3 000	?	10%	20	?	?
Mr. Jones	£4 000	£6 000	?	20%	5	?	?

Now calculate the Gross-Profit Percentage and the Net-Profit Percentage (correct to one decimal place) 'bearing in mind that general administration expenses are Mr. Smith £1 850, Mr. Jones £2 350.

4. Fill in the missing parts of the following table.

	Opening Stock	Closing Stock	Average Stock	Mark-up	Rate of Turnover	Gross Profit	Sales Figure
Mr. Giles	£5 000	£7 000	?	10%	15	?	?
Mr. Slocum	£6 000	£9 000	?	20%	10	?	?

Now calculate the Gross-Profit Percentage and the Net-Profit Percentage (correct to one decimal place) bearing in mind that general administration expenses are Mr. Giles £3 500, Mr. Slocum £4 550.

5. Here is A. Tyler's Balance Sheet. You are to answer the questions below (with calculations if needed).

Balance Sheet
(as at December 31st, 19. .)

Capital		£	Fixed Assets		£
At Start		28 000	Goodwill		1 000
add Additions during		1 000	Premises		18 000
year		29 000	Plant and Machinery		12 000
add Net Profit	8 300		Motor Vehicles		2 000
less Drawings	3 600	4 700			
	a)	33 700			33 000
Long-term Liabilities			Current Assets		
Mortgage		5 000	Stock	4 596	
			Debtors	1 274	
Current Liabilities			Cash at Bank	1 381	
Creditors	1 614		Cash in Hand	72	
Accrued Charges	97		Payments in Advance	88	
		1 711			7 411
		£40 411			£40 411

(a) What is the capital owned by the proprietor?
(b) What is the capital employed in the business?
(c) What is the working capital?
(d) What is the liquid capital?
(e) Work out the acid test ratio (correct to 2 places of decimals).
(f) Work out the return on capital invested (correct to one decimal place) assuming that Tyler could earn £4 000 a year in an alternative position with none of the responsibilities of a small businessman. The extra capital was contributed on January 1st.

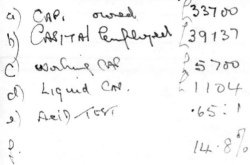

a) CAP, owned   £33700
b) CASITAL Employed   £39137
c) working CAP   £5700
d) Liquid CAP.   £1104
e) ACID TEST   ·65 : 1

p.   14·8%

6. Here is R. Montgomery's Balance Sheet. You are to answer the questions below (with calculations if needed).

Balance Sheet
(as at December 31st, 19. .)

Capital		£	Fixed Assets		£
At Start		40 000	Goodwill		500
add Additions during			Premises		36 000
year		2 000	Plant and Machinery		18 500
add Net Profit	12 750	42 000	Motor Vehicles		8 850
less Drawings	4 250	8 500			63 850
		50 500			
Long-term Liabilities			Current Assets		
Mortgage		15 000	Stock	7 864	
			Debtors	2 976	
Current Liabilities			Cash at Bank	3 281	
Creditors	12 950		Cash in Hand	475	
Accrued Charges	158		Payments in Advance	162	
		13 108			14 758
		£78 608			£78 608

(a) What is the capital owned by the proprietor?

(b) What is the capital employed in the business?

(c) What is the working capital?

(d) What is the liquid capital?

(e) Work out the acid test ratio (correct to 2 places of decimals).

(f) Work out the return on capital invested, assuming that Montgomery could earn £6 000 a year in an alternative position with none of the responsibilities of a small businessman. The extra capital is to be regarded for the purposes of this calculation as being introduced on January 1st.

Sundry Other Matters

24.1 Partnerships

There are many circumstances in which a partnership seems to be the best type of business unit. For example, in family businesses it is sometimes helpful to recognize the merits of various interested parties by designating them as partners in the business. Names such as Harrison Bros., Sorrell & Son, and Scammell & Nephew are common. In the professions, such as medicine and law, a partnership is often the only satisfactory form of business unit, for limited companies are not permitted by some professional bodies. Moreover a single person rarely has all the expertise required to offer a fully comprehensive service.

The chief reasons for forming partnerships may be listed as follows:

(a) In order to bring more capital into an enterprise, so that improved machinery, equipment and buildings may be obtained.

(b) In order to broaden the knowledge and experience available, and thus to offer a more comprehensive service to the public. Thus lawyers who specialize respectively in divorce, motor-accident, criminal and conveyancing law may form a partnership to pool their knowledge and experience in these fields.

(c) In order to unite wisdom and experience with youth and vitality. A doctor of mature years may seek a young and active partner who will take on the more strenuous part of the practice; the younger man will benefit by having the senior colleague's greater knowledge put at his disposal.

(d) In order to reduce the onerous responsibilities of a one-man business, where it is often impossible to take time off, and where sickness can endanger the very existence of the business.

Agreements between Partners

Early partnerships were often called 'common ventures' or 'joint ventures', which conveys the idea that all business is to some extent an adventure in the way of trade, and no doubt many were inaugurated with a mere handshake. There is in fact no legal requirement to have an agreement in writing. Partnerships may be held to have existed by the courts if either partner can prove:

(a) an oral agreement (proved by witnesses), or

(b) a systematic course of dealing together by way of engaging in trade or the provision of professional services, or

(c) a written agreement, whether formal (drawn up by a solicitor in deed form) or informal (a mere undertaking in writing), to be associated with one another.

Clearly the formal Partnership Deed is most desirable, since a lawyer experienced in these matters will bring to the partners' attention many points that have caused controversy in similar situations in the past. Even where people agree to work together at the start of a partnership, there is no guarantee that disagreement will not arise at a later date.

Matters to be included in a Partnership Deed

The following major points should be included in any partnership agreement:

(*a*) The amount of capital to be contributed by each partner.

(*b*) Whether this capital is to earn interest for the partner, and if so at what rate per cent. Usually it is desirable to give interest on capital if the amounts contributed are unequal. This prevents the partner contributing the greater sum from developing a sense of grievance.

(*c*) Whether any partner is to receive a salary, and if so how much. It often happens that a young man contributes very little to a partnership in capital, but a great deal in health, strength and energy. This contribution should be recognized as one entitling the young man to a reward in the form of a basic salary.

(*d*) The ratio for sharing profits and losses. Simple fractions are usually adopted, such as half and half, two-thirds to one-third, or three-fifths to two-fifths.

(*e*) The date the partnership shall commence, and the duration of the partnership. Where the duration is to be 'at will', i.e. indefinitely, some mention should be made of what is to happen if one of the partners dies. The heirs of the deceased partner will be anxious to obtain their rightful share of his estate, and so perhaps will the Inland Revenue authorities. If assets have to be sold to realize funds to meet such demands, the whole enterprise may collapse. It is therefore a wise precaution to insure your partner's life (and he yours), so that if he dies you will receive a sum of money which can be used to settle any claims on the business. More of this on page 127.

(*f*) How much each partner is permitted to take as 'drawings' each month or week, and whether interest is to be paid on these drawings.

(*g*) In the event of disputes, how the dispute shall be resolved. Some partners specify a particular person to act as arbitrator; others simply agree on how an arbitrator should be chosen if and when the need arises, perhaps a bank manager for financial issues and a solicitor for legal points.

The Partnership Act of 1890

Partnership law was codified in 1890, that is to say the legal cases on which the law had formerly depended were enacted as a formal set of rules by Parliament, and modified in line with current thought at that time. It was an age when legislators still believed that controls in business affairs were largely undesirable. The Act therefore established rules to which reference could be made as a last resort, when partners had failed to agree on how the particular point in question was to be settled. It should be emphasized that the rules stated below are only used in the rare cases where partners have entered into no clear arrangements with one another on the point concerned, and then only as a last resort. Any original agreement, however informal, to behave differently from what was suggested in the Act will always be upheld by the courts.

(*a*) All partners are entitled to contribute equally to the capital of the firm. They must share equally in the profits and contribute equally to the losses.

(*b*) No partner may have a salary.

(*c*) No partner may have interest on capital.

(*d*) A partner loaning money to the firm, over and above his capital contribution, is entitled to interest at 5 per cent per annum.

(*e*) Any partner may see and copy the books of the firm, which must be kept at the ordinary place of business.

(*f*) No new partner may be introduced without the general consent of all the partners.

Nowadays the vast majority of partnerships include clauses in their agreements which replace some or all of these rules.

24.2 Private Limited Companies

Limited companies carry out the vast majority of business activities in the free-enterprise countries of the world. There are over half a million 'private' limited companies and about 3 000 'public' limited companies in the United Kingdom alone. The popularity of companies is explained by the *limited liability* which the shareholder has. Whereas a sole trader, or a partner, is liable to the full extent of his personal wealth for all the obligations of the business, the liability of the shareholder is limited to the value of his shareholding. He cannot be held personally liable for the debts of the business in excess of the nominal value of the shares he has purchased, or agreed to purchase. Before this concession was made by Parliament in 1855, the liability of shareholders was unlimited and, if their company collapsed, they were held fully liable for the debts of the company even though they were not directors of the company and had no chance of influencing personally the conduct of its affairs. Small investors could find themselves thrown into the debtors' prisons just because they owned a share in a company which had failed.

If the shareholders are now freed from liability for the debts of the business, who can be held liable? The answer is—no one. Creditors can only hope for repayment to the extent that the contributed capital will allow. This is plainly a position that creditors would wish to avoid, and so Parliament enacted that every company must display, immediately after its name, the word *Limited*. This is a warning to suppliers to check on the financial soundness of a company before doing business with it. Readers may think that a Limited Company is a sound and reliable organization. Of course the majority are, but many have only £100 or less as the capital to which creditors may look should the company get into difficulties. It is unwise to supply goods in large quantities to companies where the capital is insufficient to cover the order. The registered share capital of a limited company can be discovered from the records which are open to examination (for a nominal fee) at Company House in London, and Cardiff. The company's current balance sheet merits careful study in this context, for there is always a risk that losses over the years have eroded the initial capital almost entirely.

Forming a Company

The chief advantage of forming a company is the one explained above —limited liability. If the business gets into difficulties you are only liable to the extent of the capital you have contributed, and not to the full extent of your personal wealth.

Forming a company is a fairly simple process which in theory anyone can perform. In practice it is better to use the services of an expert. Some firms specialise in registering companies to meet the exact needs of the businessman. They also usually have a stock of companies already registered, 'ready-made' companies, which by a simple transfer process can be made available to any one requiring a company. Such a firm is Gray's Inn Company Formations Ltd., whose address is given in the Foreword of this book. Alternatively your local accountant will advise you on these matters.

Limited companies have to operate within a much tighter framework of law than that which governs the sole-trader or partnership enterprise. This means that the book-keeping requirements are considerably stricter. If you are running your business as a company, you should make a careful study of the Companies Acts, 1948-81. *Success in Principles of Accounting* by Geoffrey Whitehead (published by John Murray Ltd), deals simply with the 'Final Accounts' of companies.

24.3 Some Book-keeping Difficulties

The Simplex Advice Bureau answers many queries from businessmen about a wide variety of topics. Its function is not to give general advice on business problems, for this is the function of the accountant, and would also require a licence from the Director General of Fair Trading. It aims only to help businessmen who are having difficulty keeping their records, using the various Simplex books. Some of the problems raised in recent years recur again and again, and are obviously of general interest, especially to those setting up in business for the first time. It is hoped that the following selection of points raised will be helpful. In each edition of this book further points are being added in a new Chapter Twenty-six, on the Simplex Advice Bureau.

Adjustments: An explanation of simple adjustments has been given in Section 21.6. A further aspect of adjustments is important if accounts are being prepared on an 'Accruals' basis with receipts and payments being adjusted to give the correct totals of sales and purchases for the year. How do we calculate the correct figures for these items. The answers are as follows.

Purchases: Take the total payments in the financial year to suppliers. From this total we deduct the amounts owed to suppliers at the start of the year (because we will have paid them in the first month or two of the year). We then add on the sums owed to trade creditors for goods supplied during the year but not yet paid. So the formula is:

Purchases for year = Payment during year − trade creditors at start + trade creditors at end of year.

Note that the word trade creditors' refers to *suppliers* to whom we owe money—not expense creditors such as light and heat bills due etc.

Sales: Take the total receipts for the year from customers. From this total we deduct the debtors figure at the start of the year, for these debtors who paid us during the year were paying us for goods sold to them in the previous trading period. We then add the trade debtors at the end of the year, who have been sold goods but have not yet paid for them. So the formula is:

Sales for year = Receipts during year − trade debtors at start + trade debtors at end.

Bad Debts. The aim in book-keeping is to achieve two results, a perfectly accurate profit figure and a perfectly honest Balance Sheet which does state truthfully what the assets and the liabilities of the business are. If we allow bad debts to continue unrecognised we defeat both these objects. The loss suffered by bad debts is not included in the Profit and Loss Account—so that profits are overstated—while the debtors which appear on the Balance Sheet include some who are never going to pay. Our assets are therefore overstated.

The best way to prevent this situation is to appraise the Debtors at regular intervals. Business specialists like Kalamazoo Ltd., do offer simple check-up systems for keeping debtors constantly under review.

Once a month take the Debtors' Record Book and consider the debts still outstanding. Bad debtors should be approached for payment and certainly should not be allowed any further credit. If a debtor cannot pay it may help to offer to accept less than the full debt—i.e. cut your losses. If the debtor is unable to pay anything, the question is whether to accept the loss and take no further action or to pursue the matter through the legal process of bankruptcy. It depends very much on our assessment of the situation as to what action we take. Generally the best principle is to pursue an unprincipled debtor relentlessly, in the general interests of the business community, while taking no action against hard-luck cases.

As far as book-keeping is concerned, the bad debt is written off in the Profit and Loss Account, and removed from the list of debtors so that the figure of Debtors on the Balance Sheet is reduced to the correct figure of known, reliable debtors.

Balance Sheets. One of the commonest complaints by businessmen using the Simplex, or any other system is that they cannot get their Balance Sheet to balance. Goethe, one of the greatest minds of his age and one of the supreme geniuses of all time once described book-keeping as the sublimest creation of mankind, for the Balance Sheet will only work out if the book-keeping has been perfect. It is a fact though that the Balance Sheet is a comparatively recent invention, and many businessmen did not bother at all about it. For the first thirty years of its use the Simplex System did not even have a Balance Sheet in it. Today the Inland Revenue is more interested than formerly in seeing a Balance Sheet, and it is certainly desirable that one should be prepared each year.

The preparation of the Balance Sheet in this edition has been fully described in two places, Section 9.4 and Section 21.4. It is hoped that the explanations given there will enable the reader to prepare his Balance Sheet properly and thus join Goethe in appreciating the finest point in book-keeping.

Book-Tokens, Gift Tokens etc. These special ways of selling cause problems both in book-keeping and in VAT records. The trouble is that when we take money by selling a token, we actually receive the money for the value of the token, but we do not supply the goods. When a customer spends his token we give up the goods, but all we really receive is the token, which we then have to redeem with the organisers of the scheme. The rule is that when we sell the token the value of the token itself is not "Takings" in the ordinary sense of Sales, the only part of the sale which is takings is the few pence we charge for the card. When we redeem other people's tokens, supplying goods to the face value of the token, this is 'takings' or 'sales', but we shall not actually receive the money until we redeem the token with the organisation which issues the cards.

When dealing with the 'Special Schemes' for Retailers the Customs and Excise Department goes to considerable trouble in the 'Schemes' booklets to point out that if these items are not dealt with properly the retailer may pay too much tax.

Buying a Business. The purchase of a business is one of the most important decisions in a businessman's life and it should not be entered into lightly. It may be advisable to take legal advice about it, and to call in a local valuer who will appraise the business, assess the Balance Sheet and accounts of the previous owner and advise about any valuation to be placed on goodwill (see below). It is false economy to save money on a valuer's fees if you do not have sufficient expertise yourself. Never accept things at their face value, and ask plenty of searching questions about the property, the stock, the neighbourhood, the clientèle etc. The law says "Let the buyer beware". Thus if you ask the seller to state in writing that the building is free from woodworm deliberate failure to declare the worm-eaten nature of the premises constitutes a fraudulent misrepresentation, which is actionable. If you don't even ask such a question you have only yourself to blame.

When purchasing a business take the Balance Sheet of the previous owner and consider carefully the assets shown. Using the Balance Sheet in Figure 21.6 as an example (see page 111) the question might be asked 'Are the premises worth £15 000?' If not, why not? A long list of points made in a letter to the seller drawing attention to the state of the roof, the re-pointing necessary, the poor state of the shop-front, the antiquated plumbing etc. etc., is likely to bring him into a reasonable state of mind about the true value of the property. Similarly the fixtures, the motor vehicles (if they are being taken over), the Stock and the Debtors should be closely appraised.

Cash Flow. There are several aspects of cash flow which are of interest to businessmen. The term refers in general to the way in which liquid funds (money) move in and out of the business, and the need to keep control of it so that funds are always available to meet requirements. Stocking-up with goods to meet busy periods brings about heavy cash flows out of the business, while at times of heavy selling the buying function may be reduced to a minimum so that cash flows into the business are greater than outlays. Part of this inflow is the profits we are making, but whether these profits are available in cash form depends upon the uses to which the cash flows are put. If we have surplus cash available and decide to use it to purchase motor vehicles we cannot later complain if there are no funds to pay out as profits. It is wise to plan ahead with a Cash Forecast, using two columns for each month, a Budget Column and an 'Actual' Column. An example is shown in Fig. 24.1. Clearly 'Other Payments', and 'Capital Items' could be given in greater detail. Time lags have to be taken into account, especially on such matters as 'Debts Collected' and 'Payments for Business Stock'. It is usual to plan six months ahead, and roll the plan forward every two months.

When the actual receipts and payments are made the figures can be inserted in the 'Actual' column. They can then be compared with the budget, and the difference accounted for. An excess payment for business stock might be explained by a favourable opportunity which arose due to the bankruptcy of another trader. It might have to be explained by higher prices, and the budgets in the months ahead might need to be adjusted, and a check made on selling prices to ensure that these higher costs were passed on to consumers wherever possible.

Wherever possible **cash flow smoothing** should be carried out. This means that where we have payments which can be moved to another part of the year when funds are readily available we should do so. Thus annual payments for car tax, car insurance, other types of insurance, pension fund payments etc., can be moved around by agreement with the organisation concerned. To move your motor vehicle insurance to a different part of the year only requires a letter to the insurance company and agreement on an interim payment to provide cover for the few months before the annual payment is paid again on the rearranged date. Similarly new capital expenditure can be put off until the best time for payment.

Deposit Accounts. Since a firm's payments and receipts are always paid out of and paid into a Current Account those who have a Deposit Account sometimes wonder how this fits into the Simplex System of book-keeping. It is also made a little more difficult because a Deposit Account may be in the firm's name, or in the proprietor's own name and not regarded as part of the firm's assets.

Imagining a sum of £200 transferred from Deposit Account to Current Account the rules are as follows:

Deposit Account part of the Firm's Assets

(i) Enter the £200 as "Other Receipts", write 'Transfer from Deposit Account' in the Particulars column and put the £200 into the Paid to Bank section of your Weekly Page.

Cash Flow	January Budget (£)	January Actual (£)	February Budget (£)	February Actual (£)	March Budget (£)	March Actual (£)
1. Cash Balance (cash & bank)	580		1,297		−1,053	
RECEIPTS:						
2. Sales in cash	2,347		1,800		3,600	
3. Debts collected	150		350		220	
4. Other receipts	420		420		420	
5. Extra capital contributed	–		–		1,000	
6. Total receipts (add 2-5)	2,917		2,570		5,240	
7. Total cash available (1+6)	3,497		3,867		4,187	
PAYMENTS:						
8. Payments for business stock	1,340		3,500		2,200	
9. Wages	420		420		450	
10. Other Payments	260		580		580	
11. Capital items	–		240		–	
12. External payments (add 8-11)	2,020		4,740		3,230	
13. Drawings	180		180		180	
14. Total payments	2,200		4,920		3,410	
15. Final Cash Balance (7-14)	1,297		Deficit −1,053 Note: New capital £1,000 Ask for £500 overdraft		777	

Fig. 24.1. Budgeting for Cash Flow

(ii) At the back of the Simplex D book is a summary called 'Movements in and out of Deposit Account'. You should enter the £200 in this summary as a withdrawal and also deduct the sum on your actual Deposit Account book to keep that record straight. Not all banks give Deposit Account customers a paying-in book for the Deposit Account, in which case you must wait until you get a Bank statement for the account.

Deposit Account not part of the Firm's Assets

(i) Enter the £200 in 'Other Receipts', write 'Extra Capital Contributed' in the 'Particulars' column and put the £200 in the 'Paid to Bank' section.

(ii) Carry the extra capital contributed into the "Summary of Other Receipts" at the back of the book, where it will be added to the Capital at the end of the year (thus balancing up the £200 which is in the Bank Account, or has been spent to some useful purpose).

When money is taken out of the Current Account and put in a Deposit Account the best thing to do is to enter it in the 'Payments Other than for Stock' section of the weekly page—Deposit Account £350·00 going out of the Cash or Bank column as preferred. If the Deposit Account is part of the firm's assets it should be entered on one of the spare lines in the 'Payments other than for Stock' section. If it is being put into the owner's private Deposit Account it should be entered on the line marked 'Drawings'.

Direct Debits. In the last few years the 'Direct Debit' system has become more and more popular with large scale organisations who much prefer this method of collecting money due to them rather than the 'Standing Order' system or 'Credit Transfer' which has traditionally been used. It is certainly much more convenient in these inflationary times for such payments as rates and water rates, where a standing order is inappropriate because the amount payable changes every year. With a 'credit transfer' you tell the Bank to pay your creditor by crediting his account with the sum due to him specified in your standing order. With a 'direct debit' the creditor tells the Bank to debit your account with the amount due to it.

Certain safeguards are built into the system, for example the creditor must have your consent to the arrangement and usually asks you to sign a form agreeing to the stated system. They also should let you know in some appropriate way how much they are demanding from you before they actually do ask the bank to debit your account, so that you can protest if you do not agree. They will also usually deal sympathetically with complaints about the system.

The point traders may not be aware of is of course that in agreeing to this arrangement the trader leaves it to the creditor to pick the moment for the transfer, and gives up his own rights to decide when payment shall be made. It follows that if rates are payable on the first day of January you will probably pay them on that date, whether it suits you or not. Tied garages and similar organisations find that Head Office debits their full debt at the earliest possible moment, whereas the small trader very often finds it difficult to get payments from large firms, who are full of tricks to delay payment. This does not mean the system is necessarily bad. If an agreed average date is arrived at, which is fair to both parties there can be no objection to the system.

Employees. Sometimes businessmen, tired of the endless task of keeping tax records etc, feel it would be a sound policy to make their employees become 'self-employed' persons responsible for their own affairs. This is particularly so where the business is run in such situations as the staffing of stalls in street markets all over a county. The trouble with adopting such a policy is that the onerous burden afflicting the employer will now afflict each of his staff. It is fairly certain that at least some of them will not wish to take on the extra worry, and the extra uncertainty, connected with self-employment. Honest, hard-working staff are hard to find, and even one or two lost may mean time, expense, losses with unreliable replacements etc. Employees can easily get into difficulties if they have to stamp their own cards for National Insurance or save up their Income Tax payments. When the 'lump' started in the building industry, and most employees became self-employed sub-contractors, the Inland Revenue lost a great deal of money. The law was changed and the Contractors had to deduct a set percentage of tax on all payments, which would be adjusted later with the 'self-employed person' if the Inland Revenue could find him. So the employer finished up doing the work anyway. Generally speaking the adoption of a simple system like the Simplex Wages Book will reduce the burden of these records, and the link with reliable, loyal employees of proven honesty should be preserved.

Goodwill. When purchasing a business it is usual to pay an extra sum, over and above the value of the assets, for the goodwill of the business. It is to compensate the previous owner for his hard work in the past since some of the new owner's profits in the future will be earned by the hard work of the previous owner because of the goodwill the public bear him.

How much should be paid for Goodwill is always a matter for negotiation; the seller will naturally claim as large a sum as possible and the buyer will try to pay as little as he/she can. Goodwill is often called an intangible asset, one that you cannot touch. Whether Mrs. Smith, Jones and Robinson do bear a trader goodwill is almost impossible to prove. If the business records are available for the last—say—five years, and show a growing turnover and rising profitability than Goodwill probably does exist. Of course inflation must be taken into account, a rising turnover may only reflect higher general prices and in real terms the business might actually be declining. If the previous owner cannot produce convincing figures it is advisable to pay only a nominal sum for goodwill, and a local valuer who knows the trends of business in the area should be consulted if the sum asked seems excessive.

As far as book-keeping is concerned Goodwill is a strange asset. Suppose we pay £2 000 for Goodwill. It is a fixed asset (really an intangible asset), but in fact of course no-one does bear *us* any goodwill. The £2 000 has been paid for the Goodwill local people feel to the *previous* owner. For this reason is it usual to write off Goodwill out of the Profits (as a type of Drawings; not on the Profit and Loss Account). Usually we reduce it by about one quarter each year for the first four years. By the time Goodwill is reduced to nothing on the Balance Sheet people have grown to know and trust us, and do bear us some Goodwill. So accountants talk about the paradox of Goodwill. When it is worth most on the

Balance Sheet it is really worth nothing, and when it is valued at nothing on the Balance Sheet it is quite valuable.

Insurance Claims. When for some reason we suffer a loss, against which we have insured, and make a genuine claim which is conceded by the insurer, book-keeping problems arise. The sum paid as compensation will be an 'Other Receipt' and go into the Daily Page in the 'Other Receipts' section. The problem is to decide how this loss, and the compensation, should be treated in the books. Let us take one or two examples:

(i) *Losses of Business Stock.* Imagine that business stock valued at £500 has been damaged in a fire, and the claim of £500 is paid. The money coming in for the claim will be an 'Other Receipt' as explained above. How shall we write off the damaged stock. The answer is that we don't need to write it off at all. Just put the ashes in the dustbin and forget them. The reason why no action needs to be taken is that Stock is only taken at the end of the year when we do the stock-taking. When we come to 'take stock' at the end of the year, the missing stock will not be there to count, and so the loss will be taken at this point. We cannot count what is not there, and so our Closing Stock figure will be £500 short.

(ii) *Losses of Fixtures and Fittings.* In this case we must make a note of the decline in value due to the fire. The £500 compensation in the Bank account will off-set the reduced Balanced Sheet value of the fittings. Write on the Balance Sheet 'less losses due to fire £500'. Of course if we spend the money on buying new fittings this will be a Capital Item in the 'Payments other than for Stock' section of the weekly page, and the Fixtures will be increased again by this new Capital Expenditure.

Investments. If a businessman buys investments they are frequently part of his private transactions and not part of the business activities at all. There are however two reasons why it is sometimes advisable to buy investments for the business. These are:

(i) *As a Sinking Fund.* Suppose we depreciate machinery each year by 10 per cent. This reduces the value of the machinery on the books, and also reduces the profits made, so that the owner does not take out more from the business than he has really earned. An amount of assets—possibly in money form—is left in the business as a result and it gives the appearance that plenty of money is available. We should really put this money in a safe place so that one fine day, when we need new machinery, it will be available from a source outside the business. We could put it in a deposit account, or in a Building Society, or we could buy investments. Any interest or dividends earned should also be invested. If we do not do this the surplus money may be spent on unneccessary assets—plush furniture for example. Even worse, someone might think he should have a wage increase out of it. If we do not create this sinking fund, to store the money for our new machinery, we shall face problems in the future and may go out of business altogether.

(ii) *To earn income from surplus funds.* Suppose that for some years trade has been brisk, we have ploughed back profits into extra stock etc. and earned good profits from the turnover. A slight 'sneeze' in the economy suggests we cut back on stocks and consolidate our position for a while. Reduced stocks means spare cash is available. We shall now make less profits for turnover is down. The spare cash will not earn money. As a result our total profitability must decline. If this cash is promptly invested as it becomes available instead of merely raising our bank balances we shall get at least some return on it and thus avoid too large a decline in our **Return on Capital Invested.**

Loans. The Simplex D book now includes a special summary at the back for loans made available and their repayments.

The method of recording money borrowed is quite simple. Let us imagine £500 borrowed from a Bank. Clearly all the Bank does is put the money into our Account, and we are free to use it as we think best. To make the entries proceed as shown in Fig. 24.2. The steps are:

(i) Enter the £500 in 'Other Receipts' on your daily page and write "Loan from Bank" in the particulars column.

(ii) Enter the £500 in the Paid to Bank column. In fact of course you never do handle the money, the Banker just credits it in your account, but we have to make the book-keeping entry.

(iii) You now have the money in your account, and can spend it. If you spend it on Stock enter it in the Payments for Business Stock. If you use it for other things like capital items enter it on the 'Capital Items' line in 'Payments other than for Stock'.

(iv) Now carry the £500 in the 'Other Receipts' column to the Loans summary at the back of the book, and also enter there the interest (£100 in the example shown). This interest is a loss of the business and must also go in the Sundries column of your 'Summary of Payments for Expenses'. At the end of the year a fair proportion of it can be written off the Profit and Loss Account.

(v) When you make the repayments each month (probably you will find them deducted on your account when you ask for a Bank Statement) put them in the 'Payments other than for Stock' section on a separate line and carry them to the summary for loans. You cannot charge them to the Profit and Loss Account as they are not losses. The only part of them that is a loss is the interest payable—which we have dealt with in (iv) above.

An extremely valuable book for those wishing to secure funds for a business is the booklet "Money for Business" published jointly by the Bank of England and the City Communications Centre. The cost is £1 at the time of writing and it may be obtained from either the Bank of England, London EC2R 8AH, or the City Communication Centre, 7th Floor, Stock Exchange, London EC2N 1HP. The book gives a comprehensive explanation of the sources of finance available, and offers much helpful advice. One of the chief points it makes is the need for the businessman to prepare in advance a good case for the loan he needs, which shows exactly why finance is required. The book is a mine of information on the subject and well worth studying if loan availability is of concern to you.

Manufacturing Accounts. When a firm is engaged in manufacturing it needs a Manufacturing Account as well as a Trading Account and Profit and Loss Account. This can be drawn up on a separate sheet of paper and clipped in the Simplex Account Book. It is usually prepared in two parts, a *Prime Cost Section*

SUMMARY OF LOANS AND REPAYMENTS		
LOAN FROM: Loanshire Bank Ltd.		

DATE	LOAN		
1. 1. 19--	AMOUNT OF LOAN ARRANGED	500	00
	INTEREST AS AGREED	100	00
	repayable over 2 years	600	00
	@ £ 25 per month.		

DATE	REPAYMENTS	AMOUNT	
1. 2. 19--	Loanshire Bank Ltd.	25	00
1. 3. 19--	—do—	25	00

Fig. 24.2 *The Summary of Loans*

and a *Cost of Manufactured Goods Section*. The Prime Cost Section deals with the costs of manufacture as far as the basic raw materials, wages and other direct costs are concerned. These costs are actually embodied in the product, and become part of the finished articles. The Cost of Manufactured Goods Section starts with the prime costs (found in the Prime Cost Section) and adds to them all the overhead costs which, while not embodied in the finished produce directly, have nevertheless to be recovered from the sale of the produce when it is eventually sold.

One special point about manufacturing is that we always have three lots of stocks when we manufacture.

These are as follows:

(*a*) Stock of Raw Materials.
(*b*) Stock of Work-in-progress; sometimes called Partly-finished Goods.
(*c*) Stock of Finished Goods.

When valuing work-in-progress it is best to consider the situation at closing time on the last day of the financial year. When the factory stops work some raw material at the start of the production process has just been brought in the door and work has barely begun on it. By contrast at the other end production has almost been completed and the last few items are almost ready to be packed and despatched. Clearly some partly finished goods are more valuable than others for more value has been added to them. The usual way to deal with this is to take an average value—half completed—and count all work in progress as being half complete.

A typical Manufacturing Account is shown in Fig. 24.3, and the Trading Account is also shown to show how the Manufacturing Account leads into the Trading Account, and then into the Profit and Loss Account and Balance Sheet.

Self Employed Stamps. If business funds are used to buy self-employed stamps their value must be treated as 'drawings' since these are a use of the businessman's profits to meet his personal expenses, and are not the same as the employer's National Insurance contributions for employees.

Stock Losses. As explained above (see Insurance Claims) any loss of stock results in a smaller stock figure at stock-taking time. Therefore any loss of stock, whether it is due to theft, passing-out, breakages or the perishable nature of the goods must not be written off as a loss. To do this would mean the loss was taken into account twice. The loss is automatically taken into account when we count stock, and it isn't there to be counted.

Note: The Manufacturing Account below is continued overleaf.

T. JONES
MANUFACTURING ACCOUNT
(for year ending December 31st, 19..)
PRIME COST SECTION

		£		£
RAW MATERIALS			By Prime Costs (carried to	
To Stock at Start		7,250	Cost of Manufactured	
To Purchases	15,520		Goods Section)	33,580
Less Returns	850			
		14,670		
		21,920		
Less Closing Stock		840		
Cost of Raw Materials used		21,080		
LABOUR				
Wages		12,500		
		£33,580		£33,580

COST OF MANUFACTURED GOODS SECTION

	£		£
To Prime Costs	33,580	By Cost of Manufactured	
OVERHEADS		Goods (transferred to	
To Power	468	Trading Account)	42,902
" Salaries	3,940		
" Rent and Rates	480		
" Lighting	854		
" Repairs	660		
" Depreciation	2,720		
	9,122		
	42,702		
WORK IN PROGRESS			
To Stock at Start	1,850		
Less Closing Stock	1,650		
	200		
	£42,902		£42,902

A Manufacturing Account

TRADING ACCOUNT

(for year ending December 31st, 19..)

		£		£
To Opening Stock of			By Sales	79,250
Finished Goods		7,050	Less Returns In	250
To Cost of Manufactured				
Goods		42,902	Net Turnover	79,000
		49,952		
Less Closing Stock		5,680		
Cost of Stock Sold		44,272		
To Warehouse				
Wages	5,250			
" Warehouse				
Rates	495	5,745		
Cost of Sales		50,017		
Gross Profit		28,983		
		£79,000		£79,000

PROFIT AND LOSS ACCOUNT

(for year ending December 31st, 19..)

		By Gross Profit	28,983

Fig. 24.3. A Manufacturer's Trading Account, etc.

The Simplex Club Accounts Book

25.1 Introduction

Businessmen often act as treasurers for local clubs and societies of every sort, so it is not inappropriate to introduce as the final chapter of this book a special accounts system which has been designed for George Vyner Ltd., by the author, to meet the needs of Clubs and Societies. Bank managers, accountants and others who read this chapter might like to advise the treasurers of clubs whose accounts they appraise of the existence of the Simplex Accounts Book for Clubs and 'School Fund' Treasurers. It is quite inexpensive, includes one year's accounts and the summaries at the end lead straight into the 'Final Accounts' i.e. Receipts and Payments Account of the club-to-be presented to the members at the Annual General Meeting. The book is available from George Vyner Ltd. at the address shown in the Foreword.

25.2 Clubs as Non-Profit-Making Bodies

The distinctive feature of club-accounts is that these organisations are non-profit-making, though many of them do in fact make profits. The point is that the organisation comes into existence for other reasons, notably to provide some centre of activity and organise functions which are of interest to the members. Thus the local Bowls Club will have its greens, club house, refreshment-making equipment etc, and will run competitions and organise meetings etc, of interest to the members. In the course of these activities it will receive a good deal of income, and make a great many payments on the members' behalf. At the end of the year it may have made a profit on some activities, but these were not deliberately aimed at. We therefore do not regard them as profits, but as '*surpluses*', excess amounts contributed by the members, surplus to the needs of the club. Similarly, if at the end of the year 'payments' exceed 'receipts' this will not be called a 'loss', but a '*deficiency*'.

The person in charge of accounts is called the *treasurer* and he will naturally be anxious to avoid a deficit on the year's accounts. He may not be keen to amass a large surplus, preferring that members enjoy their simple pleasures as economically as possible, but it may be club policy to build up adequate reserves to provide for the replacement or improvement of assets from time to time.

25.3 The Accounts of a Club

The accounts of a club therefore consist of a record of 'receipts' and 'payments'. One of the receipts for example is 'Subscriptions from Members' and another would be 'Refreshment Income'. Payments would be made for Equipment (a capital expense) and 'Refreshment Materials' (a revenue expense) would be another.

The Simplex Club Account Book has space for all the receipts and payments of the club, on a monthly basis. The amounts received and paid are analysed off under various headings so that similar items can be collected together and monthly totals are built up under these various headings. These records occupy 36 of the 48 pages, and are explained below, and illustrated in Figs. 25.1 and 25.2.

Each month the various totals for receipts and payments are taken to summaries on the Summary of Receipts and Payments page at the back of the book, while a Monthly Bank Report and Monthly Cash Report are also prepared in the usual Simplex way. See Figs. 25.2 and 25.3 for these summaries. The Cash Report each month should of course agree with the Cash in Hand, while a Bank Reconciliation Statement (see Unit 16) should be drawn up from time to time.

Finally the totals of the 'Summaries' for the whole year are used to prepare the Receipts and Payments Account of the Club, which is presented to the members of the Society at the Annual General Meeting (A.G.M.).

Let us now look at these sections of the book in detail.

25.4 The Receipts of the Club

Fig. 25.1 shows the 'receipts' page of the Club Account Book.

Amounts received are entered in the 'Cash' or 'Cheque' Column (Cols 10 and 11) and analysed off into appropriate columns, (Cols 1-9). Some columns have printed headings, others are left blank to enable the treasurer to write in suitable classes of expenditure. The receipts are totalled monthly and may be cross-totalled to check for accuracy. Columns 1-9 should total when cross-totalled to the same total as Columns 10 and 11. The totals are then carried to the Summary at the back of the book. (See Fig. 25.3).

25.5 The Payments of the Club

Fig. 25.2 shows the 'payments' page of the Club Accounts Book.

Again the payments are entered either in the Cash or Bank columns and analysed off into appropriate headings of expenditure. Once again these are totalled at the end of the month and cross-totalled to check for accuracy before being carried to the Summary of Payments at the back of the book. (See Fig. 25.3).

25.6 The Monthly Cash and Bank Reports

These are exactly the same as the Simplex Weekly Reports in the Simplex D book already described. As shown in Fig. 25.2 they present no difficulty to the treasurer and give him/her a monthly check on the accuracy of the book-keeping. As mentioned earlier the Cash Report should agree with the total of cash in hand, while the Bank Report must be periodically checked by comparison with a Bank Statement and the preparation of a Bank Reconciliation Statement.

Receipts for the month (in cash and by cheque)

Month of JANUARY   Year 19 76

Date	Details	P.C.V.	1 Subs. £ p	2 Donations £ p	3 Refr. Sales £ p	4 Raffles £ p	5 Theatre Visit £ p	6 £ p	7 £ p	8 Misc. £ p	9 Cash drawn from bank £ p	10 In Cash £ p	11 By Cheque £ p
												Amount Received	
JAN 4	Subscriptions 5 members		10 00									10 00	
5	Gift - Mrs Clark			5 25									5 25
11	Refreshments				3 25							3 25	
12	Subs Jones + Family		6 00										6 00
18	Refreshments				3 55							3 55	
19	Theatre visit						8 50						8 50
25	Refreshments				2 80							2 80	
26	Subs Brown + Smith		4 00									4 00	
30	Refreshments				2 95							2 95	
30	Raffle + Refreshments				4 20	2 45						6 65	
31	Cash from Bank										10 00	10 00	
	Totals (cross-tot to check)		20 00	5 25	16 75	2 45	8 50				10 00	43 20	19 75

Analysis Columns — You may head the spare columns to suit your own club or school

If entries have been analysed correctly total of columns 1-9 will equal total of columns 10 and 11.
At the end of the month carry the 1-8 column totals to the 'Summary' pages at the end of the book. Use the totals of columns 10 and 11 in the cash and bank reports opposite.

Fig. 25.1 *The Receipts of the Club*

Payments for the month *(in cash and by cheque)* — Month of JANUARY 1976

Date	Details	P.C.V.	1 Equipment £ p	2 Refreshments £ p	3 Stationery £ p	4 Theatre Visit £ p	5 Raffle Prizes £ p	6	7	8 Misc.	9 Cheques for cash £ p	10 In Cash £ p	11 By cheque £ p
JAN 9	Table Tennis Table		24 50										24 50
10	Refreshments			1 40								1 40	
17	"			1 55								1 55	
19	Duplicating Paper				1 85							1 85	
20	Theatre Visits					9 25							9 25
25	Refreshments			1 42								1 42	
29	"			2 05								2 05	
30	Raffle Prizes						1 85					1 85	
30	Out Board Lighting		15 00									15 00	
31	Cash from Bank										10 00		10 00
	Totals (Cross-tot to check)		39 50	6 42	1 85	9 25	1 85				10 00	25 12	43 75

Analysis Columns — you may head the spare columns to suit your own club or school

Paid to Bank

Date	Cash	Cheques
January 6	10 00	5 25
" 13		6 00
" 20		8 50
Total	10 00	19 75

Monthly Bank Report

	£ p
Opening balance from last month	86 45
Add total paid to bank in month	29 75
Total	116 20
Less { Total Payments (ch) 43 75, Bank st. orders (if any) —, Bank charges (if any) — } Total	43 75
Balance at bank at end of month	72 45
Was a Bank Reconciliation done	Yes/No

Monthly Cash Report

	£ p
Cash in hand on 1st day	2 45
Add Total cash received in month	43 20
Total	45 65
Less { Total cash payments 25 12, Cash paid to bank 10 00 } Total	35 12
Cash balance carried forward	10 53
which should agree with	
Cash Balance (as counted) on last day	10 53

© George Vyner Ltd
2 and 4 Woodhead Road
Honley, Huddersfield

Fig. 25.2 The Payments of the Club and the Cash and Bank Reports.

SUMMARY OF MONTHLY RECEIPTS

Month	1 Subscriptions		2 Donations		3 Refreshment Sales		4		5		6		7		8	
	£	p	£	p	£	p	£	p	£	p	£	p	£	p	£	p
January																
February																
March																
April																
May																
June																
July																
August																
September																
October																
November																
December																
Total																

SUMMARY OF MONTHLY PAYMENTS

Month	1 Equipment		2 Refreshment Purchases		3		4		5		6		7		8	
	£	p	£	p	£	p	£	p	£	p	£	p	£	p	£	p
January																
February																
March																
April																
May																
June																
July																
August																
September																
October																
November																
December																
Total																

Cash in hand at start of year £ .
Cash in hand at end of year £ .

Cash at bank at start of year £ .
Cash at bank at end of year £ .

Stock in hand at start of year £ .
Stock in hand at end of year £ .

Schedule of Assets	£	p
Value of Club/School Fund Assets at start of year		
Items Purchased during year.		
1.		
2.		
3.		
4.		
5.		
6.		
7.		
8.		
9.		
10.		
11.		
12.		

Memorandum – A re-order form is provided on Page 43 of this book.

Fig. 25.3 *Summaries at the end of the Simplex Club Accounts Book.*

25.7 The Annual General Meeting

At the Annual General Meeting the treasurer must account to the members for the conduct of the Club's financial affairs. He does this by presenting them with a Receipts and Payments Account which shows the members what the balance was at the start of the year, the receipts and payments during the year and concludes with the final balance at the end of the year. The balance of cash in hand should be available at the meeting for checking if required, and a Bank Reconciliation Statement should have been prepared as at the last day of the financial year.

If the Club has appointed auditors from among the members they should be asked to check the records for the year, and sign the statement submitted to the members. If duplicating equipment is available sufficient copies should be produced to meet the needs of the members in attendance. Fig. 25.4 shows a typical Receipts and Payment Account prepared in the Simplex Club Accounts Book.

RECEIPTS and PAYMENTS A/c
Annual General Meeting
Year ending 31st March   19 76

Receipts	£	p	Payments	£	p
Opening Balances at Start of Year:			Col. 1 Equipment	62	50
Cash in Hand	3	54	Col. 2 Refreshment Purchases	250	00
Cash at Bank	86	45	Col. 3 Trip to France	719	25
Col. 1 Subscriptions	142	50	Col. 4 Xmas Parties	56	50
Col. 2 Donations	5	50	Col. 5 Funeral Expenses	5	25
Col. 3 Refreshment Sales	286	45	Col. 6 O.A.P. Charity Donation	10	00
Col. 4 Trip to France	735	60	Col. 7 —		
Col. 5 Xmas Parties	48	24	Col. 8 Miscellaneous	3	64
Col. 6 —			Closing Balances at end of year:		
Col. 7 —			Cash in Hand	4	62
Col. 8 Miscellaneous	1	84	Cash at Bank	198	36
	£ 1310	12		£ 1310	12

Auditors' names_____

and Signatures:_____

Treasurer's Name_____

and Signature:_____

Notes:

(i) The Cash of £4.62 is available at the meeting – also the Bank Statement for inspection by members wishing to see it.

(ii) On refreshments, it appears that very little profit was made but as the purchases also covered entertainment to visiting teams this is not surprising.

(iii) A stock of refreshments valued at £26 is available (at the start of the year stocks were only £4). Other assets include camping equipment valued at £350, stored on the premises.

(iv) Creditors. A debt for repairing windows broken in the recent burglary is outstanding £7·25.

(v) There are no debtors.

Fig. 25.4 *The Final Accounts of the Club, ready for the Annual General Meeting.*

25.8 The Club's Membership Record

A membership record is essential for club purposes, and the last three pages of the Simplex Club Accounts Book are devoted to a membership record, such as is illustrated in Fig. 25.5.

Membership Register

Where the organisation using this book is a club, a register of the paid up membership may be kept here.

No.	Date paid	Name	No.	Date paid	Name	No.	Date paid	Name

Fig. 25.5 *The Club's Membership Registers.*

25.9 Exercises on Club Receipts and Payments Accounts

1. The following sums of money were received and paid by the Treasurer of the University Cricket Club during the season April-September, 19. .. On April 1st the club had a Cash Balance of £55 brought forward from the previous season.

Moneys Received: Subscriptions £125·00; Donations £100; Refreshment sales £178; Sales of ties and blazer badges £165·50; Grant from University Student Body £50·00.

Moneys Spent: Postage £14·65; Refreshment expenses £125·00; Gift to groundsman £50·00; New equipment £386·50; Secretary's honorarium £25·00.

Draw up the Receipts and Payments Accounts for the year, for submission to the Annual General Meeting on September 30th, 19. .. Bring out clearly the Cash Balance on September 30th.

2. The following particulars are supplied to you by the Treasurer of the Leyside Tennis Society, who asks you to draw up a Receipts and Payments Account. Take into account the point he makes in the note below the figures.

Cash Balances March 1st	£13·50
October 31st	£7·84
Bank Balances March 1st	£48·24
October 31st	£138·24

Receipts during Season: Subscriptions £150·00; Sale of spectators tickets £129·50; Entrance charges to functions £112·85; Competition fees £48·50; Refreshment sales £95·80; Donations during season £135·99.

Payments during Season: Refreshment materials £125·50; Nets and waterproof sheeting £186·50; Groundsmans charges £136·65; Postage £18·50; Stationery £14·85; Light and heat £21·50; Secretary's expenses £84·80.

Note: A debt is owing for equipment £42·00 which is to be included in the above costs as it will be paid at once by cheque, the bank balance being reduced accordingly.

3. The King's Head Darts Club has the following receipts and payments for the year ended December 31st, 19. . .

Receipts: Membership Subscriptions £28·50; Donation from publican £25·00; Coach tickets £184·80; Collections £18·50; Share of prize money for club funds £66·50.

Payments: Coach expenses £184·00; Equipment £38·50; Competition entry fees £30·00; Entertainment to guest teams £68·50; Donations to charity £15·00.

The opening cash balance was £24·56. Work out the Receipts and Payments Account for the Annual General Meeting bringing out clearly the closing cash balance.

4. The Miller's Pool Carnival Society has receipts and payments during carnival year as follows. The Committee was only set up on the 1st January and had no opening balances.

Receipts: Grant from Council £120·00; Donations from local businessmen £520·00; Collections from carnival £1 728·60; Proceeds of collection of trading stamps £758·56; Proceeds of sale of used postage stamps £236·50; Waste paper collections £956·35.

Payments: Carnival expenses £826·30; Refreshments on carnival day £186·45; Donation to Dr. Barnado's Homes £1 580; Donation to Help the Aged £500·00; Save the Children Fund £1 000.

Work out the Receipts and Payment Account for the Annual General Meeting and the cash balance in hand on December 31st, 19. . .

The Simplex Advice Bureau—Problems Answered

26.1 The Simplex Advice Bureau

In order to help the proprietors of small businesses who have decided to use the Simplex System, George Vyner Ltd operate an Advice Bureau. The aim is to help those who are having difficulty with their book-keeping—we cannot give financial advice or tax advice since this is the province of the accountant. In order to give financial advice in the United Kingdom it is necessary to register with the Office of Fair Trading. The Director General of Fair Trading has given his opinion that the type of services we are rendering does not call for registration but clearly we must avoid giving advice which should properly come from a professional, and registered, consultant.

Many of the points raised by our correspondents are of general interest, and we intend at each new revision of this book to add any matters which have been found to give difficulty since the last revision of the book. They are not arranged in any particular order.

26.2 Purchase of Stock on Taking-over a Business

When stock is purchased on taking over a business it is important to recognise that the purchase price must include an element of VAT which is in effect input tax. Thus where goods are being taken over at cost price, to the value of £2 300, the trader should insist on it being recognised that this figure in fact includes VAT. This means that the seller must issue a tax invoice for the sale, even though the goods are being passed on at a figure which does not include the seller's normal margin of profit.

The seller must account for the VAT received as output tax, but this need not concern the buyer. The buyer's purpose is to be able to reclaim the input tax claimed, for which proof of payment is available in the form of a tax invoice. If the VAT rate is 15% as at the time of writing, then 3/23 (the VAT fraction) of this £2 300 is VAT. 3/23 of £2 300 is £300, and this is VAT input tax for the new trader, which is recoverable.

26.3 What to do with a Credit Note

When a credit note is received for goods returned it is in effect a reduction in the charge previously made. It depends what this charge was for, as to the remedial action that should be taken. If it was a charge for business stock, the credit note may be deducted from the cost of the next supply made, and this will mean that the total charge made for 'Payments for Business Stock' will be reduced to the correct figure. If the credit note is for a capital item, or a service supplied and no further purchase is to be made it should be followed by a refund of the amount due back from the supplier. This should be entered as an 'Other Receipt' and carried to the summary page concerned, in red ink—where it will reduce the capital assets purchased during the year, or the charge for services (expenses) paid during the year.

26.4 Depreciation

Every asset wears out in the course of time and depreciates in value over the years. The amount of the depreciation on the asset is therefore a legitimate charge against the profits of the business, which can be written off in the Profit and Loss account. However, this process need not really concern business people today, since whatever we deduct for depreciation is completely disregarded by the Inland Revenue, which adds it back on again as if we had never deducted it. Instead of depreciation, a system of capital allowances is given, which may be much more beneficial to the business. These are of four types, first year allowances, initial allowances, writing down allowances and balancing charges. Exact details of these allowances should be checked in *Income Tax Simplified* (see page 126), since they do tend to change slightly each year.

The first two are rather similar. First Year allowances give the trader a 100% first year allowance on plant and equipment, but not on private motors cars or certain 'shared assets'. Initial allowances give a 75% allowance on expenditure on buildings in Enterprize Zones. Clearly these allowances are very helpful to the business person who is making profits, since they enable a full recovery of the expenditure to be claimed against tax. They are less helpful to a business which is not profitable, and consequently these allowances may be disclaimed or only claimed to the extent that they are beneficial. The rest passes into a 'Pool of Expenditure' on which **writing-down allowances** may be claimed in later years. These are at a rate of 25 per cent. Motor vehicles purchased are also dealt with in a similar way.

At the end of the financial year it is therefore advisable when submitting accounts to the Inland Revenue to state what you wish to claim as allowances for the financial year. Thus a statement 'I have spent £360 on various capital items this year, please give me a 100% allowance for this expenditure' would be sensible for a profitable business. For a business which was making losses, it would be sensible to ask for the sum to be taken to the 'Pool of Expenditure' so that the 'writing-down' allowance could bring a benefit in future years.

There are special rules about things like cars or any other capital expense which is part business and part domestic. You can't get 100 per cent relief on these anyway and the tax man will give you the allowance to which you are entitled.

Finally, the system of capital allowances could work very unfairly on the Inland Revenue if a person who had been given a 100 per cent allowance then sold the item at its fair market price. To safeguard the revenue if you sell something on which you have claimed capital allowance the proceeds must be notified to the Inspector. He will set this against any pool you have left—thus reducing the pool. If this wipes out the pool completely the extra will be added to your profit and you will pay tax on it—because you had tax relief on it before —so it is only fair you should suffer tax now you have disposed of the equipment.

26.5 Sales on Credit Cards (Barclaycard, Access etc.)

Some traders are unsure what entries to make for credit card sales. The difficulty arises because the credit card company is entitled to make a 'service charge' monthly. The procedure is as follows:

(i) The actual voucher issued when goods are sold is exactly like a cheque, and should be treated as such on the Simplex receipts section. Enter the total for cheques and vouchers in the Gross Daily Takings (cheques) column and pay them into the bank in the usual way. The full value of these vouchers will be credited to your bank account in about three days (the same time as it takes to clear a cheque).

(ii) Once a month you will receive a statement from the Barclaycard office (or other credit card company) notifying you of the service charge payable, which will be deducted from your account by the direct debit system. You should enter this on one of the lines in your 'Payments other than for Stock' section, and carry it to a column in the Summary of Payments for Expenses. At the end of the year the total of this column will be deducted from the profits in the Profit and Loss Account.

26.6 Dealing with a Loan

Loans present considerable problems to businesses, from a book-keeping point of view, quite apart from the major problem of repaying them. Where a sum of money is borrowed over a period of years, and repaid by equal instalments, the repayments in the first year are nearly all interest, and very little repayment of capital. As the years pass the amount of each repayment that is interest falls, and the amount that is capital repaid rises.

Imagine a businessman who borrows £12 000 from a finance company at a flat rate of interest of 12 per cent per annum, over 7 years. This means that he must repay £12 000 + 84% (7 × 12%) of £12 000 = £22 080. If this is repaid in 84 monthly instalments each instalment will be £262·86. The interest being repaid will be an expense of the business and deductible on the Profit and Loss account. The capital repayment will not be deductible as an expense of the business.

The trouble is to know how much of the £262·86 is interest and how much is capital being repaid. As with all loans in the early months it is nearly all interest and very little capital repayment. Later—in 6 years time—it will be very little interest and nearly all capital. The difficulty arises from the difficulty of not knowing the true rate of interest, since a flat rate of interest is usually only about half the true rate. Fortunately it is now necessary for the finance company to reveal the true rate of interest on the loan. Let us imagine that this is stated to be

24 per cent. We can now answer the question 'How much of the first month's instalment is interest'. The answer is

Interest = Original Loan × True rate of interest ÷ 100 ÷ 12
= £12 000 × 24 ÷ 100 ÷ 12
= £240 interest

We have to divide by twelve in the calculation because we only want the interest for one month. So of the £262·86 repaid in the first month only £22·86 is capital; the other £240 is interest.

In the second month the amount of the actual capital still on loan is £12 000 − £22·86 = £11 977·14. This month the interest will be:

Interest = £11 977·14 × 24 ÷ 100 ÷ 12
= £239.54

Therefore the capital repaid = £262·86 − £239·54
= £23.32

Each month when this calculation has been done you should take the interest amount to a special column headed 'Interest' in the Summary of Payments for expenses.

By the end of the year there will be over £2 000 to deduct from the profits for interest paid on the loan.

26.7 Items Purchased on Access/Barclaycard

Where a business person buys items for business use on Access or Barclaycard a problem arises since the actual payment does not occur until the account is rendered by the Head Office of Access or Barclaycard. You will find the following rules helpful:

(i) When you make a Barclaycard purchase you are given the customer's copy of the slip. (If you eventually register for VAT you may need to ask for a VAT invoice as well—or at least a till receipt which is recognised as valid for VAT purposes). Return to your Simplex D Book and enter this purchase in one of the columns (either Purchases for Business Stock) or Purchases other than for Stock. However, since the money has not gone out yet put brackets round it, i.e. (£45·60) and do not add it in to your total cash payments for that week.

(ii) When you carry the entries to the summaries at the back of the book enter these ones as if they had actually been paid, but put some little sign against it so that you know it has not been paid—the best sign is CR to let you know it is on credit really. This might look like this

Sundries
CR 45·60

(iii) When you actually receive your monthly account go through it together with your Simplex D Book and tick up the letters CR against all these items which are listed on the statement. Thus if the £45·60 shown above was entered on the statement you would tick up the CR on the summary page.

(iv) You may also find some interest entered on the statement. If your card is purely for business use, enter the amount of this interest in the weekly page for the current week, and put brackets round it:

Barclaycard interest (1·62)

When you enter that in the summary page put CR by it but tick it up right away because it is on the statement.

(v) Now you only have to enter the payment you are making on the day you actually make it. This will be a week or two later no doubt. Whether you pay only a part of it or the full amount enter it in the 'Payments other than for Stock' column. This item will not have brackets round it and will be added in to your cash or bank total—because of course it is money going out—but you will not post it to any summary because it has already been entered in little bits in the summary pages as you entered the original slips.

26.8 Break-even Points

It is quite common to see references in business magazines to 'break-even' points, and business persons often write in to the Simplex Advice Bureau asking how they can tell when they have broken even. It is a long story really, but briefly we may say as follows:

(i) We break even when we have covered our total costs, and from that point on everything extra we receive is profit.

(ii) Total costs are made up of 'fixed costs' and 'variable costs'. To explain variable costs first, they are the costs incurred in making our product, and they are called 'variable' because they vary with output. So if I make pizzas with pizza pastry costing ten pence and other items costing 10 pence, and if the labour cost is 5 pence the variable costs of my pizzas are 25 pence each. So long as I sell them for more than 25 pence I shall make a profit on any particular pizza. Let us say I sell them for 50 pence. Then I have covered my variable costs, and have 25 pence left over. This 25 pence is called the 'contribution'.

(iii) To what does it contribute? The answer is it is a contribution towards covering my fixed costs (often called overheads), and once they are covered, and I have broken-even, they are profits of the business. Fixed costs must now be explained. They are the costs that have to be borne whatever the output of the business. Thus I need a factory whether I make 1 000 pizzas or 100 000 pizzas. I need a managing director, a lorry for distribution purposes etc., etc. These are all part of the 'fixed costs', which do not vary directly with output—though I might need a bigger lorry if output grows. Suppose my total fixed costs are £2 000 and I sell 1 pizza. I have a contribution of 25 pence towards my fixed costs and no profit. I shall need to sell 8 000 pizzas to cover my fixed costs, so 8 000 pizzas is my break-even point. After that I shall begin to make a profit.

This can best be followed by looking at the break-even chart in Fig. 26.1

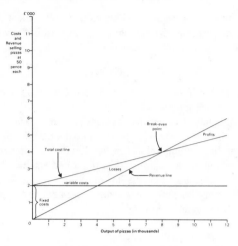

Fig. 26.1 *A break-even chart*

Notes: (i) As the output of pizzas rises from 0-12 000 the variable costs increase by 25 pence per pizza. As these are incurred over and above the fixed costs we see the total cost line sloping up towards the £5 000 (£2 000 fixed and £3 000 variable).

(ii) At the same time revenue from the sale of pizzas is rising; £1 000 from 2 000 pizzas, £2 000 from 4 000 pizzas etc.

(iii) Break-even point is at £4 000, where the sale of 8 000 pizzas brings in £4 000, which exactly covers £2 000 fixed costs and £2 000 variable costs.

(iv) After that point we have profits being made and at 12 000 pizzas we get profits of £1 000, since revenues are £6 000 and costs £5 000.

26.9 How to deal with American Express vouchers

American Express use a different system from Barclaycard and Access. They send the trader who has paid in vouchers a cheque for the net value of the vouchers (ie the value of the vouchers less charges). VAT on the original sales is therefore included in the value of the cheque.

It is best not to enter the value of the vouchers at all until you get the credit notification back from AMEX. You then make the following entries.

(*a*) Enter the *full value of the vouchers* in the Daily Takings (cheques) column, and the words AMEX takings in the particulars column.

(*b*) Enter the *full value of the vouchers* in the Paid to Bank column (although you do not have a cheque for that amount, since the cheque you have received is only the net value).

(*c*) Enter the AMEX charges in the Payments Other than for Stock section as 'AMEX' commission, in the cheques column. The result is that the sum paid to bank less the commission is the same as the net value of the cheque that has actually reached the bank.

26.10 How to Deal with Enterprise Allowances

Your Enterprise Allowance of £40 a week is paid in fortnightly lumps of £80 by credit transfer into your bank account. Like all such transfers you only become aware of it when you get your monthly bank statement. Do *not* make any entries until you receive the bank statement. If you have not asked your bank for a regular monthly statement do so at once.

When you get your statement go through it and find the entries for the Enterprise Allowance. They will normally come to £160 a month, but very rarely there might be three payments in the month, ie £240. Enter this in the Other Receipts section and write 'Enterprise Allowance' in the 'particulars' column. Do this in the week you receive the Bank Statement; do not try to go back and alter your records by entering each £80 in the week it was transferred into your Bank account. Enter the total for the month in the Current Week's entries. You should also enter the total of the enterprise allowance in the 'Paid to Bank' section.

Now carry it to the Summary of Other Receipts at the back of the book, in the column 'Miscellaneous Receipts'. This will bring the figure in to the Profit and Loss Account at the end of the year—because it has to be included as 'Takings' for tax purposes. We have added a special line to the Profit and Loss Account in the latest edition of Simplex D to remind you that the Enterprise Allowance must appear as taxable income.

The entry of the Enterprise Allowance is therefore really one of the things you do as part of your 'Bank Reconciliation' each month. If you are not familiar with the bank reconciliation process and do not know how to draw up a Bank Reconciliation Statement the whole process is fully explained in Chapter 16 of this book.

26.11 Overdrafts and the Simplex System

Some people worry about the book-keeping records needed when an overdraft is sanctioned by the bank. There is really no need to make any entry at all—though if you wish to remind yourself when it was agreed you could write at the top of the weekly page, or in some clear space on the weekly page 'Overdraft for £??? sanctioned—to be reviewed on . . . . . . 19. .'. There is no real impact on the business except that you may go 'into the red' on the Weekly Bank Report—see Example 2 at the front of the Simplex D Account book. Do not forget that once you go into overdraft you will not only have bank charges to pay for each cheque you write, but also you will have interest deducted from time to time on your Bank Statement. Watch for these items when you receive a bank statement and enter them at once in the current week on your weekly page—carrying them to the Summary of Expenses at the back of the book.

26.12 Keeping Separate Bank Accounts for Personal and Business Items

A great many people get into difficulties with bank accounts because they muddle up personal and business items. It is highly desirable to run separate bank accounts—preferably with different banks if you live in an area which is well served for banking purposes. Since most of us start up with a bank's help and bankers do not like to lose customers there can be an initial difficulty in changing to another bank. To avoid this at least get clearly separate accounts for business and personal use with your present banker and avoid using the wrong cheque book. It is also very helpful to have a separate deposit account for VAT and Inland Revenue money. Put your tax away in the deposit account every week or month, and you will always have it available on the due date. When it is time to pay you simply transfer enough out of the Deposit Account and into the Current Account and pay it by cheque at once. The Deposit Account earns interest, which is of course a little profit for the business.

26.13 Thefts and Burglaries

Thefts and burglaries present a variety of problems to traders, and some of them are raised in this section.

Theft of Stock: Theft of stock by shoplifters and by 'passing out'—staff giving goods to friends—call for action with the police, but no book-keeping records are needed. The reason is that the stock losses are taken into account for the final accounts of the business when we count the stock (and the stolen items are not there). We have a smaller stock than we should have, which raises the cost of stock sold and lowers the profits. We do not need to 'write off' the stolen stock, because if we did that we would be taking the loss twice. All such losses are taken into account when we count the stock.

Theft of Cash: If cash is stolen from the tills it does present a problem because it means you are left with a 'Difference on the Books' at the end of the week. The Simplex Weekly Page on Page 8 shows that if the 'Cash balance on books' differs from the 'Cash in hand—as counted' it gives rise to a 'Difference on Books'. If that difference appears regularly the Inland Revenue take a poor view of it and will almost certainly take the view that it is undeclared drawings, and will add it on to your profits as taxable income. This might seem a bit unfair, but it is up to you to keep proper records and trace theft if it is occurring. You cannot just pretend it is mistakes in giving customers change—staff training is also your responsibility. If you have staff who are stealing from you get the police in and frighten the life out of them. If you can pin down a member of staff charge them, and try to get a written admission of the amount embezzled over the past months. Submit this as firm evidence of a loss explaining a 'difference on books' to the Inland Revenue at the end of the year.

Burglaries and Insurance Claims: Burglaries—and indeed other events like fires and floods—require the preparation of insurance claims. The method adopted is to establish what is known and hence deduce the unknown—the amount of the loss. We can usually establish (a) the value of stock at the start of the financial period and (b) the purchases during the period. We can also usually calculate the sales during the period. When these have been reduced to cost price by removing the profit margin we only have to count the stock that is left (or value it in the case of a fire or flood). The amount of the claim is then found by the following formula. Some imaginary figures have been used.

	£
Stock at start—say	10 000
Add Purchases during the period	32 500
	42 500
Deduct Sales at cost price	25 000
Stock that should be left	17 500
Stock actually left	3 200
Amount of claim	£14 300

We may need to add any expenses (such as the valuer's charges) to this claim.

26.14 Stock-taking

At the end of any trading period it is necessary to value the stock in hand so that the final accounts can be worked out. It is also a good idea to hold unscheduled and surprise stock-taking sessions to check the availability of both stock and capital assets—particularly if such things as tools etc, are likely to be pilfered. The method in both cases is to draw up an inventory of stock—a list of every stock item, preferably in some sensible order (such as the order in which they appear on the shelves). This is a chore the first time it is done, but on subsequent occasions it can simply be photocopied and any extra items added at the end. It is best if the items can be on loose leaf sheets retained in a lever arch file, for easy extraction and photo copying. There should be a place at the top of the page to record the date of the stock check and columns for recording the actual stock as counted. Personal supervision, or the supervision of a reliable person, is always advisable on any sort of stock-taking and random checks are desirable. Thus if there is a record on the sheet of pocket calculators—counted as being 15—ask to see the 15 and count them as a random check. Managers frequently exaggerate stock counts—leaving the losses (or thefts) to be discovered next time around.

26.15 Improving Premises—the Capitalisation of a Revenue Expense

Many small businesses do repair jobs to their own premises, and these are legitimate expenses of the business and can be deducted from the profits at the end of the year. However, if you finish up by *improving* the premises, or the fixtures and fittings you have; you cannot count these as business expenses which are deductible from the profits—you have to take the extra value on as capital assets of the business (and you may then be entitled to some capital allowance from the tax inspector).

Let us consider two cases.

(a) You do some repairs, using materials from your ordinary business stock, and paying your workers some wages. The repairs are just repairs, not improvements. In this case you need not make any special entries in the books —all the entries are done already. The materials you used are entered in the Payments for Business Stock and as you cannot sell them now (having used

them) this loss will be suffered at the end of the year. The wages you paid will be entered in the wages section of your Payments. Other than for Stock and so they need not be entered again. The work done is not a VAT output, so no invoice needs to be issued and no VAT has to be recorded. The business expense has been recorded as extra purchases and extra wages and could be left to go through the books under those headings. If you really want to do so at the end of the year you could reduce the Purchases by the amount of materials used, and reduce the wages by the amount paid to the workers who did the work, and put these amounts in instead as Repairs and Renewals.

(b) In the second case the work done and the materials used result in an improvement to the value of the property. Here you will have to do what is called 'capitalising a revenue expense'. This means you must make up your mind how much value has been added to the premises as a result of the work. Let us suppose you use £100 materials and £200 labour and it results in a £500 increase in value. You have therefore made a bit of profit on yourself (or really the workers you employ).

The book-keeping entries are as follows:

(a) Deduct £100 from materials—you will have to do this in the Summary of Payments for Business Stock. Make a small entry *in red ink* on the summary —£100 business improvements.

(b) Deduct £200 from wages—you will need to do this in the Summary of Expenses for year—make a small red ink entry in the wages column—£200 business improvements.

(c) The £200 profit presents a little problem. It could be argued that it is not a revenue profit but a capital profit, since it is not a profit in the ordinary way of business. If you decide to treat it as a capital profit do not enter it at the end of the year as a 'miscellaneous receipt' in the Profit and Loss Account (where it will be taxable) but put in the 'Extra capital contributed' as a capital profit. Tell the Inland Revenue what you have done and hope they will treat you kindly.

(d) Now you only have to enter in the Summary of Capital Expenses in the year £500 as 'Business Improvements £500'. Don't forget to tell the Inland Revenue about this as it will entitle you to a capital allowance.

(e) This is not a VAT output, so no VAT entries are required.

The result is that on one side of the Balance Sheet we have an increase in the value of the premises of £500. On the Capital Account we have an increase of £200—the capital profit and an increase in the net profit of £300 (because the expenses have been reduced in the Trading Account (Purchases £100 less) and in the Profit and Loss Account (Wages £200 less). These expenses have been capitalised.

26.16 VAT and the Simplex D Account Book

We sometimes get accountants who complain about the way VAT is done in the Simplex D Account Book and it is true that we have adopted a simpler system than most accountants use. The reason is that many users of the Simplex System are busy traders and don't make out VAT invoices for outputs and there is little point in analysing VAT out of each day's takings.

The way VAT works in the Simplex D Account Book is as follows:

(a) Sales (Daily Takings) and Purchases (Payments for Business Stock) are recorded gross.

(b) When these figures are entered in the Trading Account they give a Gross Profit which is larger than it should be (Gross Profit + VAT).

(c) When taken into the Profit and Loss Account this Gross Profit is set against

    (i)   The expenses (inclusive of VAT)

    (ii) The payment to the VAT man (Output Tax—Input Tax)

    (iii) The VAT on capital items

This removes all the VAT that is in the Gross Profit and reduces it to a Net Profit free of VAT.

26.17 Cash Refunds by the Business

On occasions we may make cash refunds to customers either because they have returned goods or because they have cancelled orders for services (such as driving lessons). We have to record these payments somewhere, and as they are really a reduction in 'Takings' they must in some way be taken to the Weekly Summary of Takings and *deducted from it*. The best method is to use one of the spare lines in Payments other than for Stock to record the refund. Then carry this item not to the Summary of Expenses at the back of the book, but to the Summary of Takings. Enter it in red—keep a red ball point pen handy for such entries—very small, above the weekly takings figure and deduct it from the quarterly total.

A simpler way if a till is being used is to make the refund direct from the till, which automatically reduces the 'daily takings', but the disadvantage is we have no clear record of the refund.

26.18 Cash Refunds to the Business

On occasions we may get a refund to the business, for a variety of reasons. In each case the refund should be entered in the other Receipts column, with an explanation in the Particulars column. Examples might be:

(a) Refund from the VAT man (this will be made direct to the bank account and will be found when you get a bank statement).

(b) Refund for the return of business stock by the business.

(c) Refund of an expense (as when an author who does a mailing about his book has the postage refunded by the publisher).

The refunds now have to be dealt with as far as the summaries are concerned:

(a) The refund from the VAT man will be collected in the VAT repayments column in the Summary of Miscellaneous Receipts.

(b) The refund for returned Business Stock will have to be entered as a reduction in the Summary of Payments for Goods Purchased. Enter it in red above the current week's entry, and *deduct it* from the quarterly total at the end of the quarter.

(c) The refund of an expense will similarly have to be entered in red on the Summary of Miscellaneous Expenses—and *deducted* from the total at the end of the quarter.

Answers to Exercises

Unit Two
Numerical answers not required.

Unit Three
Numerical answers not required.

Unit Four
1. Total Takings; cash £1 777·35; cheques £73·65; Other Receipts £500; Paid to Bank cash £950; cheques £573·65.
2. Total Takings; cash £1 275·90; cheques £100·00; Other Receipts £52·00; Paid to Bank cash £450·00; cheques £152·00.
3. Total Takings; cash £1 525·25; cheques £118·45; Other Receipts £18·25; Paid to Bank cash £631·55; cheques £544·00; Other Receipts £57·00; Paid to Bank: cheques £586·50.

Unit Five
1. Total payments: cash £31·25, cheques £202·24.
2. Total payments: cash £67·05, cheques £41·05.
3. Total payments: cash £12·81, cheques £291·99.
4. Total payments: cash £51·05, cheques £51·45.

Unit Six
1. Total payments: cash £108·90, cheques £138·25.
2. Total payments: cash £153·44, cheques £289·16.
3. Total payments: cash £48·74, cheques £149·10.

Unit Seven
1. Closing Balance in Bank £1 880·01.
2. Closing Balance in Bank £3 207·56.
3. Closing Balance in Bank £3 213·97.
4. Closing Cash Balance £30·27.
5. Closing Cash Balance £33·86.
6. Closing Cash Balance £107·00.

Unit Nine
1. Balance Sheet total £27 830·00.
2. Balance Sheet total £22 370·00.
3. Capital £21 280, Balance Sheet total £33 980.
4. Capital £54 760, Balance Sheet total £68 960.

Unit Ten
1. Books of R. Johnson: Daily takings £1 198·75; Bank balance £3 064·36; Cash balance £704·28.
2. Books of Mary Shaw: Daily takings £1 384·55 (including cheques) Bank balance £4 063·03; Cash balance £566·23.

Unit Eleven
1. Books of R. Coppersmith: Daily takings £1 303·50; Bank balance £4 237·87; Cash balance £49·45.
2. Books of Anne Overton: Daily takings (including cheques) £1 570·09; Bank balance £2 353·44; Cash balance £237·09.

Unit Twelve
1. Books of A. Upson: Daily takings £2 001·45; Bank balance £3 926·31; Cash balance £1 312·38.
2. Books of M. Grainger: Daily takings (including cheques) £453·21; Bank balance £1 943·91; Cash balance £282·45.

Unit Thirteen
1. Books of M. Lucas: Daily takings (including cheques) £693·80; Bank balance £221·23; Cash balance £257·42.
2. Books of R. Tobermory: Daily takings (including cheques) £195·00; Bank balance £572·91; Cash balance £72·50.

Unit Fourteen
1. Books of M. Reagen: Daily takings (including cheques) £340·00; Bank balance £4 571·73; Cash balance £127·20.
2. Books of Pat Sterling: Daily takings (including cheques) £461·00; Bank balance £1 989·00; Cash balance £53·70.

Unit Fifteen
No exercises in this unit.

Unit Sixteen
The exercises in this unit are self correcting, since the Bank Reconciliation Statement has to come out to the figure given in the exercise.

Unit Seventeen
1. Nett Wages A = £54·44; B = £53·23; C = £34·17.
2. Nett Wages G = £64·23; H = £59·55; J = £53·75.
3. Nett Wages P = £56·36; Q = £52·52; R = £45·50.
4. Nett Wages X = £54·85; Y = £78·93; Z = £50·95.

Unit Eighteen
No exercises in this unit.

Unit Nineteen
No exercises in this unit.

Unit Twenty
No exercises in this unit.

Unit Twenty-one

1. Books of Tom Price: Gross Profit £16 500·00; Net Profit £9 713·50; Balance Sheet totals £15 994·50.
2. Books of Brian Wood: Gross Profit £11 900·00; Net Profit £5 122·50; Balance Sheet totals £16 260·85.
3. Books of A. Fashionable: Gross Profit £15 425·00; Net Profit £4 216·25; Balance Sheet totals £26 436·87.
4. Books of Julia Browne: Gross Profit £18 955·00; Net Profit £5 451·45; Balance Sheet totals £26 234·40.
5. Books of Smith & Jones: Current Accounts, Smith £3 200, Jones £1 400; Balance Sheet totals £24 085·50.
6. Books of Brewer & Stillman: Current Accounts, Brewer £1 450·00, Stillman £100·00; Balance Sheet totals £25 575·75.

Unit Twenty-Two

No exercises in this unit.

Unit Twenty-Three

1. Net Profits (a) £4 800 (b) £8 400 (c) £5 250 (d) £7 000; Gross Profit Percentages (a) 35·7% (b) 45·3% (c) 32·7% (d) 27·9%; Net Profit Percentages (a) 11·4% (b) 22·1% (c) 20·2% (d) 10·3%.
2. Net Profits (a) £2 500 (b) £1 950 (c) £3 600 (d) £3 000 (e) £3 400; Gross Profit Percentages (a) 48·5% (b) 49·4% (c) 65·3% (d) 73·8% (e) 35·8%; Net Profit Percentages (a) 30·3% (b) 25·3% (c) 37·9% (d) 46·2% (e) 25·7%.
3. Average Stock Smith £2 500, Jones £5 000; Gross Profit, Smith £5 000, Jones £5 000; Sales Figure Smith £55 000, Jones £30 000; Gross Profit Percentages Smith 9·1%, Jones 16·7%; Net Profit Percentages Smith 5·7%, Jones 8·8%.
4. Average Stock Giles £6 000, Slocum £7 500; Gross Profit Giles £9 000, Slocum £15 000; Sales Giles £99 000, Slocum £90 000; Gross Profit Percentage Giles 9·1%, Slocum 16·7%; Net Profit Percentage Giles 5·6%, Slocum 11·6%.
5. Capital owned £33 700; Capital employed £39 137; Working capital £5 700; Liquid capital £1 104; Acid-test ratio = ·65:1; Return on Capital Invested = 14·8%.
6. Capital owned £50 500; Capital employed = £75 632; Working capital £1 650; Liquid capital = £6 894, Acid test ratio is ·53:1 (Montgomery is in a very illiquid position indeed). Return on Capital Invested = 16·1%.

Unit Twenty-Four

No exercises in this unit.

Unit Twenty-Five

1. Cash balance £72·35.
2. Total of Receipts and Payments Account £734·38.
3. Cash balance £11·86.
4. Cash balance £227·26.

Unit Twenty-Six

No exercises in this unit.

Index